THE PHILOSOPHY OF SCIENCE

OXFORD BROOKES
UNIVERSITY
LIBRARY

THE PHILOSOPHY OF SCIENCE

Science and Objectivity

George Couvalis

SAGE Publications
London • Thousand Oaks • New Delhi

ISBN 0-7619-5100-8 (hbk)
ISBN 0-7619-5101-6 (pbk)
© George Couvalis 1997
First published 1997
Reprinted 1999

Apart from any fair dealing for the purposes of research or private study, or criticism or review, as permitted under the Copyright, Designs and Patents Act, 1988, this publication may be reproduced, stored or transmitted in any form, or by any means, only with the prior permission in writing of the publishers, or in the case of reprographic reproduction, in accordance with the terms of licences issued by the Copyright Licensing Agency. Inquiries concerning reproduction outside those terms should be sent to the publishers.

ACC. NO. 91526002 FUND THEOP
LOC ET CATEGORY STAN PRICE £24.99
13 DEC 2010
CLASS No 501 COU
OXFORD BROOKES UNIVERSITY LIBRARY

SAGE Publications Ltd
1 Oliver's Yard,
55 City Road
London EC1Y 1SP

SAGE Publications Inc
2455 Teller Road
Thousand Oaks,
California 91320

SAGE Publications India Pvt. Ltd
B–42 Panchsheel Enclave
PO Box 4109
New Delhi 110 017

British Library Cataloguing in Publication data
A catalogue record for this book is available from the British Library

Printed on paper from sustainable sources

Typeset by Photoprint Ltd., Torquay, Devon
Printed digitally and bound in Great Britain by
Lightning Source UK Ltd., Milton Keynes, Bedfordshire

Contents

Preface

Striking features of the modern era are the growth of scientific knowledge and the growth of the power and influence of the natural sciences. The natural sciences have been widely used as a model for many kinds of human activities and regarded as the acme of human achievement. They have also been widely reviled for distorting human life and veiling crucially important truths. Yet many textbooks on the philosophy of the natural sciences are either unnecessarily technical or simplistic. In addition, many of them fail clearly to connect with fields of general interest, such as epistemology, metaphysics and ethics. Despite this, the philosophy of science has rightly had and continues to have an important influence both within and outside philosophy. A danger posed by its indirect influence is that half understood or dubious views are taken up and used to defend outrageous claims. Sociologists, literary critics and historians are among the worst offenders, but philosophers are by no means immune. There is thus a need for a textbook, for higher education students and academics who have some philosophical knowledge, which presents material in a sophisticated but non-technical manner.

I have tried to meet this need here by discussing central arguments in the literature in a way that makes clear their relevance to a wide range of issues and corrects dubious interpretations of them. I also vigorously present a view of my own as it is important in these times to defend objectivity and realism. The philosophy of science has become too much a technical domain that only indirectly contributes to areas to which it is relevant. It should be intelligently discussed in the mainstream of philosophical thought, as it was in the eighteenth and nineteenth centuries.

The book often refers to important developments in the history of science. Readers do not need to understand any more of either the science or the history than is explained in the text to understand the philosophical relevance of the material discussed. In addition, while the text works through a large number of ideas derived from a variety of sources, I list at the end of every chapter some suggested texts for further reading which require little background knowledge, as well as some texts which require more background. Material referred to in the main text but not in the lists of further reading is generally more suitable for detailed research. However, many of the items listed can be read with profit by any intelligent reader, and people attempting to read this material should not be intimidated by jargon or technical notation. Often key points become clear if one continues reading. In any case, a quick look at encyclopaedias of science and technology or in *The Encyclopaedia of Philosophy* will often clarify things. The notes to the text take up issues which may be of concern to people who know the philosophical, historical, or scientific literature well. Students should feel free to ignore them.

Acknowledgements

There are a large number of people I wish to thank. I particularly wish to thank Linda Burns for her useful comments and for coping with me while I was writing. Josep Corbi, Tobies Grimaltos, Graham Nerlich, Belinda Paterson and Ian Ravenscroft have been particularly kind in providing me with helpful comments on many aspects of the book. Richard Brown, Greg Currie, Marty Davies, Gerard O'Brien, Ian Hunt, Pamela Lyon, Chris Mortensen, Ken Sievers and Peter Woolcock have also provided me with useful comments. Sandra Egege proofread the manuscript with great thoroughness. The participants in the Flinders/ Adelaide research seminar series and my students have also made useful suggestions. Catherine Dale, Sally Fraser and Karen Gordon have provided me with some valuable administrative help.

The Department of Epistemology and Metaphysics at the University of Valencia in Spain provided me with a congenial place in which to begin work on the manuscript. I would like to thank the members of the department for their kindness and their comments. Mercedes Torrevejano provided me with every facility a visitor could wish for. Josep Corbi, Carmen Fayos, Alfredo Garriga and Tobies Grimaltos were particularly kind.

The National Technical University of Athens provided with me with administrative help, a room and helpful feedback. I thank the staff and students there, particularly Pantelis Nicolacopoulos.

Introduction

The methodology, metaphysical assumptions and ideals of rational conduct which underpin the natural sciences have long been of interest to philosophers. In the seventeenth century, the philosopher-scientist René Descartes used the science of geometry as a model of how best to conduct an inquiry. John Locke thought that by acting as a philosophical under-labourer to Newton he could discover how we come to know anything and how we learn truths about the fundamental structure of the world. As it became obvious that Newtonian mechanics was incredibly successful in producing verifiable predictions, Locke's strategy seemed to be the correct one to many thinkers. During the Enlightenment, many philosophers came to think that the proper application of scientific method would lead us to an understanding not only of the external world but also of human nature. They believed that the knowledge acquired would provide guidance as to the ethical principles we should follow and lead to the construction of the correct social system. Science, they thought, would come to replace metaphysics, ethics and political philosophy.

Yet in the eighteenth century, philosophy itself began to undermine this vision. The philosopher David Hume, in an attempt to found a scientific study of human nature, discovered he could not justify elementary principles of scientific method or ethics. Hume's ideas were ultimately to have a great impact in epistemology. Hume discovered that predictions about the unobserved behaviour of objects could neither be proved to be true nor even proved to be probable on the basis of knowledge of their past behaviour; for example, that the sun has risen in the past an enormous number of times is insufficient evidence to prove true or even probable the statement that it will rise tomorrow. However, a basic part of scientific method seems to be drawing conclusions about unobserved objects on the basis of knowledge of observed objects. What Hume discovered is sometimes called *the problem of induction* because the reasoning by which we arrive at truths about unobserved instances of things from truths about observed instances of things is called inductive reasoning. Hume did not think that there was a serious problem with inductive reasoning *per se*; he treated what he had discovered as merely posing a puzzle about how it is that we know things through inductive reasoning. However, he thought the fact that there exists such a puzzle means that scientific laws, which seem to be primarily useful and informative because they tell us about the unobserved behaviour of objects, cannot be known to be true solely on the basis of reason or experience. In contrast to Hume, other thinkers who became aware of the puzzle of induction concluded that Newtonian mechanics, which was widely thought to be the pinnacle of human knowledge, is nothing more than speculation.

Hume was also to have a great impact on ethics. He found what he thought was an unbridgeable gap between knowledge of the natural world and knowledge of proper motives for action – a gap that seemed to make morality a prisoner of arational passions. He argued it is not possible to prove any claim about what is morally right from any statement about human nature and the natural world, but merely to engage someone's emotions. If, for example, one could show that people are naturally greedy, then nothing follows logically about what should be done about this. One person may conclude that we should all be killed and another that we should all be restrained by laws: neither of them would be making a mistake in reasoning, and most people would be swayed one way rather than another by their natural dispositions and desires. This train of reasoning suggested to Hume that the very idea of founding ethics and political philosophy on scientific knowledge was absurd.

In response to what he thought he had discovered, Hume grounded the sciences on habit and instinct, and ethics on passion and tradition. By grounding both the sciences and ethics on arational forces, he provided romantic and theological thinkers (whose pretensions he would have despised) with an excuse for claiming dubious sentiments, tastes and metaphysical principles to be as sound as the laws of the natural sciences.

Although Hume's arguments and conclusions had some impact, they were not generally accepted by philosophers in the eighteenth and nineteenth centuries. Instead, Immanuel Kant and John Stuart Mill developed philosophical accounts of scientific method, which were refined by their followers and which seemed to bypass the problems Hume had raised. Further, developments in the sciences seemed to demonstrate that Hume's scepticism was an overreaction to the grandiose expectations of the Enlightenment.

Kant and his followers claimed to have solved Hume's puzzles without admitting absurdities by arguing that some judgements were the necessary underpinning of all coherent beliefs about the world. By their account, to attempt to doubt such judgements was not to be sceptical but to lapse into incoherence. They argued that these beliefs included the basic laws of Newtonian mechanics and the axioms of Euclidean geometry as well as basic principles which justified reasoning from truths about observed things to truths about unobserved things. Kantians also tried to untie Hume's other Gordian knot by arguing ethics to be a separate domain that was supported by different but equally adequate justificatory principles. They argued that while ethical truths could not be derived from truths about human beings or about the natural world, our reason itself could be used to ground ethics in a different way.

Empirically minded thinkers preferred Mill's more modest attempts to vindicate science through a new understanding of the nature of induction and of scientific laws, and to vindicate ethics by appealing to our feelings and intuitions. Mill argued that science was a self-correcting enterprise which did not need ultimate foundations, and in which principles of reasoning from observables to unobservables are gradually improved. In ethics, he stated, the desires and intuitions of people provided as much of a foundation as was necessary; a scientific justification of ethics may be impossible, but an appeal to human nature gave us a way of producing acceptable principles.

To many philosophers and ordinary people, however, advances in the sciences were much more important than Kant's and Mill's philosophical vindications. The predictive success of Newtonian mechanics proved to be enormous, culminating in the discovery of the planet Neptune by the savant Leverrier in the position he had predicted on the basis of Newton's laws. Further, the sciences of chemistry, geology and biology were able to provide plausible explanations, and sometimes predictions, of a whole range of phenomena. Such successes seemed to make philosophical justifications of the sciences unnecessary and speculative, and to make scepticism about the sciences arcane.

Just as scientific knowledge seemed secure, a series of unanticipated events seemed to have plotted to destroy it. In the late eighteenth century mathematicians raised doubts about whether Euclidean geometry was necessarily true. In the late nineteenth century, Leverrier's work turned out, as the philosopher Norwood Hanson (1962) has said, to be not only the zenith but also the nadir of Newtonian theory, though this was not understood at the time. While trying to repeat his success in predicting the existence of a new planet by working on an odd feature of the orbit of Mercury, Leverrier repeatedly failed in his predictions. Then, using ideas derived from Hume, Mach showed that many of Newton's metaphysical assumptions about space were dubious. Very late in the nineteenth century Michelson and Morley produced experimental evidence that, contrary to Newtonian expectation, light did not spread through space by using an elusive substance. Finally, soon after the beginning of the twentieth century Albert Einstein, who began by attempting to modify Newtonian theory, produced a startling new account of the fundamental laws of physics. Einstein's account was simpler and more experimentally satisfactory than Newtonian mechanics and within it Newtonian laws were at best useful approximations. As experimental work was done to test Einstein's predictions, it became obvious that Newtonian mechanics was sometimes wildly wrong.

The philosophical importance of Einstein's work can hardly be exaggerated. A supposed proof of the truth of basic principles underlying

Newton's laws had been produced by Kant as part of his program for a viable metaphysics. The failure of this proof rendered Kant's program suspect. Worse problems were produced for the Kantian picture by later developments in physics. Einstein showed that his new theories were compatible with the idea that space had the structure described by Riemannian geometry, which was a different geometry to the one which Kant had claimed was necessarily true. Einstein also argued that since space was more simply modelled by Riemannian geometry, space was likely to be Riemannian rather than Euclidean. In Riemannian geometry, apparently necessary propositions of Euclidean geometry – such as three angles of a triangle add up to one hundred and eighty degrees – are false. Kantianism seemed to lie in ruins. Hume's puzzle about how we can know truths about unobserved things on the basis of our observations seemed to acquire a new force, presenting a serious problem for defenders of the rationality of science.

Empiricist accounts, such as that of Mill, were somewhat bruised by events. Mill and other empiricists had sometimes talked as if inductive reasoning could be conclusive; yet Newtonian mechanics, apparently the most inductively supported hypothesis anyone had produced, was seen to be false. Nevertheless, much in modest empiricist accounts might be worth preserving. Empiricist accounts of deductive logic were deficient; however, a number of logicians in the late nineteenth and early twentieth centuries, principally Gottlob Frege and Bertrand Russsell, achieved enormous advances in formalizing deductive reasoning so as to make it like algebra. During the 1930s a group of philosophers called the 'logical positivists' developed an empiricist account that used the new formal techniques to produce a daring new view of the nature of science, logic and language. They hoped to eliminate metaphysics from the domain of significant discourse by proposing an account of the nature of meaning according to which terms derive much of their meaning directly from experience. Ethical language expressed emotion, they said, and did not describe features of the world. However, the logical positivists were neither able to produce an account of language which eliminated metaphysics, nor were they able to deal with Hume's puzzle of how we can come to know truths about unobservables on the basis of truths about observables. Their attempts to modify deductive formalisms so as to develop an inductive formalism to deal with Hume's puzzle failed. Their great merit was to have set rigorous standards of philosophical argumentation and honest criticism. Our understanding of the depth of their failures is due largely to the power of their own critique of their most deeply held assumptions.

Enter Karl Popper, whose influential ideas will be discussed throughout this book. Working against the logical positivists from the outset, he attempted to marry some Kantian ideas with empiricist method while using important elements from the new deductive logic. He argued that all statements are theoretical and contain metaphysical elements, so that scientific laws cannot be derived from experience. Even a simple statement like 'I see a swan in the lake in front of me' involves various theories: that the thing I see is not a decoy, that I am not hallucinating, that I can recognize swans, and so on. Theories, Popper says, are the result of the innate tendency of creatures to impose order on the world and are, thus, creations of the mind. Further, what keeps science rational is not some logical method for justifying theories about the unobserved but the fact that scientific theories can be shown to be false. On this basis, risky and bold conjectures are to be preferred to cautious statements because such conjectures, whether they fail or succeed, advance science enormously. In Popper's view, the lesson to be learned from the failure of Newtonian mechanics is science is a risky but rational enterprise.

Popper also introduces ethical elements into his discussions of scientific method. Popper's defence of the view that all beliefs are fallible arises from a concern to defend free inquiry and democracy against totalitarian tendencies. By his account, criticism is always important in establishing the shortcomings of hypotheses, and even the best-tested hypothesis is not immune to problems. One can never tell from which direction fruitful criticism will come, so suppression of views is dangerous. All conjectures, including political conjectures, are risky. If even the best-tested scientific theories can fail, surely this is even more true of social and political theories. Yet political activists will unjustifiably risk the lives of many unwilling participants on the basis of quite dubious claims. They will do this, according to Popper, because of a natural human tendency to render our favourite views immune from falsification by hedging them with *ad hoc* modifications. This tendency to dogmatism has an important role to play in the early development of children, but it can become dangerous. The critical and fallibilist tradition of the sciences, in which refutations are taken seriously and conjectures are regarded as risky, thus has much to contribute to a democratic society.

Popper's ideas have been developed and criticized in great detail, and have influenced theorists working in many areas, ranging from economics to art theory. Within the sciences themselves, they are used to argue for various methodological standards. In palaeontology, for example, the claim that certain West Australian rocks contain the earliest fossils has been attacked because its proponents failed to put it in a falsifiable form. Popper is cited by both sides in the debate. Popper's work has been thought by many scientists and philosophers to protect the objectivity and rationality of science. But Popperianism has important problems and influential rivals.

Popperians have had great trouble in producing a convincing solution to Hume's puzzle, for it seems that by their account we cannot know that any proposed scientific law is even likely to be true. Thus, it seems that past experience can provide us with no basis for action. It seems that if we believe Popper, we might as well try riding a broomstick as getting on a bus to get home from work. But this is preposterous. As a consequence, many philosophers have claimed that Popper's view leads to an extreme scepticism about science and does not solve Hume's puzzle.

Popperianism has influential rivals in ideas developed by Paul Feyerabend, who started out sympathetic to Popper's ideas, and by Thomas Kuhn, a physicist who became a historian of science. Kuhn and Feyerabend invoke some of Popper's ideas to criticize some of his most basic claims, such as that science leads to a cumulative growth of knowledge. They claim that if we accept, as Popper does, that all statements are theory-laden and that they contain metaphysical elements, it becomes impossible to justify simple objective tests for theories because one is testing theories against theories, not against the facts. Further, if two theories differ radically in their fundamental metaphysical assumptions, it will become impossible rationally to compare them without using unwarranted standards. It turns out, by this account, that the so-called growth of science has often not been cumulative but has occurred in radical breaks, in which new theories introduce new methodological standards and new metaphysical assumptions to an extent which makes simple objective comparison with older theories impossible. For instance, according to Aristotle's theory of the world, men are pre-adapted to perceive the world correctly under normal conditions. This means that evidence about the nature of the heavens obtained by using telescopes is dubious unless it agrees with what the normal man would perceive with his naked eyes. Feyerabend claims that because of this Galileo could not legitimately use his telescopic observations against the medieval geocentric account of the heavens since that account relied on Aristotle's metaphysics and theory of perception.

Kuhn supports his claims with historical studies of scientific revolutions, which he claims show that science undergoes crises that can only be resolved when practitioners radically change their standards for assessing theories. In his view, science only works cumulatively if it operates with a series of unquestioned assumptions and procedures that are regarded as normal. Abandoning such assumptions and procedures, which sometimes happens in science, produces changes that are so revolutionary that one can talk of changing one's world-view. A simple objective comparison of the very different methodological prescriptions and metaphysical theories which were held before and after a scientific revolution becomes impossible.

While Kuhn thinks there are problems for simplistic views of how science can be objective, he has stressed that his view allows for progress of a certain kind in science. In order for scientific theories to develop so that they can be used to solve a wide range of theoretical problems and be of some use in practical contexts, it is necessary that practitioners put aside discussions of unresolvable fundamental problems. On the other hand, such problems cannot be put aside forever. When a scientific theory cannot plausibly answer many of the theoretical questions the scientific community as a whole thinks it should answer, and is of little use in solving important practical problems, it is time to try working with different fundamental assumptions and different sets of procedures. No rules can be formulated as to when to abandon older approaches, and none can be formulated as to how to proceed in formulating new assumptions. Different scientists will give differing weights to the problems a theory cannot easily solve. Nevertheless, Kuhn stresses that scientists do not proceed irrationally or arationally. Medieval geocentric astronomy was eventually abandoned because, as time went on, the rival heliocentric picture was better able to solve practical and theoretical problems such as predicting the paths of the planets accurately and explaining the behaviour of comets. Kuhn thinks that science does progress in the sense that successive theories tend to solve more problems than their predecessors; however, he does not think that newer theories can be said to be more true than their predecessors or to solve more fundamental problems. A cumulative growth of knowledge of the kind that Popper describes does not occur according to Kuhn.

Feyerabend argues for the more radical view that there is no such thing as scientific method, at least as philosophers understand the term 'method', and that science has illegitimately acquired a dominant position in our culture, even though it is objectively no better than witchcraft. He argues that what makes theories true is completely internal to the world picture of which they are a part. 'The goddess Athene inspired me with strength' is a true observation statement for a Homeric Greek; it is false or nonsense for later Greek thinkers. Feyerabend is a relativist in terms of the truth of theories, and he does not think that they can be objectively justified. As a result of his relativism, he calls for science to be put under democratic control and for its grip on our society to be loosened through a separation of the state from science. If citizens want to go to faith healers, the state should not prevent such healers from becoming practising doctors. If citizens want voodoo to be taught in universities and schools, there is no objective reason why it should not be taught. He accuses Popper and other rationalists of being 'ratio fascists' who want to impose a particular type of rationality on other cultures but disguise their imperialism with fine phrases.

Following in the footsteps of Kuhn and Feyerabend, other thinkers have developed pictures of the sciences that present social and political factors as crucial in understanding the resolution of scientific controversies. Barry Barnes and David Bloor (1982), for example, say that scientific data never logically imply that one theory is better than another; what ultimately determines whether a scientific theory is accepted is that one group wins a political struggle. The evidence for a theory is never sufficient to provide objective grounds for thinking that it is better than its rivals. To explain why one theory became accepted and its rivals rejected, it becomes necessary to appeal to other factors. If

Barnes and Bloor are right, theories are not and cannot be objectively justified on the basis of the evidence. Helen Longino (1990) argues that while some observational data are true, the interpretation of those data inevitably involves choices because the data, by themselves, do not imply any particular theory. The choice as to how to interpret data may be legitimately made by appealing to values. Consider, for example, data which show male–female differences in certain abilities. According to Longino, a feminist may legitimately take those differences to be environmentally rather than biologically caused, based on her system of values. Scientific theories cannot be objectively justified by methods which show them to be likely to be true.

Among recent writers there is a further and weaker criticism of the objectivity of science. According to this criticism, which has been put with considerable force by Bas van Fraassen and others, science does give us ever-increasing knowledge of observable features of the world and is, therefore, of enormous practical use. However, science is of very limited philosophical interest as it does not offer us knowledge of unobservable features of the world, such as the true underlying causes of events. This means that the hope of earlier philosophers that science would play an important role in resolving metaphysical problems is unfounded. Our ideas about unobservables cannot be objectively justified.

In this book, I argue that science is pragmatically useful, gives us some understanding of important physical and metaphysical aspects of the world, and to some degree follows a critical ideal which it is important to understand and whose spirit is worth emulating. The grandiose claims of the philosophers of the seventeenth century were not completely mistaken. However, I concede that much can be learnt from the critics of science. Science, and indeed scientific method itself, is fallible and has often been an accomplice of repressive traditions. Further, science does not give us knowledge of ethical truths. Thus, many of our important beliefs about science have to be revised in the light of criticism.

Science is supposedly grounded on experience and experiment. I start by discussing the claim that experience is theory-laden in ways which make the objective testing of theories impossible. I argue that neither experience nor descriptions of the world are theory-laden in any sense that poses problems for objectively testing theories. Science supposedly uses experience as evidence for the existence of general truths about the world. Hume's puzzle seems to pose an important problem for this claim, for it suggests that no interesting generalization about the world can be justified. For this reason, I turn to discussing solutions to Hume's puzzle after discussing theory-ladenness. I maintain that Hume's puzzle poses no problem for science. Some reasoning from the observed to the unobserved is unproblematic, so we can justify some generalizations about the world. In the course of my discussion of solutions to Hume's puzzle, I argue that epistemology needs to be revised in important ways in order to deal with it. We do not need precise definitions or methods of reasoning which conform to precisely defined and law-like patterns. After discussing Hume's puzzle, the discussion turns to Kuhn's critique of science. I argue that Kuhn is wrong and that, by relying on fairly secure observations, scientists can use vaguely defined but objectively justified standards to produce an increasing knowledge of truths about the world. My discussion of Kuhn leads to a consideration of Feyerabend's more radical claims. I maintain that Feyerabend's relativism is incoherent and his historical account is shoddy. However, I argue that his ethical arguments deserve to be taken seriously. The role of science in the modern world is deeply problematical and there are many reasons for thinking that science should be under the control of the members of a free society. I then turn to the accounts of the role of social influences and values on science provided by Barnes and Bloor, and Longino. I argue that there are many problems with those accounts and that, in so far as they are correct, they do not threaten the objectivity of scientific knowledge. Finally, I turn to the problem of how much science can teach us about the world. Contrary to Bas van Fraassen and others, I maintain that we learn a great deal about the unobservable features of the world from science, so that it has important implications for metaphysics.

Throughout the book, I argue that two problems underlie the criticisms of the credentials of science. The first problem is the critics are implicitly working with the false idea that the only kind of knowledge worthy of the name is knowledge that uses and is based on precise distinctions and statements, is absolutely unchallengeable, and is established by methods that conform to formal, law-like, patterns. This idea has caused almost endless mischief throughout the history of Western philosophy. It occurs in Descartes's famous *Discourse on the Method*, and was revived in this century because enormous advances in formal logic mesmerized philosophers by seeming to offer them the possibility that they would be able to give a precise account of the basis and nature of all types of justifiable reasoning. The idea underlies the work of the critics of science in the same way as it underlies the arguments of the most dogmatic defenders of science. I will be criticizing this idea throughout the text.

The second problem is that some philosophers take too little notice of common-sense principles of reasoning, allowing themselves to be seduced by a philosophical argument which uses apparently plausible premises and sound logical techniques to arrive at an absurd conclusion. The apparently powerful philosophical arguments of the ancient philosopher Zeno for the impossibility of motion were taken seriously by his disciples who should, instead, have used them to attack either the inadequacy of his argumentative techniques or his assumptions. The history of philosophy is littered with arguments leading to absurd conclusions, which sound good but are obviously false – although it can take generations to figure out precisely what is wrong with the arguments. Unfortunately, rather than treating such arguments as entertaining puzzles, some philosophers have a lamentable tendency to take them seriously in the name of objectivity. The fact that some of their predecessors took other seemingly powerful philosophical arguments seriously and were shown to be wrong should have made much more of an impact in philosophy than it has. When dealing with apparently flawless arguments for a seemingly irrational or absurd claim, the common-sense rule of thumb is to start by asking: given the deplorable failure rate of apparently flawless philosophical arguments, is it likely that the conclusion of this argument is true? Typically, we will be able to note that the conclusion is highly unlikely to be true as it implies many things which are very likely to be false. This should be taken to indicate that something is wrong with the argument and that it poses a mere puzzle rather than a serious problem. I shall be arguing that many of the arguments which purport to undermine the objectivity of scientific knowledge actually pose only puzzles.

1
Theory and Observation

It is widely believed that many scientific theories have been justified objectively and that we know they give us a true picture of the world. In contrast, the claims of philosophers and the pronouncements of religions, no matter how plausible, are widely believed to be speculative and dubitable. The belief that many scientific theories have been justified objectively is allied to the view that scientific theories can be justified by observation because observation gives us direct access to the world. Taking this view, science provides an ideal method for acquiring knowledge which should be emulated whenever possible – the answer to the central problem of epistemology, 'how can we get knowledge?', is 'follow the methods of science as much as possible'.

A radically different view of observation holds that all observation is deeply permeated by theories, so it does not provide us with direct access to the world. This is the view that all observation is *theory-laden*. Arguments for this view have been put by many philosophers.

If all observation is theory-laden, the objectivity of scientific research might be undermined, for it seems that we may well be unable to tell whether our perceptions accurately capture aspects of the world. To deal with the problem of whether scientific theories can be justified objectively, I need to consider the three main claims which are used to support theory-ladenness and discuss their consequences. These three claims are:

1 all experience is permeated by theories;
2 theories direct our observations, tell us which observations are significant, and indicate how they are significant;
3 all statements about what we observe are theoretical and cannot be derived from our experience.

I shall argue that these claims are incorrect or misleading but, even if they were correct, scientific theories could be tested objectively.

1 The influence of theory on experience

The arguments for the theory-ladenness of experience

The first claim is that all experience is permeated by theories. This claim is often defended by pointing out that our experience sometimes dramatically changes, even though the perceptual stimulus remains the same,

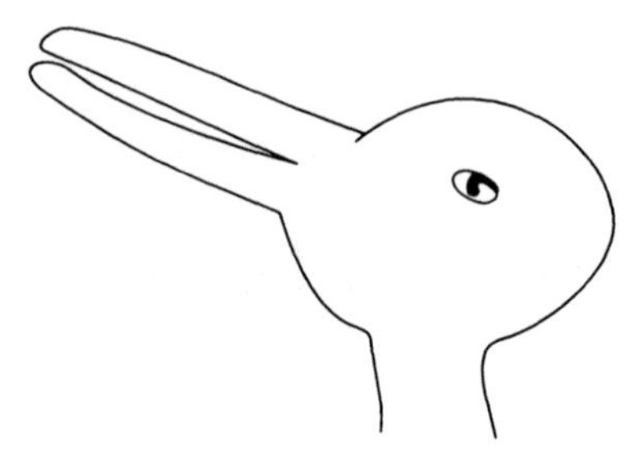

Figure 1.1 *The duck-rabbit drawing*

and arguing that this change is dependent on interpreting the stimulus theoretically. Consider the famous case of the duck-rabbit (see figure 1.1). The drawing remains the same, yet it will sometimes look like a picture of a duck and sometimes like a picture of a rabbit. Many people find that they can easily make the image look like one or the other. This seems to indicate that our ideas about what we want to see, or about what we expect to see, change how things look. It seems that those who want or expect to see a duck, see a duck, and that those who want or expect to see a rabbit, see a rabbit. Apparently we can change from seeing a duck to seeing a rabbit merely by changing what we want or expect to see.

A second argument for the first claim points out that sometimes the way an item looks does not reflect how it really is and argues that the best explanation for this phenomenon is that theories permeate experience. A famous case of this kind is supposed to be the Müller-Lyer illusion (see Figure 1.2). People typically report that the two lines look like they are of different length. But if we measure them with a ruler, we find that they are of the same length. It is often said that our beliefs about rooms with right-angled corners lead us to experience the Müller-Lyer diagram in a false way, that is, we have come to expect lines with corners with certain angles to be further away than they really are, and hence to look smaller. Some researchers have claimed that certain groups of people in Africa do not suffer from illusions like this one. They suggest that perhaps the different background of such people means that they have theoretical beliefs which make them immune to those illusions.[1]

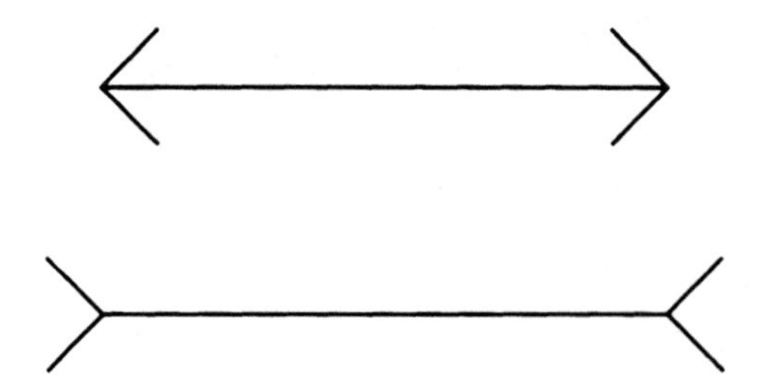

Figure 1.2 *The Müller-Lyer illusion*

Some philosophers have said that illusions like the duck-rabbit and the Müller-Lyer show that the effects of theories deeply affect scientific observation. For example, they maintain that Copernicus and Ptolemy really had quite different experiences when they watched the sunrise. Because Copernicus believed the horizon falls, his experience was of the horizon falling; because Ptolemy believed the sun rises, his experience was of the sun rising (Hanson, 1958). If these philosophers are right, then it appears to be impossible to test theories objectively, for it is impossible to appeal to observations which have not been contaminated by the very theories which are supposed to be tested through experience. Both Copernicus and Ptolemy may have thought their theories were justified by how the world looked, but the way the world looked would have been so deeply affected by their theories that it would be impossible to tell whether what they were seeing was a product of their theories or a feature of the world.

Critical discussion

My first criticism of the claim that experience is penetrated by theory is, even if it is correct, there are limits to perceptual plasticity and this means that many theories can still be objectively tested through experience. We can make the duck-rabbit drawing look like a drawing of either a duck or a rabbit, but simple experiments the reader can carry out will show that we cannot get it to look like much else. No matter what we expect to see or want to see, we cannot get the duck-rabbit drawing to look like the Parthenon, the Sydney Opera House or a teacup. We cannot even make it look like a real duck as opposed to a drawing of a duck. This means the claim that the duck-rabbit drawing is really the Parthenon is refuted by experience; no matter how hard we might try to make the drawing look like the Greek building, we fail (Brown, 1979: 93–4).

My second criticism of the arguments for the theory-ladenness of experience is that, in any case, a perceptual stimulus can only be plausibly said to be capable of looking more than one way in situations in which we are either perceiving a two-dimensional item (such as a drawing) as a representation of something else or perceiving something under poor conditions (for example, when we see an object at night or when we examine it quickly). That our experience is untrustworthy under poor conditions does not imply that it is always affected by theories, and so does not imply it cannot be used to test theories objectively. In situations in which we carefully examine something in bright light, walk around it, etc., we seem to be unable to make the object look different. In such situations, our experience can be used to objectively test theories. This does not mean, of course, the appearance of things is never deceptive under ideal conditions – perhaps a stick seen through clear and well-lit water will look bent. However, it does mean that *our beliefs* are not determining the way things look, so at least one source of error can be eliminated.

This second criticism finds some support in everyday experience, but its force may be thought to be blunted by the fact that much of science relies on observations which are not made under ideal conditions. When we study the planets or tiny objects, we often use telescopes and microscopes which do not present us with bright and sharp three-dimensional images. In such cases, we have to practise to make the images at all crisp. It may be argued that we need to use theory to make our images crisp and, as a result, we can unwittingly make our images include things which do not exist. This may explain, for example, why Galileo, though an experienced observer, drew two large moons rather than rings when looking at Saturn. Thus, a sceptic about science may say there is a serious problem in trying objectively to test theories about distant or small objects through experience, as our observations of such objects are contaminated by our preconceptions.

However, I can strengthen my second criticism to deal with this problem. First, when images sharpen as we practise, it is not at all clear whether theory plays an important role. In the absence of other evidence, it is just as plausible that the changes are brought about solely by localized mechanisms in the eye or brain which adjust over time. To understand this point, consider the parallel case of entering a dark room after being in bright sunlight. At first we cannot see anything clearly, but after a while we begin to distinguish various objects; yet this process seems to have nothing to do with theory. Second, even when theory seems to play some role, for example when our visual field changes to include the white blood cell in the upper left corner of the slide after we have been told to look for it, it is not clear that the theory is acting as anything more than a device for directing our attention to a particular area – something which we might have done anyway given more time or which could have been done by shining a bright light on that spot. (Note that I am only talking about *experiencing* the blood cell, not about *knowing* that it is a blood cell.) There is no evidence that theory problematically permeates experience as opposed to merely helping us focus on some aspect of the world. Third, examples which are supposed to show that we see images of non-existent things when we expect to see them, may well turn out to be examples of us compensating for the lack of sharpness of images through our descriptions and not of us changing experience through belief. (It might well be the case that Galileo, who was using a telescope which focused badly and produced a great deal of chromatic aberration, could not resolve the image of Saturn's rings and guessed that they were moons.) Anyone who has used a telescope or microscope knows that some images simply will not resolve and that frustration can lead us to fudge results.

My three subsidiary arguments imply that there is no good reason to believe that careful observations through instruments are contaminated by theories. As far as we can tell, scientists can objectively test theories about small objects and about distant objects by relying only on stable and sharp images produced by instruments and by resisting the impulse to fudge results. To strengthen my three subsidiary arguments, I need to move on to my third criticism of the first claim, which is: the best explanation available of changes in the way a stimulus looks says that such changes have nothing to do with theory. This explanation has been developed in detail by Jerry Fodor, so I shall turn now to his story.

Fodor begins by pointing out that when we experience items in a way that has been distorted by mental processes, the evidence indicates the distortions do not depend on one's beliefs. He argues this means that theory-ladenness is refuted and not supported by such experiences. He concentrates on the Müller-Lyer illusion, though his argument applies to similar cases: whether we believe (hold the theory that) the two lines are equal or unequal when we observe the Müller-Lyer diagram, they continue to look unequal. This means our beliefs cannot be causing them to look unequal.

Fodor explains the illusions in question by using his modularity theory of mind which, he claims, better fits the empirical evidence than explanations which involve theory-ladenness. According to the modularity theory, the mind has separate modules which process information. Modules cannot be influenced by other modules in their basic functioning (which is either innately specified, or partly innately specified and partly specified by environmental training) – Fodor makes this point by saying modules are *encapsulated*. Information can be acquired from such modules by a central processing unit which has linguistic beliefs and can make reasoned judgements about such information, but the kinds of reports the modules give are not affected by those beliefs.

An example of a module might be the visual processing system. By Fodor's account, this module is either hard-wired or becomes hard-wired through training in a particular environment. It can be directed by the central unit to give information about what is happening in a particular spatial area, but the perceptual reports it gives are not influenced by the beliefs of the central unit. For example, people brought up in an environment with lots of corners with 90° angles, such as rooms in modern Western buildings, may suffer from the Müller-Lyer illusion; on the other hand, people brought up in round African huts may not. It may be possible to make the African people suffer from the illusion by making them move about in Western rooms for some time, but this would have nothing important to do with their beliefs about those rooms. A young cat's visual module would also adjust to our rooms over time through being trained in them. The key point is that the adjustment does not occur through a top-down process in which the language module passes the 'correct' theory to the visual module.[2]

Fodor thinks the most plausible explanation of why illusions are recalcitrant is that it is useful for the survival of animals to have fairly unintelligent and quickly functioning perceptual processing modules. Such modules provide experiences which tend rapidly to fix true beliefs about the world. Linguistic beliefs are subject to all sorts of speculative theoretical influences and if such beliefs affected all experiences, animals would have trouble surviving (Fodor, 1984).

Fodor's account occupies a kind of middle ground between a simplistic empiricism which sees perception as unintelligent absorption of information and a view which holds that highly intelligent processing systems transform perceptual stimuli. The modular units which provide us with perceptual information are intelligent in the sense that they process perceptual stimuli. This means our perception is structured in various ways. However, the modular units do not use theories in the central processing module to structure information.

At first sight it would seem that Fodor has difficulty in explaining how certain items, such as the duck-rabbit drawing, sometimes seem to look one way and sometimes the other. A plausible explanation of this phenomenon is that our belief that we see a drawing of a rabbit makes it look like a rabbit. However, Fodor argues that a better explanation is that the change in the apparent image is triggered by changing the point on which we focus (1988). By focusing on one point we make the image look like what English speakers call a rabbit-like image, while by focusing on another point we make it look like what English speakers call a duck-like image – whatever we believe (and even if we have never heard of ducks or rabbits!). Fodor's argument here implicitly relies on well known psychological evidence that our ability to change illusions is, at least, inhibited when we cannot change the point on which we focus.

The details of Fodor's proposal are controversial as subjects can make illusions decrease in intensity, a phenomenon which requires explanation.[3] For our purposes, however, we can ignore these controversies and concentrate on the arguments for the encapsulation of the mechanisms involved. For Fodor to criticize theory-ladenness, it would be sufficient for him to show that the mechanisms do not seem to be affected by our theories. I take it that the sorts of theories we have in mind here are fairly general views about the world which are articulated, or presuppositions of such views which are not articulated but which are clearly present.[4] An example would be Copernicus's theory. Fodor makes two claims: first, there is no evidence that holding Copernicus's theory affects one's experience, and second, the recalcitrant nature of one's experiences suggests the opposite. Fodor's account is consistent with the fact that if we concentrate on the horizon when the moon is rising, the moon will seem to be moving and the Earth will seem to be still, even though we *know* that the Earth is moving very quickly and the moon is still.

Even if we were to say that beliefs which are solely about an individual item are theories (for example, the belief that one is seeing a drawing of a rabbit in front of one), Fodor's view seems to provide an explanation of the evidence which fits at least as well as explanations involving theory-ladenness, and which can more easily explain recalcitrant illusions. Of course, if we call any kind of low-level cognitive processing theoretical, it is true but trivial that all experience is permeated by theory.

I should explain here that in defending Fodor I am not trying to defend the thesis that experience is totally unstructured, or that our understanding of it uses no conceptual categories at all. In Fodor's fuller account, the higher processing module contributes terms which are hierarchically organized into families of natural kind terms, ordered from the very specific to the very general. Some of the terms in these hierarchies are roughly midway and Fodor calls these 'basic categories'. For example, 'bird' is halfway between 'animal' and 'black crow'. According to Fodor these concepts are phenomenologically salient in the sense that they are triggered by encounter with their instances. Confronted with the average bird we will naturally see it as a bird. Basic categories are observational in the sense that normal unassisted subjects will recognize things as belonging to those groups. It is important to stress three things: first, Fodor thinks it is a matter of empirical research as to which categories are basic. Second, the language of basic categories is not an impoverished language which merely describes experiences, but a realist one in the sense that using that language and perceiving items involves one in assuming the existence of space, time, matter, etc. Third, using that language does not presuppose any particular theory about the universe or the nature of space, time, matter, etc.[5]

Fodor puts a good case for saying our everyday experience of the world yields something which may be called the Basic Observational Fragment of sense perception. It is basic in the sense that it provides a common ground to which various theorists can appeal to test their theories. It is also independent of the beliefs of particular theorists and reliable in the sense that normal observers will all give similar reports about what it contains.

Churchland's reply to Fodor

Paul Churchland (1988) presents various objections to Fodor's account. He claims that the sensory aspect of experience is merely the detection of causal proximal stimuli, the meaningful content of experience being totally provided by the network of our belief system. This is a very strong version of the thesis that all observation is theory-laden. His first important objection to Fodor is that Fodor does not allow for the effects theories have over time. Certainly, Churchland argues, theories do not have *immediate* effects on perception but they do have effects over time which can drastically change any aspect of experience. Contrary to what one may think from Fodor's account, the functioning of perceptual mechanisms is neither biologically hard-wired, nor completely specified by plastic mechanisms whose detailed functioning has been fixed by early training.

Churchland's first objection is problematic as he presents no good evidence that theories will have an effect on experience over time, whereas Fodor at least presents evidence that theories do not have immediate effects on experiences.[6] Further, as mentioned above, the evidence seems to be against the total plasticity of perception even in cases where some item can be perceived in two ways. That a drawing can look like a drawing of a duck or rabbit does not mean it can look like a teacup. In any case, Churchland's first argument suffers from a deeper problem. If perception is plastic to the degree he suggests, he could not provide *objective evidence* that it is so plastic. Taking Churchland's view, Fodor's supporters would, over time, gradually come to perceive *any* apparent evidence for Churchland's view in a different way. For example, on hearing a subject say, 'I have been able to change the way a table looks to make it look like a chair', the Fodorian listener would be able to make that utterance sound like 'I have not been able to make the table look like a chair'. There would be nothing wrong with this, as in Churchland's view the way things sound to us is *solely* the result of previous theoretical commitments. Experience only provides a stimulus whose content is fully determined by theory. Thus, if Churchland's view were right, Fodorians should be able to provide as much evidence for their view as Churchland can provide for his view. This means that if Churchland is arguing for complete plasticity, his view *cannot* be shown to be superior to its rival by appeal to any kind of objective evidence. This does not, of course, show that his account is false, but it does take it out of the domain of rational discussion.

Churchland's second objection to Fodor's account is more plausible. He says that Fodor wants to use the data provided by experience to test theories in an objective way. However, if Fodor is right, such data are provided by mechanisms that are not theory penetrable, but there is no reason to believe such data give a correct account of the world. When we use such data we may be condemned to a kind of universal dogmatism by our biology. Thus, if Fodor is right, experience does not give us a way of testing theories objectively. That this may be the case is shown by the fact that it appears to us that the sun is moving in relation to the Earth whereas the Copernican theory tells us that the opposite is true – that is, the horizon falls rather than the sun rises.

The main claim underlying Churchland's second objection is that if Fodor is right we may well always be misled by experience. His evidence for the claim is presumably that, according to Fodor we are sometimes misled by our experiences. There are three problems with using this evidence to defend the main claim: first that we are sometimes misled by our experiences does not mean that we may well always be misled. Second, the evidence cannot even be used in a good inductive argument because, just as there seems to be a small number of cases in which experience is misleading, there seem to be many cases in which it is not misleading. Third, the claim that we should seriously consider the possibility that we might always be misled by our experiences cannot be supported by Fodor's arguments, as those arguments will work only if our senses are sometimes reliable. For example, the way in which we know that the Müller-Lyer illusion is misleading is by checking with a ruler and finding that the two lines are, in fact, the same length. Indeed, it is difficult to see how the claim could otherwise be supported. Perhaps all Churchland wants to do is point out that if Fodor is right, it is *possible* our experience is always misleading. If so, his claim is true but uninteresting, unless Churchland gives us some reason to believe our experience *may well be* always misleading. It is possible that we are actually pink rats dreaming we are reading, but unless someone gives us some reason to believe it, the possibility is not worth worrying about as there are an infinite number of things that are logically possible – for example, it is also possible that we are never wrong in our central beliefs.

Although Churchland's second objection to Fodor fails, discussing it allows us to return to the central point of discussing the theory-ladenness of experience. The Basic Observational Fragment may be reliable, but it is also possible that it is deeply mistaken about the world. Thus, it does not constitute an infallible tribunal of appeal in scientific disputes. However, it is reasonable to put the onus on a theorist who disagrees with a part of the Basic Observational Fragment. The mechanisms which yield the Basic Observational Fragment are the products of millions of years of evolution across a wide range of environments. This is a good reason for thinking that the way the world looks is the way it is, or at least that our perceptual world is systematically related to the actual characteristics of the real world. For example, there is good reason to believe that all red objects look alike either because of a real colour property they have in common, or because of some other common property.

Conclusion

So far, we have been given no strong reasons for thinking that our experiences are ever theory-laden, and Fodor has given us a good reason for holding the opposite view. Further, the examples which have been used to support theory-ladenness involve peculiar conditions, so they cannot be used to show that all experiences are theory-laden. Finally, even if we were to accept theory-ladenness in the case of these examples, the evidence could not be used to show that such experiences are permeable by *any* theory, as the experiences can only be changed in limited ways. The upshot of all this is that the purported theory-ladenness of experience poses no serious problems for the objective testing of theories through experience. Even if limited theory-ladenness were accepted, this would only mean we would have to be cautious about which theories could be tested by using particular experiences.

However, I should be careful not to go too far. First, experimental evidence may be discovered by psychologists which provides more powerful arguments for the theory-ladenness of experience. Fodor's argument relies on empirical claims and is subject to empirical refutation. In the past, philosophers have relied too much on a priori reasoning to settle issues which properly belong in the domain of empirical disciplines. A philosopher intending to deal with the problem more thoroughly should pay close attention to experimental material. Second, to say that experience is not theory-laden is not to say that experience is never misleading. As I pointed out above, there are cases in which certain experiences are misleading. However, we know this by using other experiences, for example, the experience of running our hand down an apparently bent stick in water or of pulling it out of the water and looking at it.[7]

2 The influence of theory on what one notices

Observation is always directed by theory

The second claim is that observation is always a theory guided process – that is, it is always the case that theories direct our observations, tell us which observations are significant, and indicate how they are significant. This claim is defended by Popper (Popper, 1972: 341 ff.; 1980: 106–7). Popper argues that science is not merely a random gathering of observations, but a process in which one sets out to find data to confirm or disconfirm theories which are in the form of expectations. Scientific procedure is not like dragging a bucket through the water to see what one can pick up, but rather like scanning for something in particular with a searchlight. Someone who decides to observe will not know what to observe unless he or she has some hypothesis to test. She or he will have to use that hypothesis to pick out what to observe.

Popper intends his argument to have both a descriptive and a normative aspect. First, it is impossible for someone to observe something without some theory or theories guiding the observation process. Second, in any case, random observations would be useless for discovering or testing a hypothesis. A random search around my room might come up with observations about the colour of the third brick up on the wall, the distance my cup is from me, the fact that there is a book by Feyerabend on the shelf, the burn mark on the carpet, etc. Even if these observations were totally non-theoretical (which they are not), they would be about a cluster of things which have nothing in common, or at least nothing interesting in common, and so would not contribute to the testing of any useful hypothesis.

Popper does not intend his argument to undermine science. Yet if he is right, he may be thought to show that scientists are biased in a way which undermines objectivity because what he says may be thought to imply that we only notice things which we expect, or, more plausibly, to imply that we can only discover things which either fit or conflict with our expectations. This would seem to mean that we may miss important items which neither negate nor fit our expectations.

Critical discussion

Popper argues that saying our expectations direct our attention is not the same as saying what we attend to turns out as we expect. Indeed, the fact that we are often surprised might be taken to be evidence for the view that our hidden expectations are often frustrated by our observations. Further, Popper claims, that we may be missing some patterns in the world merely shows the search for knowledge is an epistemologically risky business; it does not show that we lack some perspective which is proper to the search for knowledge. Our search for knowledge in an infinite universe is necessarily limited but, provided we are sensitive to refuting evidence, we are being objective.

Popper is correct in saying that if our expectations direct our observations, this does not pose a problem for objectively testing theories. However, if Popper were found to be right in saying our expectations direct our observations, our search for knowledge would be very restricted and focused. We could only test theories. We would not be able to notice and investigate interesting phenomena which our senses happen to bring to our attention and which have little or nothing to do with theories which we are testing. But Popper is wrong when he says our expectations *always* direct our observations and that these expectations might be (plausibly?) put in the form of hypotheses. We are sometimes startled or intrigued by something we see, but this does not mean that we are startled or intrigued because we hold specific hypotheses. To say that we have hypotheses in such circumstances is to impute to us something far more sophisticated than the evidence warrants. We notice all kinds of unusual things – bright colours, bright lights, loud noises, etc. – which is not to say that we notice everything that is unusual. Further the history of science is full of examples of experiments that produced results which had nothing to do with the hypothesis that was being tested – experimental results which led people to discover things that the original experiments were not designed to test. People can thus be led by experimental evidence to discover things which neither fit their expectations nor refute them.

Consider the process that led to the discovery of X-rays, for example. Röntgen turned on a vacuum tube designed to produce cathode rays. To his surprise, something glowed some distance away. He thought that what he had seen was a reflection in a mirror. He turned on the tube again. This time he noticed not only the glow, but also a faint cloud moving in unison with a fluctuating discharge produced by the coil in the tube. When he struck a match, he realized the glow was produced by a screen coated with barium platinocyanide on a nearby table. Not only that, but the screen glowed even when the coated side of the screen was facing away from the tube. He knew from past experience that cathode rays, which would cause the facing side of such screens to glow, were unlikely to have bridged the gap between the tube and the bench. He took the screen and placed it at various distances beyond the tube. The screen continued to glow. Having found that whatever was coming from the vacuum tube seemed to penetrate air to a greater distance than cathode rays and apparently could penetrate the screen, he reasoned that they might also penetrate other things. At this point he recalled that, according to some recent theories, light rays may exist which could go through solid materials. He placed various kinds of obstructions in front of the vacuum tube, including a book and pieces of wood and metal, and observed that the screen continued to glow. The only material that obstructed whatever was emanating from the vacuum tube was a sheet of lead.

Röntgen then held a small disc of lead in front of the tube. To his amazement he saw the outline of the bones in his thumb and forefinger on the screen as darker shadows in the glow. This was quite unexpected and had nothing to do with what he was testing, that is whether the rays coming from the tube would penetrate lead. He later carried out a whole series of experiments directed by the problem of whether the phenomenon he was dealing with was produced by known causal agents. These experiments led him to realize that he must be dealing with a new kind of influence ('Agens') he called X-rays. He was not initially testing any hypothesis which had to do with the screen glowing. He just happened to look in that direction and observe an unusual phenomenon. Neither was he later testing the hypothesis that the bones in his hand would show up as dark shadows on the screen.[8]

Popper is right in stressing that we would not notice some among the myriad of unusual things in our environment unless some mechanism were there to direct our attention to them. (Which is not to say that the mechanisms expect them to happen, any more than a thermostat attached to a fire alarm expects to receive a particular level of heat, or heat *per se*.) However, the mechanisms probably have nothing to do with theory. For example, it need not be the case that we have worked out that creatures which produce loud noises are likely to be threatening to us, and so have primed ourselves to pay attention to loud noises. Simple mechanisms may well be doing the work – mechanisms that function to bring to our attention certain sorts of things which they detect because raising our awareness of them aids our survival. The functioning of such mechanisms could be said to be driven by theory only if one uses the term 'theory' in a very loose sense. Consider a further two points: first, unsophisticated animals which are our close biological relatives share the same propensities we have to notice unusually loud noises and bright lights; and second, we find it difficult initially to overlook unusually loud noises and bright lights even when we know they are not produced by something important to us. These facts suggest that the influence of unsophisticated mechanisms produces both our patterns of concentration in such cases and our ability to adjust our concentration when we get used to such noises. Both our ability to ignore certain things, and the fact that we seem to be forced to pay attention to them are likely to be due to mechanisms which have little to do with theory.

Some may claim my argument is misleading. Three objections could be put to it. First, it may be said the fact that we notice certain unusual things but not others shows we are primed to notice those things by theory, even though we may not expect them at all. Röntgen thought various kinds of glowing things were significant, even if he was initially looking for them in other places. He also knew of a theory which predicted the existence of a kind of light which could pass through opaque solid objects. Second, while it is true that an experimenter may constantly change both his or her hypotheses and focus of interest, it could be said that at each stage in the series of experiments he or she is testing a specific conjecture. The experimenter is thus not led by the experiment but by theory to do particular further things. Theory always precedes experiment. Third, it may be urged that we must connect our observations of unusual things with some explanatory account if they are to have any significance, and that account cannot itself come from observation.

To deal with these objections, I shall discuss the work of Ian Hacking (1983). Hacking has cogently argued that a number of scientific experimenters have been led to investigate unusual phenomena, without having theories in the sense of specific hypotheses which make predictions, and have made important discoveries as a result. Grimaldi and Hooke decided to look carefully at the shadows of opaque bodies, having heard of the surprising fact that there is some illumination in the shadow of such bodies. They found regularly spaced bands at the edge of the shadow, an important observation that preceded by more than a century the detailed development of the theory which would explain diffraction – as the phenomenon they had discovered came to be called. Diffraction posed a problem for theorizers rather than being the result of a theory. That is, Grimaldi and Hooke had no precise theory in this case, merely the vague one that unusual phenomena to do with light might be used to show something interesting about it. Further, there is no good evidence that they were primed by theory to notice what they found.

Hacking points out that the claim that theory must precede observation in science is misleadingly ambiguous. The key ambiguity is between two claims: you must have some ideas about nature and what you are observing to make useful observations, and you must have a fairly precise conjecture about the phenomena under scrutiny to make useful observations.[9] The first claim is clearly true. Grimaldi had some vague ideas about what light usually did and what might be worth observing, but he was not testing a specific theory of light or a specific conjecture about what light would do. He was merely looking closely at an odd phenomenon. He could, of course, have noticed many different things when he looked into the shadow of opaque bodies. The fact that he noticed diffraction bands, however, does not show he was looking for them in the sense that he had a belief they would be there (or even a belief they would not be there). He may well have been biologically primed to tend to select out certain sorts of things, or perhaps the conjunction of biology and early training in concentrating on certain sorts of features caused him to notice diffraction bands. His own account of the matter describes the process as not being led by a specific conjecture, so the evidence is against theory playing a key role. All too often reconstructions of historical episodes in science import background assumptions which a particular scientist may well never have held.

Hacking uses many further examples to show it is frequently the case in science that significant observations and experiments have been carried out by people who only had vague ideas about what they were doing, and who were certainly not testing specific conjectures about phenomena. Many of the useful observations about light, for example, resulted from people shining beams of light through objects at various angles to see what would happen. Observations in science have frequently not been directed by precise conjectures, but have set problems which can only be solved by precise conjectures.

This means, of course, that ultimately precise conjectures must be used, and precise connections must be made, if important scientific work is to be done with observations. Hacking's account, however, shows this only need occur in the later stages of research in an area. One might be inclined to say on the basis of this that the Popperian claim that important scientific research is driven by conjectures is essentially correct. However, Hacking rightly thinks that good research is much more driven by observation, particularly in its experimental form, than even a modified Popperian account would allow. Conjectures become more precise and they are driven to develop in a particular direction in a process in which vague ideas guide, but are also themselves guided and made more precise by observations. Interesting chance observations that neither refute nor verify conjectures change the vague direction of a research project or cause it to become more precise.

When discussing the Popperian view, it is easy to confuse a possible justification for doing something with how one came to do it. It is also easy to slip into assuming that someone must have had a particular justification for doing something. To say a particular sort of theory would justify one in doing certain things is not to say that, in fact, one did those things because one believed the theory; nor is it to say it is the only way one could justify doing those things. As Hacking points out, one can easily impute particular beliefs to people by assuming that everything they do must be the result of their holding theories. For example, one can think the reason why someone uses a microscope, and is justified in using it, is that he or she has a theory of optics. But in fact the individual may use it without ever having thought there was a need to justify its use. Further, if he or she did think its use had to be justified, he or she may have done so without reference to anything like a theory of light or a theory of optics – for example, by extrapolating from the fact that lenses of increasing magnification sharpen details we can see with the naked eye. (Hacking shows that plausible justifications for the use of the microscope existed long before optical theories could justify its use.)

Conclusion

Popper correctly argues for two important points. First, contrary to a naive version of theory-ladenness, we do not always perceive what we expect; and second, the fact that our attention is directed to specific things by theories does not mean we are not being objective. As he notes, everyday examples provide evidence that what we perceive is not merely the result of the functioning of our own mental processes and that it is possible to test our beliefs by using our experience. There may be important patterns which we may never discover because of the way our attention is directed, but this does not mean we are not testing theories objectively.

Despite Popper's insights, his view that all reaction patterns can be illuminatingly treated as conjectures is implausible, and so is the view that what one observes must either fit or clash with one's theories. One does not need conjectures in any interesting sense to be startled by something or to have one's attention drawn to it. Further, any number of conjectures could license a particular reaction pattern. In addition, the view that one must produce precise and very general conjectures to make important observations is wrong. Important observations have been made on the basis of vague ideas or as a result of trying out procedures to see what would happen.

3 All descriptions of observations are theory-laden

The third claim is that all statements about what we observe are theoretical. If the claim is correct, it may be thought to imply that we cannot test scientific theories objectively. After all, to test theories we compare descriptions of what we observe with what is predicted by those theories, so if the descriptions are mere conjectures they cannot provide objective grounds for accepting or rejecting theories.

The third claim has been defended by a number of philosophers, particularly Feyerabend (Popper, 1980; Feyerabend, 1981a: 17–43). Feyerabend holds that to test a theory we do not compare that theory with experience. Instead, we determine what would be a correct description of what is being experienced and then assess the logical relation between that description and the theory. But the description cannot be derived from experience. It is a conjecture about what is being experienced. For example, to test the hypothesis that all swans are white, we do not simply observe Australian swans (which are black) and concentrate on how they look. To produce something which is inconsistent with our hypothesis, we must formulate a statement that what we are observing is a non-white swan. But the statement that we are experiencing a non-white swan cannot be derived from experience. It is a conjecture that the cause of our experience is a swan of a particular colour rather than a powerful drug or a blow to the head.

Feyerabend's argument for the thesis that no statement about what we are observing can be derived from experience is as follows. How something looks in experience does not in any way determine the meaning of terms which correctly describe it. If experience does not determine the meaning of the terms which describe what is being experienced, there is no necessary connection between the experience of something and a true description of what is being experienced. Thus, no statement about what we are observing logically follows from how a thing looks in experience.

Feyerabend's argument takes this rather odd form because it is intended to be a critique of some logical positivists. They argue that we can be sure that some of our scientific statements are right because the meaning of descriptive terms in science is determined by experience. Thus, in their view, when we have experiences of black swan-like patches of colour which are accompanied by certain sounds and by all the other aspects of typical swans, we can be sure we are experiencing a black swan. Feyerabend maintains these positivists are wrong. Although certain terms such as 'swan' seem to be directly and obviously connected to certain experiences, the meaning of such terms is not necessarily connected to such experiences. The meaning of terms is, in fact, necessarily connected only to the items described by such terms. The term 'swan' may seem necessarily connected to a swan-like patch of colour, that is, a patch of colour which has an elegant shape of a particular kind, is black (if it is Australian), etc. However, a picture of a swan, or a mental image of a swan experienced in a hallucination, would be a swan-like patch of colour, but not a swan. Further, real swans which are seen from a peculiar angle, which have various diseases, or which have been in accidents, will not resemble swan-like patches of colour at all. 'Swan' refers to something which is not necessarily connected with any particular experience or cluster of experiences. It is about a type of bird. No experience or series of experiences will necessarily be of a bird, and how an experience should be correctly described cannot be determined from experience. Therefore, no scientific theory can be tested by appeal to experience as such.

According to Feyerabend, to assume that our descriptive terms are actually conceptually connected to experiences is like assuming that the term 'electricity' refers to the movement of pointers in old-style voltmeters – it is to confuse the particular instrument readings we typically use to detect things with the things themselves. Items in the world can be detected in any number of ways. Swans, for example, could be detected by various mechanical detectors which then produce numerical readouts about them. A congenitally blind person who has never touched a swan or had colour sensations, and who reads such readouts in braille, would be able to learn a great deal about swans – that they have a certain shape, a certain density, and so on.[10]

If Feyerabend is right, it would seem that so-called 'scientific knowledge' is dubious. Scientific hypotheses are tested against statements which are themselves merely guesses about how experience should be interpreted. If there is no necessary connection between having certain experiences and the real existence of certain states of affairs, it seems that we could just as justifiably guess the opposite to what we normally think in the presence of certain experiences. For example, it seems that after the experience of seeing what we are inclined to think is a swan, we would be perfectly justified in guessing we are observing a witch.

Critical discussion

At first sight, Feyerabend's argument seems to lead to sceptical conclusions about science. However, in so far as it is correct, it does not. While it is true that descriptions of many things we experience cannot be read off from the things themselves merely by looking, and it is also true that it is always possible we are mistaken in our descriptions, it would be wrong to suggest that all descriptions must, therefore, be theoretical in the sense that they are dubious.

First, the mere possibility we are wrong does not provide us with a reason to believe that possibility is worth worrying about, as I pointed out earlier. To say that statements about our observations are theoretical suggests they are only as certain as any piece of wild speculation and thus cannot be used to test speculative claims. However, it does not follow from the fact that we *may* be wrong that it is quite likely that we *are* wrong.

Second, contrary to the impression we might get from Feyerabend, merely looking at things is often not the way we discover the nature of things in science. We often do not use looking to identify things until either we: (a) have experimented with those kinds of things for a while and found our hypotheses to be reliable; or (b) have been trained to identify those kinds of things by a community in which others have investigated them and have set up training procedures. We realize this when we come across things which barely resemble things we have seen before. We produce conjectures about what they are on the basis of what we know about things we take to be similar. We then test these conjectures until we find some that prove to be useful in predicting what will happen. In time, these hypotheses are rightly taken to be so reliable that they are taught to children as the obvious truth, and may then seem to spring from the things themselves. Yet they have been produced through a long process of trial and error. It is not plausible to call them conjectures at this stage, though of course they *may* be wrong.

Experimentation does not usually involve just looking. It involves experimental manipulation on the basis of conjectures which are constantly modified. Predictively successful conjectures are finally incorporated into the beliefs we are inclined to take for granted. Feyerabend is right to say there is *no necessary connection* between our being inclined to think that a particular thing fits a description and the description being correct, but *it is not true* that there is no significant connection or that the connection is a mere matter of convention. Many of our inclinations are put into place through a process which is based on a rational procedure for testing hypotheses, a procedure which, when followed, gives us good grounds for accepting hypotheses. This provides us with grounds for believing the implications of our everyday linguistic inclinations until we have good reason for believing we are wrong.[11]

An objection to my second argument may be that it relies on implausible speculation about how our inclinations come about rather than a well-argued case, and that we cannot tell which of our inclinations are solidly grounded and which are the result of traditional prejudices. After all, anthropological studies seem to indicate that some peoples give bizarre descriptions of some ordinary objects. Such peoples think that other individuals are witches or that dreams are correct perceptions of objects. Since these peoples have survived for many generations, it is possible for communities to be riddled with false beliefs about everyday objects (or with false beliefs about what count as perceptible everyday objects). Everyday descriptions are thus not a reliable testing ground for theories.

I have two replies to this objection. First, it is difficult to see how we could survive for long unless many of the propositions we are inclined to believe about everyday objects of our perception are (a) true, or at least partly true; and (b) training procedures for inculcating these beliefs into the young tend to transfer true or partly true beliefs to them.

Second, even people with bizarre beliefs about everyday objects must have, as part of the content of many such beliefs, views about how those objects typically look and affect them – otherwise they would not be able to use such beliefs to deal with the world they experience. One can have a number of idle beliefs – that is, one can have some beliefs which do not have any consequences for how one should act in relation to items one experiences. But many of one's beliefs cannot be idle if one is to survive. The consequences of beliefs about many objects must thus be tied into observations which can be made in an ordinary way. Consider a gatherer from a tribe who believes that every lizard is a close relative of particular humans and came into existence in the dream-time. If he or she is to find them, cook them, etc., it is likely the gatherer will also believe that, by and large, they live and behave in the way we know them to behave. The tribal food gatherer may use a descriptive vocabulary which has many odd ontological presuppositions but that vocabulary must largely correlate with the things we would experience in the same environment if we had to survive using the same sorts of tools.

My second reply can be tied to Fodor's modularity theory. A large part of a people's descriptions, particularly the part which deals with items they experience, must have implications about the way things will typically look when they are experiencing them. A claim that we are now perceiving a witch will normally be tied to typical visual information provided by the visual processing module. Typical witches must look like the items we call humans, for instance, if the various strategies which have been used to control them are to be effective strategies of control. I do not mean by this only that linguistic descriptions used to describe humans must be implied by descriptions of witches, but also that witches must literally look like humans if the information provided by the visual processing module is to be useful for the group's survival.

The view that a linguistic statement can imply some non-linguistic thing about the way things will typically look will appear somewhat startling to those who think of all implication in terms of the logical relations between statements. But if people are to survive, they must be able to use visual information in a way that systematically connects it to linguistic statements. In any case, Nerlich has recently argued that the idea that visual information is to some degree statement-like is not as odd as it sounds. Consider the case of someone pointing to an identity kit picture in a police station and saying, 'He looked like that.' The witness is incorporating part of the visual appearance of a drawing into a statement. The policewoman listening to him would find a detailed linguistic description more confusing than useful, but she is able to use the statement to find the suspect. She can glance at the drawing, look at a man, and conclude: if the witness is trustworthy, then that's him or someone who looks just like him. Her inference uses various things, including the way the drawing looks. As she stares at the suspect, she might reasonably say to herself, 'The man at the station implied that the suspect looked like him.' If her face recognition mechanism is working correctly, etc., she will be right (Nerlich, 1992: 29–31).[12]

I should note here that, in any case, people living in other cultures seem to use many terms for everyday items which mean similar things to terms we use and are not tied, in any necessary way, to presuppositions remote from our own. As one would expect from the Fodorian account, many of these terms seem not to be deeply theory penetrated. We can be understood and survive in cultures remote from our own by learning a minimal vocabulary through ostension and through watching people's gestures. According to accounts of meaning in which the meaning of terms is necessarily and importantly tied to any remote belief, this is difficult to explain.

Theory-laden descriptions, incommensurability and objectivity

I have argued that the third claim is only partly right, as we can test theories objectively. However, even if we were to accept that every item experienced must be described in a language which is totally dependent on a problematic theory, it would still be possible to test theories objectively. I shall show this in the following text.

If we accept that all descriptions are theoretical, the first possibility which arises is that two rival theorists could disagree on some of their relevant descriptions but agree on others. But this situation would pose no particular problems for testing the theories in question, as they can be compared in the area in which they agree. Consider the following case which is adapted from a historical instance. P believes that burning is the removal of a substance, phlogiston, from a body. Q believes that burning is the addition of a substance, oxygen, to a body. P will describe burning as dephlogistication, whereas Q will describe it as combustion. Let us assume that although both call combustion 'burning', as both have different theories about the fundamental nature of burning, they must mean different things by 'burning'. (This is an implausible assumption, but I will criticize the strongest claims Feyerabend says he can justify.) Both theorists, however, agree on the meaning of the term 'weight' and on how to measure the property described. This means that P should predict that the weight of a substance decreases after what he calls burning, and Q should predict that it increases after what she calls burning. If one proceeds to test the two hypotheses, one finds that the weight of substances does increase after burning. This means the experimental evidence will produce evidence against P's theory and in favour of Q's theory.[13]

A second possibility, which prima facie poses more difficulties, is that two theorists disagree in *all* their relevant descriptions. At one stage, Feyerabend called theories whose relevant descriptions are all incompatible 'incommensurable theories', because there is no obvious external standard against which the correctness of the descriptions can be measured. He defined incommensurable theories as pairs of theories in which: (a) not a single descriptive term of either theory can be adequately defined by means of the descriptive terms of the other; and (b) the use of the concepts of either one of the theories makes the concepts of the other inapplicable. An implicit third part of the definition is that such theories cannot be rationally compared by using a third neutral theory, because all the relevant evidence has to be described in terms used by each of the theories. I will call such theories 'conceptually incommensurable' because the key feature of them is that they contain no terms which are inter-translatable. In Chapter 5, I shall discuss Feyerabend's claim that there are theories which are incommensurable in other ways.

Mary Hesse (1974), using a suggestion put by Feyerabend, argues that such theories could be rationally compared. Suppose theory X produces a prediction about an item which, when it is tested, turns out to be false even when things are described in X's terms. Suppose, in addition, that theory Y turns out successfully to have predicted that item when it is described in Y's terms. In such a case, it will be rational (all other things being equal) to prefer X to Y.

Consider Hesse's example. The Greek scientists Anaximenes and Aristotle devise an experiment to decide between their theories of free fall. Anaximenes holds that the universe is such that there is an absolute up and down in empty space. In his view, the Earth is a flattish disc suspended in empty space and objects tend to fall in a line perpendicular to and through this disc. (What keeps objects from going through the Earth is the strength of the materials of which the Earth is made. What keeps the Earth in place is that it is a flattish disc held up by a strong wind.) Aristotle holds that the Earth is a sphere situated in a universe organized in a series of concentric shells whose radii, directed towards the centre, determine the direction of fall.[14]

Assume the word 'fall' carries a different theory in each case. Suppose also that every other relevant word carries a different meaning for each scientist because their theory of the nature of the earth is different – for example 'Greece' means something different for each of them. Nevertheless, both will be able to agree on a crucial experiment because both will be able to agree that on the other side of the world from the side on which Greece is situated certain things will happen. ('Other side' and so on are, of course, understood by each in his own way.) They fly to the other side of the Earth and position themselves standing with the soles of their feet pointing towards it. They then drop a round stone from a small height (or, as Anaximines would say, 'let go of a round stone from a short distance below the Earth'). Anaximines predicts that the stone will fall. Aristotle also predicts that the stone will fall. But since they each mean something different by 'fall', what they expect to happen is different. The experiment is carried out. Anaximenes, using the vocabulary defined by his theory, mutters that the stone rises and admits his theory has problems. Aristotle is exhilarated to discover that, using the vocabulary defined by his theory, the stone falls – which is exactly what his theory predicts. All other things being equal, Aristotle's theory is preferable. The reason is that when the result of the experiment is described in its terms, it is confirmed, whereas when the result of the experiment is described in the terms of Anaximenes's theory, that theory fails to predict what happens.

Several objections could be put to the above arguments. First, the testing of theories in these cases is not properly objective. In both sorts of cases we are testing theories against events described by descriptions which may well be wrong – that is, whether theories meet or fail to meet these standards may well tell us nothing about the nature of the world. For instance, experimental results interpreted to indicate an increase in weight may well not be due to weight at all. If this were true, the phlogiston theorist might be inconsistent but this would not show anything about which explanation of burning is correct. Second, Hesse's method for comparing conceptually incommensurable theories relies on the assumption that two such theories are referring to the same items in the same world. However, this assumption is not plausible when *all* the items relevant to testing two theories are described by each conceptually incommensurable theory. The descriptions in one theory have no relevance to the descriptions in the other theory.

The first objection is mistaken. Theories which successfully predict a range of surprising facts, even if they predict those facts in the descriptive terms of some dubitable theory, are very likely to be true. The likelihood that such theories are false is very low because it would be a cosmic coincidence that theories which predict a range of facts they were not concocted to explain did not describe the world in a roughly correct way. Thus, their predictive success is good evidence that they are approximately true, and that the way in which they describe the world is roughly right. Take an example to illustrate this argument. Suppose that theorist Q's theory of burning predicts that after being burnt in a gas he calls 'oxygen', a whole range of substances will make machines which are supposed to measure weight show an increased reading. Suppose, further, that the fact that these substances do this to supposed weighing machines was not known to Q. It is merely an unexpected consequence of that theory that the weighing machines should behave as they do behave. If Q's theory turns out to be right, this is good evidence for the truth of Q's theory, and doubts about whether the weighing machines really measure weight become unreasonable. (The type of argument I use here, inference to the best explanation, is further discussed in Chapters 2 and 7.)

The second objection assumes that reference is totally fixed by the descriptive language of a theory. But this is implausible. Children learn to refer to many things because they have a natural tendency to concentrate on certain features of the world when we gesture to them (for example, by pointing). Everything may have an infinite number of features, but we are naturally primed to concentrate on some in certain contexts. If this were not true, it would not be possible for us to learn a language. This ability to fix the reference of some terms non-linguistically does not disappear when we become adults. If you use the word 'dog' while staring at cats, pointing to them, manipulating them, etc., it is plausible for us to believe that you use the word 'dog' to refer to cats (or at least to refer to something important to do with cats). After all, we are biologically similar to you, so the things we think we would be referring to, if we were acting like you, are probably the things to which you are referring. Further, the theoretical terms of a language have their reference partly fixed through being linked with the things we observe and refer to in everyday contexts (for example, fixed as things which are the causes of aspects of those things).[15]

In his later work, Feyerabend has put forward a version of this second objection where he argues that conceptually incommensurable theories must be referring to items in different worlds. He also attempts to distinguish a class of what might be called *strongly* incommensurable theories, theories in which standards of appraisal differ radically from one theory to the other and, thus, cannot be compared by an appeal to objective standards. His claims will be rebutted in Chapter 5.

Conclusion

In so far as Feyerabend's arguments have any force, they do not raise any problems for the objective testing of scientific theories. If the claim that descriptions are never necessarily connected to experiences is true, our strong inclination to describe everyday things in particular ways is typically well-grounded because it is emplaced as through the application of rational test procedures. We thus have some assurance that the statements produced are true or have a substantial truth content. As a result, we can use such statements to test theories. Those tests are not infallible, but the onus is on the sceptic to show they are problematic. In any case, we can assume statements are deeply theory-penetrated but still produce objective tests for theories.

Readers should not assume, however, that I have shown objective testing of scientific theories to be possible. There remain a number of important arguments put by Feyerabend and others against objective testing which I shall discuss in later chapters.

Further reading

Two very clear discussions of theory and observation are Hunt, 1994 and Campbell, 1988. A classic defence of a strong version of theory-ladenness is Hanson, 1958: 4–30. Churchland, 1979 is a difficult but rigorous defence of theory-ladenness. A witty though jargon-ridden critique is Fodor, 1984. Churchland, 1988 is an accessible reply to Fodor; Fodor replies in Fodor, 1988. Gilman (1991) defends Fodor by appealing to neurophysiological and psychological evidence. Karl Popper puts his view simply in Popper, 1972: 341ff. Ian Hacking presents a clear critique of Popper's view in Hacking, 1983: 149ff. Feyerabend, 1981a: 17–43 puts Feyerabend's key arguments. They are very difficult and not recommended to students. A more sympathetic account of his central claims than I give here was presented in a previous text, see Couvalis, 1989: 1–38. For an important cautionary tale about psychological and neurophysiological material, see Long, 1988. The psychological literature on illusions is enormous and largely inaccessible to lay persons.

Notes

1 Some supposed evidence for this claim is very clearly discussed in Dergowski, 1973. However, Jones and Hagen (1980) point out that on the best evidence available, the claim is highly suspect.

2 I have changed the story presented by Fodor (1984; 1985) to make it more plausible, as empirical evidence shows that a proneness to illusion is not simply hard-wired. However, the neurophysiological and psychological evidence fits well with the view that changes in our experience are not produced by changing our theories (Gilman, 1991).

3 Great care should be used in interpreting such evidence. For a salutary cautionary tale, see Long (1988).

4 The term 'theory' is used in a variety of different ways. I have avoided providing a definition of it as I think defining such terms leads to trivial semantic debates. It is clear enough what it means when it is used by Fodor.

5 Fodor, 1983: 94 ff. I am indebted to Campbell (1988).

6 Gilman (1991) points out that the evidence Churchland cites is problematic and that the neurophysiological evidence goes against Churchland's claims.

7 I should point out that Fodor and others have in any case plausibly argued that whatever the truth is about most experiences, we can objectively test theories without relying on experience except in limited ways, and perhaps without relying on it at all (Shapere, 1982; Fodor, 1991).

8 Nitske, 1971: 86–98. Quinn places emphasis on the fact, not noted by Nitske, that Röntgen was surprised by the fact that the glow also occurred on the side of the screen facing away from the tube (Quinn, 1995: 139).

9 Hacking produces a convincing case that Popper and others commit themselves to the second claim (Hacking, 1983: 155 ff.).

10 Some philosophers would object to Feyerabend's argument because they believe it assumes the existence of experiences as separate entities. By their account, what has gone wrong is that we have improperly assumed the existence of a separate class of things which form a kind of obscuring veil between us and the world. Feyerabend agrees with this objection. He casts his arguments in terms of experiences only because he is opposing people who believe in such items. His main argument can be put differently: when one observes things in the world acting in some manner, one may be inclined to think that a particular description fits those items. However, one's inclination, no matter how strong, is not evidence that those items are as described. There is no necessary connection between being inclined to describe things in certain ways and those things being as one describes them.

11 My view has much in common with the method of grounding epistemology developed in Goldman, 1986. Popper and Feyerabend have developed accounts which are like mine in certain respects. However, for them, the use of inclinations to develop tests for theories is ultimately a matter of conventions that either: (a) have no particular grounding but guarantee falsifiability (Popper, 1980; 1972); or (b) provide a pragmatically useful test procedure (Feyerabend, 1981a).

12 Obviously, 'looks like' is not logically transitive, but when it is used in conjunction with psychological mechanisms which are shared by the people involved, this is unimportant.

13 Readers who know the history of the discovery of oxygen will know my account to be oversimplified. The increase in weight which occurs after burning was discovered by phlogistonists and used by Lavoisier to develop the oxygen theory. It is not a good test case for the oxygen theory because that theory had been specifically developed to explain it. However, such historical details are irrelevant to the claim that even if all descriptions are

theory-penetrated, this does not rule out finding some test which will bear out the predictions of one theory and refute the other.

14 Hesse's interpretation of the theories of Anaximenes and Aristotle is dubious. This does not matter here.

15 Quine has pointed out that there is a sense in which my behaviour is logically compatible with *any* hypothesis about the meaning of a term, but the same is, of course, true of any words I use. In any case, that my behaviour is logically compatible with some hypothesis does not mean it is the best hypothesis about my behaviour. Your behaviour in the 'dog/cat' example is logically compatible with the view that the term 'dog' is about something behind you which you have never seen; but it is not plausible to interpret the term to be about that thing in the absence of other evidence.

2

Induction and Probability

Many scientific theories contain generalizations, that is, statements which say that all items of a certain type have certain properties. Newton's theory of mechanics contains laws which are generalizations. An example is his first law, which says that all objects which are not acted upon by a force will continue forever in a state of rest or uniform straight-line motion. Pasteur's germ theory contains generalizations, such as all infectious diseases are caused by micro-organisms. Generalizations like these play an essential part in science, which seeks to explain and predict the behaviour of things by using them. The behaviour of satellites in Earth orbits is in part explained and predicted by Newton's first law. The reduction in the incidence of infectious diseases which occurs when doctors wash their hands in chemicals that kill micro-organisms is in part explained by Pasteur's generalization.

The generalizations which have come to be widely accepted by scientists deal with both the past and the future, and go way beyond what has been observed. Some of them deal with the behaviour of entities which are unobservable to the naked eye, such as viruses and atoms. Yet scientists and the general public have a great deal of confidence in them. It is commonly assumed that these generalizations have been justified by using some reliable procedure. In modern times it has been widely believed that this procedure is one which allows us to justify them on the basis of true statements about how things look in experience. Philosophers have tried to discover the nature of this procedure because they have thought that it can be used to expand our knowledge enormously.

Statements are justified if they have been inferred from other true statements by a procedure which ensures that they are at least likely to be approximately true. The most reliable procedure known for justifying statements on the basis of other known statements is to reason *deductively.* In a deductive inference, we can infer a statement Q with complete confidence from a statement (or statements) P because Q must be true if P is true. In such a case, Q is said to *follow* from P and the inference *P, therefore Q,* is said to be *valid*. (Note that 'deductive', 'follow' and 'valid' do not mean in logic what they mean in ordinary language.) For example, if it is true that all dogs are mammals and Regina is a dog, it must be true that Regina is a mammal. It follows that Regina is a mammal and the inference is valid. In a deductive inference, if we know that a statement is true, any statement which we can validly infer from it cannot fail to be true.

It might be thought that if deductive reasoning is the most reliable procedure known for justifying statements on the basis of other known statements, scientists must use it to justify generalizations. However, while deductive reasoning can justify some statements by clarifying what is implied by complicated statements we already know, it cannot justify statements which go beyond our informational base. From the knowledge that all bodies at rest will remain at rest unless acted upon by a force (which is a part of Newton's first law) and the knowledge that the Earth is a body, we can justify through deductive reasoning the statement that if the Earth is at rest, then it will remain in this state unless acted upon by a force. But since we cannot be acquainted with all possible bodies, deductive reasoning will not allow us to justify the first law from any knowledge we might acquire through experience.

This poses a problem. Scientists can apparently justify some generalizations by appealing to experience, and it seems whatever procedure they use has enormous potential. They cannot justify these generalizations by using deductive reasoning. How then are they able to justify them? A very plausible suggestion, put by Newton and many other scientists, is that scientists are able to justify generalizations by using *inductive* reasoning.

Inductive reasoning is a family of procedures by which we infer that some statement S is true from the fact that some other statement (or statements) R is (or are) true. There are three important features of inductive inferences: (a) it is never the case that S deductively follows from R – that is, it is not a necessary truth that if R is true, S is true; (b) S always contains information that R does not contain; and (c) R always seems to provide some support for S. The most basic type of inductive reasoning is simple enumerative induction, in which we infer a statement about the properties a type of thing has from relatively few instances, and from an absence of known counter-instances. In simple enumerative induction, we pay no regard to the type of thing we are dealing with. For example, we might infer that all ravens are black from 500 ravens which are black and from the fact that no non-black raven has been found.

Many scientists and philosophers have argued that inductive reasoning is not only used by scientists to justify theories, but that it is essential to our survival. Unless we know many everyday generalizations – such as bread nourishes or fires burn us – we cannot survive. But it seems we only know them by reasoning inductively. It seems that we only know bread nourishes because it has always nourished people in the past, and this justifies the conclusion that bread always nourishes. It seems we only know fires burn because people who got very close to fires in the past always got burnt and this justifies the conclusion that all fires burn.

In the eighteenth century, Hume highlighted an important puzzle about inductive reasoning. The puzzle is that it seems inductive reasoning cannot justify a conclusion on the basis of true premises. Hume argued in roughly the following way. The premises in inductive reasoning can neither guarantee that a conclusion is true, nor even guarantee that it is probably true. If inductive reasoning cannot guarantee the truth of a conclusion or even its probability, then it seems that it cannot justify a conclusion. By contrast, it is obvious that deductive reasoning can justify a conclusion because in deductive reasoning the conclusion must be true if the premises are true, so the truth of the premises guarantees the truth of the conclusion.

By Hume's account, inductive reasoning can neither guarantee that a conclusion is true, nor even guarantee that it is probably true, because inductive reasoning has two features. The first feature is that it is always possible that the premises are true and the conclusion false. This means that however well supported some generalization appears to be, it could still be wrong. To see that this feature of inductive reasoning can produce real problems for our knowledge, consider the many known examples of conclusions which were apparently justified inductively, but which are false. For instance, until the seventeenth century Australians thought that all humans were black. There are reports of how astonished they were to see white people for the first time. It seems that from the premise that all of the large number of humans they had seen were black, they had inferred that all humans are black. However, the generalization that all humans are black is false.

The second feature is that inductive reasoning cannot guarantee that a conclusion is probably true. We can only guarantee the probability of a conclusion on the basis of premises by using deductive reasoning because only such reasoning can show that it must be true that a conclusion is probable. For example, if we have the information that a box of chalk contains eight white pieces of chalk and two of an unknown colour, then we can know that in one random choice, we are likely to pick a white one. We can know this because it follows from the information we have been given that there is at least a probability of 8/10 that we will pick a white piece if our single choice is random. This means we could justify the conclusion that we will pick a white piece in one random choice, because we know that conclusion is probably true. But when we reason inductively, we do not know what proportion of the total population of a certain type of thing we have examined and neither do we know if the things we have examined are a random or representative sample of that type. It might well be the case that the things we have examined of a particular type are only a small proportion of the total number, and that they are quite unrepresentative.[1] Assume, for example, that I am an aboriginal Australian living in the early seventeenth century. Every human I and my remote ancestors have ever seen was black. I might have reasoned inductively that it is probable that all humans are black. I might even have noted that skin colour does not seem to vary with climate, since the inhabitants of the Australian snow fields are as black as those of hot deserts. Yet the sample of people in the world I and my ancestors have seen is confined to a particular geographical area, and is quite unrepresentative of the peoples of the world, many of whom are non-black.

Hume dealt primarily with simple enumerative induction. However, he thought that it is always true in inductive reasoning that the premises cannot even guarantee the probability of a conclusion. In contrast, he thought that the premises in deductive reasoning can guarantee the truth of a conclusion. By his account, this could pose a problem about our knowledge of the world because there is no way to justify informative generalizations about the world except by induction. Hume's reasoning went something like this. The generalization that fires burn or the generalizations of science are not necessary truths because it is conceivable that such generalizations are false. It is conceivable that fires do not burn or that Newton's first law is false. So, such generalizations can only be justified by appeal to experience. But the only way to justify them by appeal to experience is by induction. However, if induction cannot even guarantee the probability of a conclusion on the basis of true premises, how can it be used to justify such generalizations?

Hume argued that philosophers who think we need to show that a type of reasoning is cogent to legitimately use that type of reasoning are stuck with the problem of showing that induction is cogent. He thought the problem was a serious one for such philosophers because the only available ways of showing that induction is cogent are circular.

To grasp why Hume thought that the only ways to show the cogency of induction presuppose the cogency of induction, consider an example. One supposed justification for induction is that most generalizations defended by induction in the past have turned out to be true, so it is likely that generalizations defended by induction in the future will be true. If this justification is to be adequate, it must be true that the future is likely to be like the past in relevant respects But it seems that we could only know that the future is likely to be like the past in relevant respects by using induction. After all, we have not yet experienced the future. Further, since the generalizations we are concerned with are about both the future and the past, we could not even know from experience that most of the generalizations which were tested in the past are true overall. We could only know that the part of the generalizations which deals with the past is true. But this seems to mean that we could not even know the truth of the premise in the supposed justification without using induction.

Hume's puzzle was not taken to pose a problem by many philosophers in the eighteenth and nineteenth centuries. Newton's mechanics had remarkable predictive power and was not shown to be false. Kant presented an account of how Newton's mechanics could be defended which suggested it consisted of necessary truths, and John Stuart Mill and others presented a much more sophisticated account of how induction might work. This suggested Hume's arguments had only undermined a simplistic variety of inductive reasoning and that scientific generalizations were secure because they were either necessary truths or were established by more elaborate inductive justifications than those discussed by Hume. Hume's puzzle appeared to be of interest only to absurdly sceptical philosophers. But when it became clear that Newton's mechanics is false, Hume's puzzle was taken much more seriously. Newton's mechanics could not be necessarily true, and so Kant's method for justifying it was taken to be obviously wrong. Further, the failure of Newton's mechanics is not at all surprising if Hume's puzzle is thought to raise a serious problem about what justifies us in relying on induction. More elaborate varieties of inductive reasoning obviously do not ensure that our conclusions will be true if our premises are true.

Hume's puzzle has been argued by some philosophers to pose a serious problem for our scientific knowledge. Karl Popper argues that Hume showed induction cannot be used to demonstrate that scientific generalizations are true or likely to be true. Scientific generalizations are guesses which might well be shown to be radically mistaken at any time. We can know that they are true of the past, but we have no way of knowing whether they are true overall or even likely to be true overall. We cannot even know they are likely to be approximately true overall. If Popper is right, it seems that much supposed scientific knowledge is not justified objectively. I will discuss Popper's attempt to deal with Hume's puzzle in the next chapter. In this chapter, I will discuss some other attempts to deal with the puzzle and what implications can be reasonably drawn from the existence of the puzzle. I will examine three attempts to argue that it does not pose a problem:

1 Hume's arationalist response;
2 appealing to a formal account of confirmation; and
3 appealing to an intuitively plausible notion of probability.

I will be arguing that Hume's puzzle does not pose a problem for our scientific knowledge.

1 Hume's arationalist response

Arationalist responses to epistemological puzzles about beliefs, practices, or types of reasoning concede that they cannot be justified by appealing to something more fundamental. But they hold that this does not matter as philosophical objections to them are absurd, and are thus less warranted than those beliefs or practices. Hume's response to the puzzle of induction is sometimes of this kind. He begins by arguing it is impossible to show that induction is cogent except by using induction. He continues by attempting to explain why we might think that induction is cogent in terms of a natural disposition imaginatively to complete temporal sequences of events we have experienced the moment we perceive the first member of the sequence. We form a habit of expecting, and indeed almost imagining, y straight after x because we have invariably experienced y coming straight after x. We thus are deluded into thinking y must follow x, when in fact it need not. However, even though he says we are deluded, Hume later recognizes that it would be impossible for us to survive without the disposition which generates the supposed illusion. He thus seems caught, because he can only explain why it would be impossible for us to survive by assuming that induction is really cogent. He argues that whatever is going on should not be taken too seriously. He praises the vulgar who believe in the efficacy of induction, and attacks philosophers who think that the premises and logical structure of philosophical arguments are more reliable than common sense. To follow philosophical arguments against common sense is obviously a crazy way to a short life.

Hume thus holds it is not induction that is put into doubt by the puzzle but the philosophical argument which leads to the puzzle. Something (perhaps undiscoverable) must be wrong with either the premises or the reasoning which is used to arrive at the view that inductive reasoning might never be able to justify a conclusion.[2] There is an important central thread to his line of thought which is worth teasing out. Whatever conclusion he comes to, he is not going to give up the view that inductive reasoning can justify a conclusion as its obvious practical efficacy makes a belief in the cogency of induction more reasonable than virtually anything else. Implicit in some of his discussion seems to be the idea that he would even accept that some contradictions are true rather than give up his belief in the cogency of induction. After all, accepting some contradictions would have consequences only in areas remote from our everyday lives, so it seems we could live while adhering to them.

You can see why some theologians thought they could use Hume to defend, though not justify, their adherence to deeply held but irrational beliefs. If the cogency of induction cannot be shown to be justified even though we can reasonably believe that induction is cogent, why cannot adherence to a religious doctrine be unjustified but reasonable? An outraged philosopher may say that Hume's response to the puzzle of induction allows theologians to claim their unjustified or irrational beliefs can be held legitimately. Yet though Hume's response is not grounded on anything more fundamental than our deeply held convictions, it is both sensible and does not offer support to irrationalists. Hume is only defending a kind of reasoning which he believes we will *all* recognize to be essential to living any kind of long life. If Hume is right, if we continue to act in our daily lives it will be because we believe induction is cogent. To pretend to doubt that it is cogent while continuing to live our lives would involve us in a pragmatic contradiction in which we continue to act as though it is cogent while verbally claiming that its cogency could reasonably be rejected. This is not the case with theological beliefs; many of us recognize that we could live our lives without them. In any case, Hume is not implying we should accept contradictions. The strongest thing he could plausibly say is, if it came to a choice between accepting some contradictions and rejecting induction; he (and indeed all of us) would and should accept the contradictions.[3] But this is very different from saying that we should accept contradictions in general, or that any bizarre belief is equally as plausible as a belief in the cogency of induction.

What may strike readers as odd about Hume's response is that it relies on a kind of unquestioning adherence to a belief which we cannot seriously doubt because of our natural tendencies. Surely, someone might object, a philosopher should follow through an argument from solidly based premises even if he or she does not like the result; further, if a philosopher is to stop at some principle or premise it should be self-validating – like the statement Descartes claimed to be self-validating, namely that if I am thinking I cannot doubt that I exist. To appeal to psychological tendencies or baseless instincts is to give way to some minimal form of irrationality, even if it is not giving way to bizarre theological assumptions.

This objection assumes that legitimately to use a type of reasoning, we must be able to justify using it through manifestly true statements. But what if there are no such statements available? Hume thought he had discovered that there are no such statements available in the case of induction. As serious inductive scepticism is not a realistic option, he thought he could reasonably argue that if an inductive sceptic continues using induction, he or she is being a hypocrite. But Hume's argument does not stop with this. He goes on to suggest the result produced by the arguments for inductive scepticism can reasonably be turned against the philosophical assumptions and methods which justify it. If an argument leads to a conclusion that goes against claims which seem to everyone more plausible than its premises or its underlying logical principles, then there is something wrong with the argument. We do not need to know what is wrong with it to reject its conclusion.

Consider a parallel case. Some of Zeno's paradoxical arguments seem to show, on the basis of obviously true premises, that motion is impossible. Yet most of the Greeks and their successors rationally concluded, on the basis of experience, that the argument merely poses an intellectually interesting paradox. That is, they concluded that the argument must be faulty even though we do not know what is wrong with it. In concluding this, they decided that the knowledge they gained from experience was more deeply grounded than their intuitions about motion or about logic. In some of his work, Hume endorses this attitude. He argues that it is some philosophical techniques and assumptions that are brought into doubt by puzzles such as the so-called 'problem of induction', not induction itself. Philosophers seem to produce no successful predictions and apparently plausible arguments put by them are constantly being contested by similarly plausible arguments. When they question apparently very plausible scientific theories, one can properly conclude that they are the ones who are very likely to be in the wrong.

In a sense, Hume argues in a question-begging way; but in the absence of indubitably true statements, we must argue in this way. If Hume is right, we have no grounds for assuming the conclusions of philosophical arguments are more likely to be false than very basic common-sense beliefs, but the choice has already been made through our fundamental natural tendencies which we know to be generally epistemically reliable. In any case, suppose we assume philosophical arguments against induction work and that the premises of those arguments cannot seriously be doubted. We would then be arguing that there is a real problem with induction on the basis of premises which are in fact groundless and, thus, begging the question against Hume.

Conclusion

While Hume fails to solve the puzzle he raises, he is right to stress that we do not seem to act as if the puzzle were a problem. It seems that no one really believes that scepticism about induction is reasonable. To claim there is a problem of induction is inconsistent with the commitments we display through our actions. We would be committed to thinking there is a problem if we thought that the conclusions ratified by philosophical arguments were as well-grounded as those produced by induction from experience. However, we do not think this. So, it is sensible to think that nothing more than an intellectually interesting paradox is raised by Hume's puzzle about inductive reasoning. However, to say this is not to say that we are able to justify induction or know exactly how it works. Solving the puzzle of induction and trying to figure out exactly how inductive reasoning works seem still to be legitimate pursuits. Further, we may discover we do not need to accept that any type of induction works in order to show that relying on theories endorsed by science is rational. After all, the case of induction is not quite like the case of Zeno's paradoxes. We *see* objects moving before us. However, when we assume scientific theories are rendered plausible by induction, we rely on the claims of famous scientists and on our own inability to imagine alternative ways of justifying scientific theories – we do not see ourselves reasoning inductively.

In the next two sections of this chapter, I shall discuss some attempts to figure out how cogent inductive reasoning works which also constitute attempts to solve the puzzle of induction. In Chapter 3, I shall discuss an attempt to show that we can reasonably accept and rely on some scientific theories without believing that inductive reasoning is cogent.

2 Confirmation

Hempel and Goodman

A number of philosophers have suggested that true observation statements about instances confirm a generalization about those instances. This amounts to suggesting that we can justify a hypothesis by simple enumerative induction. For instance, the true observation statement that Abraham is a black raven confirms the hypothesis that all ravens are black.

Some time ago, the logical positivist philosopher Carl Hempel tried to develop a formal logic of confirmation which would explicate what is involved in simple enumerative induction through a formal account of the relations between statements. What was driving him was the view that induction would be partly vindicated if he could show confirmation could be explicated in formal terms. He thought that if he could give a formal account of confirmation, this would be evidence that cogent inductive inferences exist because it would show that confirmation can be described by using objective criteria (Hempel, 1965: 8–10). Hempel hoped that a formal logic of confirmation might be added to standard systems of formal deductive logic which had been developed with great success earlier this century. It seemed that those systems offered the hope that we might be able to understand the nature of all cogent inference in terms of a formal account of the relations between statements.

An explanation of what Hempel was trying to do, for those readers who know little about formal logic, may be helpful here. A formal account of a type of inference is one in which the specific subject matter of the statements involved is unimportant. It does not matter whether the statements in the inference deal with ravens or shoes, black things or spotty pink things. Logicians describe this feature by saying that a formal account of validity or inductive cogency is one in which the validity or inductive cogency of inferences is due purely to their *logical form*.

Consider a type of inference to illustrate the notion of logical form. Suppose we define '>' to stand for 'if . . . then . . .', and '~' to stand for 'it is not the case that . . .' It seems to turn out that we can prove on the basis of some basic rules of standard formal deductive logic that for any two statements 'a' and 'b', the inference 'a > b; ~ b; therefore ~ a', is valid. Now suppose I want to know if a particular inference is valid. For instance, the inference 'If I put the iron in the fire, then it is hot; it is not the case that the iron is hot; therefore, it is not the case that I put the iron in the fire' is valid. I can substitute the symbol 'P' for 'I put the iron in the fire' and the symbol 'Q' for 'it is hot'. In symbols, the inference is 'P > Q; ~ Q; therefore ~ P'. It turns out this inference has a form which has been proved to be valid in the deductive formal system, so it must be valid. 'P' is a symbol of type a, and 'Q' is a symbol of type b. Of course, we already know intuitively that this inference is valid. But it seems that formal logic will allow us to use a fairly simple objective procedure to prove a vast range of inferences are valid without ever considering the specific content of the statements contained in the inferences.

Hempel thought that reasoning which can justify statements on the basis of other statements never depends for its cogency on the specific content of statements. If so, Hempel reasoned, this must be true of cogent inductive inferences. He thus set out to try to describe a formal system for capturing what is involved in simple enumerative induction.

Hempel begins his discussion with a very plausible proposal put by Nicod, that statements like 'all ravens are black' are confirmed by true statements about observations like 'Abraham is a black raven'. Hempel understands this to mean that any purported scientific generalization of the logical form '(x) (Ax > Bx)' is confirmed by any true observation statement of the form 'Aa&Ba'. (Note: '(x)' means 'for all x'; 'Ax' means 'x is an A'; 'A' is any predicate; 'a' is the name of some thing; and '&' means 'and'. Hempel is saying that any statement of the form 'for all x, if x is an A, then x is a B' is confirmed by a true observation statement of the form 'a is both an A and a B'.) Suppose P stands for the property of being a raven, Q stands for being black, and p is Abraham. On Hempel's translation of English into formal logic, Nicod's proposal would imply that '(x) (Px > Qx)' is confirmed by the true observation statement 'Pp&Qp'.

Hempel points out, in deductive logic it is a rule that whatever implies a statement also implies any statement which is logically equivalent to it. In standard formal deductive logic '(x) (Px > Qx)' is logically equivalent to '(x) (~ Qx > ~ Px)', so whatever implies '(x) (Px > Qx)' also implies '(x) (~ Qx > ~ Px)'. That is to say, 'All ravens are black' and 'all non-black things are non-ravens' are logically equivalent, so whatever implies 'all ravens are black' implies 'all non-black things are non-ravens'. The reason why this rule exists is that statements which are logically equivalent to other statements seem to have the same content because they are both true under the same conditions and false under the same conditions. 'All ravens are black' and 'all non-black things are non-ravens' will both be true when there are no non-black ravens, and false if there is a single instance of a non-black raven. Hempel argues that Nicod's proposal about confirmation will have to be expanded to include the rule that whatever confirms a statement confirms any statement which is equivalent to it in standard formal deductive logic. Thus, what confirms '(x) (Px > Qx)' also confirms '(x) (~ Qx > ~ Px)'. But, Hempel shows, expanding Nicod's proposal in this way leads to a serious problem.

The problem arises because equivalence is a symmetrical (that is, two-way) relationship, so whatever confirms '$(x)\ (\sim Qx > \sim Px)$' also confirms '$(x)\ (Px > Qx)$'. This implies that '$\sim Qa \& \sim Pa$' confirms '$(x)\ (\sim Qx > \sim Px)$', and so confirms '$(x)\ (Px > Qx)$'. However, as Hempel indicates, this seems to mean that any true observation statement describing a non-black thing which is a non-raven would confirm 'all ravens are black'. Thus, I can now look at my white coffee cup, Mabel, produce the true observation statement 'Mabel is a non-black, non-raven', and so confirm the statement 'all ravens are black'. But, obviously, this conclusion is absurd.

Hempel's apparently rigorous account of confirmation seems to tell us that a ridiculous indoor ornithology, which does not even involve studying birds, could justify general statements about birds as much as studying birds would. The fact that Hempel's intuitively rigorous account of confirmation seems to lead to the conclusion that indoor ornithology, which does not involve studying ravens confirms generalizations about ravens has been called 'the paradox of the ravens'. Many attempts have been made to resolve the paradox of the ravens and a number of similar paradoxes. The purported solutions have not been found convincing by many philosophers. Hempel seems to think that if a convincing solution cannot be found, this poses a problem for the cogency of inductive reasoning. However, it can only pose a problem for the cogency of inductive reasoning if we think, as Hempel does, that all cogent reasoning is purely formal. If we think the specific content of statements is importantly involved in cogent inductive reasoning, it is not clear that Hempel has raised a problem for inductive reasoning. For, as the statements would normally be understood, they deal with different things. The statement 'all ravens are black' is about ravens. The statement 'all non-black things are non-ravens' is about non-black things, so does not deal with ravens at all. This is true even though if they were translated into formal logic according to widely used conventions, they would turn out to be logically equivalent.[4] As we will see later in this chapter and in Chapter 3, in some accounts of induction what a statement is about is crucial to whether an inductive inference involving that statement can be cogent.

Let me now turn to a further paradox which I think can only be solved by admitting that attempts to produce a formal account of cogent enumerative induction will fail. The paradox was produced by Nelson Goodman (1965). According to Hempel's and similar accounts, the scientific generalization 'all emeralds are green' is confirmed by 'Great Mogul is a green emerald'. As the statement 'all emeralds are green' is an example of a scientific generalization, it must be taken to mean that all emeralds – now, in the past and in the future – are green. If confirmation is purely formal, then any statements of the same form as 'all emeralds are green', and which have any subject or any predicate at all, should follow the same rule. Consider the predicate 'grue', defined in the following way. Before 2020, things are grue if they are green; after 2020, things are grue if they are blue. It seems that the same observations which would license us to confirm the statement 'all emeralds are green' will also license us to confirm the statement that they are all grue. But the statements 'all emeralds are green' and 'all emeralds are grue' are inconsistent. Saying all emeralds are grue predicts that they are all blue after 2020, whereas saying all emeralds are green predicts that they are not. Clearly this is absurd, for if confirmation is a way of justifying statements objectively, we should not be able to confirm statements which are very different from one another by using the same observations. Goodman points out, of course, that if confirmation were purely formal, we could produce any number of different statements inconsistent with 'all emeralds are green' which are confirmed through the same observations.

Goodman tries to deal with this paradox by arguing that while confirmation is a relation between evidence and hypothesis, our definition of that relation can legitimately use other relevant knowledge. In particular, it can use knowledge of the outcome of past predictions. He says the statements in cogent inductive inferences only contain predicates which have been long used in unrefuted generalizations. For instance: the inference from the fact that all of the large number of emeralds we have encountered are green to the conclusion that all emeralds are green is cogent. But the inference from the fact that a large number of emeralds we have encountered are grue to the conclusion that all emeralds are grue is not cogent, as 'grue' is an untried predicate. Unlike 'green', 'grue' has not been used in a large number of unrefuted generalizations (Goodman, 1965: 59 ff.).

To follow Goodman's solution is, in effect, to give up the search for a purely formal account of confirmation. If he is right, confirmation might still be a relation between evidence and hypothesis because we only need to use other evidence to determine whether such a relation exists. But this would still mean that a formal account of the conditions under which the relation holds cannot be given. It will not be the case that the formal structure of statements alone determines whether a statement is confirmed by other statements. The specific predicates used in the statements must also denote a property which is one over which past enumerative inductive inferences seem to have been successful.

There are two unsatisfactory aspects of Goodman's solution. First, it is not plausible that it is something about the predicates used in an inference which makes it likely that all things in a particular group have something in common. The predicate 'black' is a well tried predicate but, even if I had seen a large number of humans and they had all been black, I would not have been warranted in inferring that all humans are black from my experience. This is because humans are animals and animals of the same species often differ widely in their colour (think of dogs, for example).[5] The second problem is Goodman does not explain why inferences over statements that use predicates which have been used in apparently successful inductions in the past should turn out to be more successful.

To be fair to Goodman, he is well aware of the first problem and tries to deal with it in a manner which need not be discussed here. Hilary Kornblith has proposed a plausible solution to both problems which builds on some of Goodman's ideas but interprets them in the light of a metaphysical hypothesis. Kornblith argues that the best explanation of why only some statements with a particular logical structure can be confirmed by observing instances is that those statements are about things which belong to natural kinds. The things in a natural kind have an underlying structure in common which causes them to have a large range of common properties of particular sorts. For example, the instances of a particular mineral will all have the same hardness and specific gravity because both their underlying chemical composition and their atomic arrangement are the same. This common underlying structure means that we can securely infer from the properties of one instance of a mineral many of the properties which are possessed by all instances of that mineral. For example, all instances of the mineral corundum have the same hardness and the same specific gravity (Kornblith, 1993). (However, they do not all have the same colour. Rubies and sapphires are instances of corundum; rubies are red and sapphires are blue.)

Kornblith's account is even further from a formal account of confirmation than Goodman's, for, according to Kornblith, whether a statement can confirm another statement or not depends on whether the subject term of those statements refers to a natural kind. Thus, in Kornblith's account it is not only something about the relation between an observation statement and a generalization which makes the observation statement a confirming instance; it is also something about the structure of the things to which both statements refer.

Kornblith argues we do not reason by simple enumerative induction when we reason inductively; what we do is something like the following. We use rough rules which typically allow us to latch on to a natural kind. When we have latched on to a natural kind, we use rough rules to infer from the fact that instances of that natural kind have certain properties to the fact that all instances of that natural kind have those properties. We do not infer that all the properties of some instances of the natural kind are possessed by all its instances. Thus, we do not take large numbers of instances of any type, which have any old property, to confirm a generalization about that type of thing. If we know of a large number of clocks which have hands and none which do not have hands, we do not infer that all clocks have hands. In contrast, from a small number of sapphires which have a particular hardness, we might infer that all sapphires have a particular hardness. Having seen a large number of platypuses in zoos and none outside zoos, we do not infer that all platypuses live in zoos. However, having seen a small number of platypuses laying eggs, we might infer that all platypuses lay eggs.

I will not explain Kornblith's account of our inductive reasoning in any detail, particularly since it is similar to that of John Stuart Mill, which I discuss in detail in the next chapter.[6] For the purposes of this chapter, it is important to note that if Kornblith is right, he may have solved Hume's puzzle. The reason is that Kornblith explains how an inductive inference can be cogent without the truth of the premises deductively guaranteeing the conclusion or even deductively guaranteeing the probability of the conclusion.

Critical discussion

A possible objection to Kornblith's account is that we are unable to tell whether there are natural kinds in the universe or not unless some sort of induction is cogent, so his account cannot be used to solve Hume's puzzle. To support this objection, someone may argue in the following way. It is true that all of the many rubies or sapphires we have tested have had the same hardness and specific gravity. It is also true that in the past, all gems which have those two properties in common have had many other properties in common. We may have decided on the basis of a vast amount of information we have accumulated from chemistry that a simple explanation of why such gems all have these properties in common is that they are all instances of the mineral corundum. (All instances of a mineral have the same chemical composition and structure.) None of this shows, however, that any gems we encounter in the future with the specific gravity and hardness of past rubies and sapphires are likely to be like past rubies and sapphires in any other respects. Thus, Kornblith fails to solve Hume's puzzle.

This objection fails as it stands. If Kornblith is right, there are natural kinds and our reasoning usually allows us to be able to latch on to them. Further, if he is right, our inductive inferences are cogent because they usually involve statements which deal with certain properties of natural kinds. Even if we cannot prove we are dealing with natural kinds, we are only inclined to inductively infer a conclusion if we are dealing with a property which is in fact likely to be the result of membership of a natural kind that we have successfully identified. Our inductive inferences with true premises will thus justify some of our conclusions, whether we can prove there are natural kinds or not. The reason is our inductive reasoning will be a reliable process in the sense that conclusions we draw from premises will usually be true. We may not be able to prove there are natural kinds, but we do not need to prove this in order to reason in a cogent manner.

However, the objection can be restated to deal with this response. It may be argued we need to show in a non-inductive way that we are dealing with natural kinds in order to solve Hume's puzzle. Hume does not just want an account of what makes our inductive inferences cogent; he also wants a non-circular *justification* of that account. Certainly, it may be said, if our inductive reasoning works in the way Kornblith says, our inductive reasoning is cogent. But this does not show there are natural kinds or that our inductive reasoning is cogent.

Yet restating the objection in this way indicates that it is rather weak because Hume's demand for a non-circular argument which proves that a kind of reasoning is cogent cannot be met even by deductive reasoning. If pushed to defend the view that there are cogent deductive inferences, we can: (a) produce circular arguments which use deductive inferences to argue for the cogency of deductive inferences; (b) argue from the fact that we seem to be unable coherently to doubt deductive inferences; or (c) argue that it is impossible for deductive inferences to fail to be cogent.

If the sorts of doubts Hume raises about induction are legitimate, all three of these responses are inadequate. The first response is inadequate because by Hume's account, to use a circular argument is always to beg the question. The second response is inadequate because to appeal to our apparent inability coherently to doubt deductive reasoning is, as John Stuart Mill pointed out in the nineteenth century, merely to appeal to supposed psychological facts about us which may have nothing to do with the cogency of deductive reasoning. To produce an argument for the cogency of deductive reasoning from our apparent incapacity, we need to show that something about deductive reasoning is the cause of our incapacity. But to show this, we will presumably have to use deductive reasoning from a premise about the causes of such incapacities. Let us turn to the third strategy. Many philosophers have presented accounts which claim that deductive reasoning cannot fail to be cogent. The problem with such accounts is that to arrive at the conclusion that deductive reasoning cannot fail to be cogent, we need to use deductive reasoning from premises about the nature of deductive reasoning. So, such accounts fail to meet the kind of standard Hume says is necessary to show inductive reasoning is cogent.[7] Thus, it seems that if scepticism about induction cannot be rebutted by a circular argument, scepticism about deduction cannot be rebutted by using a circular argument either. But, I suggest, this is absurd.

That types of deductive reasoning can only be justified in a circular manner indicates it may well be that, contrary to Hume, some circular justifications of types of reasoning are unproblematic.[8] But if so, this applies to inductive reasoning as much as it does to deductive reasoning. In fact, Kornblith presents an intuitively very plausible inductive justification of scientific inductive reasoning from instances to generalizations as follows. In science, we are enormously predictively successful in using purported natural kind categories. For example, chemistry allows us successfully to predict what many of the properties of a substance will be on the basis of one or two of its properties by relying on the view that these properties are diagnostic of a natural kind with a common underlying structure. The enormous success of scientific theories which apparently refer to the properties of natural kinds would be a miracle if such natural kinds did not exist, and we did not have methods for latching on to them. Thus, natural kinds exist, and we have methods for latching on to them (Kornblith, 1993: 41).

Kornblith's argument for the existence of natural kinds and for our ability to discover them is intuitively persuasive because it uses a second type of inference to justify some inductive reasoning from instances to a generalization. This second type of inference is not deductive, for if the premises in Kornblith's argument were true, it would be possible but very unlikely that science has been highly successful even if natural kinds did not exist. This second type of inductive inference is also different from inferences which generalize from statements about instances of natural kinds. But the fact that Kornblith uses such an inference indicates that he has not explained why *all* cogent inductive inferences are cogent.

Conclusion

Philosophers who are concerned to preserve formal accounts of logic have been dissatisfied with solutions like those of Goodman and Kornblith to Hempel's paradox and the grue paradox. They attempt to solve those paradoxes in other ways. I do not have the space here to discuss their purported solutions, but none have been widely accepted. It should be noted, however, that such paradoxes can only threaten the cogency of inductive reasoning if we accept that what makes inferences cogent depends solely on the logical form of statements in them. It is not at all obvious why we should accept this. In any case, Kornblith presents a plausible account in which many inductive inferences are cogent because the statements in them deal with aspects of natural kinds. He thus shows us it is perfectly possible for inferences to be cogent in a way which does not depend solely on the logical form of statements in them. In his account, Kornblith presents a strong argument for the claims that there are natural kinds and that we have strategies for discovering natural kinds. However, his argument for these claims introduces a second type of inductive inference which is not an inference over statements which involve natural kinds. He thus fails to explain how *all* cogent inductive inferences work by using an account of natural kinds. This means he fails to solve completely Hume's puzzle. I shall now discuss this second type of inductive inference.

3 Probability and inference to the best explanation

We have seen in the previous section that one way to try to deal with Hume's puzzle is to argue that it arises because simple enumerative induction is not actually what gives us knowledge of scientific generalizations. In the nineteenth century, William Whewell and John Stuart

Mill developed accounts of inductive reasoning which claimed that the inductive reasoning involved in science is quite different from enumerative induction. I shall be discussing John Stuart Mill's account in Chapter 3. Whewell thought that a theory which predicts or explains a large number of facts which it was not produced to explain will never be false and that scientific theories can be justified by their ability to predict a large number of such facts. Whewell's account seemed to run into serious problems in the early part of the twentieth century when philosophers realized that Newton's mechanics is false, even though it predicts or explains an enormous number of facts it was not concocted to explain. In recent times, Whewell's account has been revived and modified by philosophers who use the notion of probability. They argue that a theory which predicts or explains a large number of facts it was not produced to explain is very probably approximately true.

The attempt to use the notion of probability to explain how inductive inferences work has three motivations. First, we might be able to give a plausible account of how there can be cogent inductive inferences. Second, our account might allow us to explain why some types of inductive inference provide less of a justification than others. Third, we might be able to give a formal account of induction based on the intuitively plausible axioms of mathematical probability, thereby showing that induction is as secure as deduction, or perhaps that its most contentious part is really a form of deduction.

According to some accounts that use an intuitive notion of probability, inductive inferences which can justify a conclusion work something like this. Suppose we know that some theory, T, is consistent with known facts and suppose we know that T would explain a number of facts if it were true. Assume further that we know that if T were not approximately true, it is highly unlikely that some event (or events), P, would happen. Assume we also know that P has happened. We can now infer that T is very probably approximately true. Finally, we can reasonably infer that T is approximately true. Put more schematically, by this account, the central part of a good inductive inference goes roughly like this:

Premise 1: If not approximately T, then, very probably, not P
Premise 2: P
Preliminary conclusion: So, very probably, T is approximately true
Final conclusion: Therefore, T is approximately true

(Call this schema x.)[9] Note that the only step in schema x which is clearly inductive is the last step, for it does not follow from the fact that something is very likely to be approximately true that it must be approximately true. The key previous step seems to be deductive. To see this, consider that to say 'it is very unlikely that P if not approximately T' seems to be to say the same as 'it would be very unlikely that not approximately T, if P is true'. If we know premises 1 and 2 to be true, it seems to follow that the final conclusion is likely to be true. Further, note that the inductive inference involved in the last step of schema x seems to be extremely plausible. Unlike enumerative induction, which seems problematic, the inductive inference in schema x seems intuitively to be very like a deductive inference. At any rate, it appears that if schema x captures what is involved in much warranted inductive reasoning, Hume is wrong in saying that inductive reasoning cannot guarantee the probability of a conclusion. For it appears that in arguments which follow schema x the premises do guarantee the probability of the conclusion.

Some probabilists claim to offer a plausible account of warranted inductive inference through schema x. An inference which follows schema x is sometimes called an inference to the *best explanation* of some facts which are predicted or already known. It is called an inference to the best explanation because in a schema x inference, we infer that the best explanation of T's power to predict or explain facts it was not concocted to explain is that it is very probably approximately true. Other philosophers argue that what is really involved in scientific inferences which use the notion of probability is not schema x, but an inference to the best *available* explanation. Their account goes something like this: of theories $T_1 \ldots T_n$, the best theory is the one which 'best explains' the greatest number of known facts. If a fact would be more probable if a theory were true than if any of its rivals were true, that theory 'best explains' the fact.

There are important differences between an inference which follows schema x and an inference to the best available explanation. I shall be focusing on inferences which follow schema x even when I am discussing the merits of two rival theories. That a theory is the best of a (quite possibly) bad lot, on the evidence available, gives us no grounds for thinking it advances our knowledge or can reasonably be relied on as a basis for action. This is because a theory which is the best available explanation of something may well be totally false. Thus, showing that a theory is the best available explanation does not justify the theory objectively. (However, it might justify us in doing further research on it rather than on its rivals.)

I will explain schema x inference by using an example: in the eighteenth century many chemists believed that everyday burning was the removal of a substance they called phlogiston. They adduced a number of reasons for believing the phlogiston theory, including: (a) it appeared that after such burning a substance was smaller; and (b) metals have more in common with each other than what we now call their oxides (metals are shiny, malleable, etc.). As the phlogiston theory had been constructed to explain these and other phenomena, it might be said that it was constructed by using observations. But a probabilist would argue that the fact that it fits the phenomena cannot be said to be evidence for it, as perhaps it fits only because it was constructed to fit. There is thus nothing surprising in the fact that it fits. It is quite likely that these features would be there if some other theory were true. For example, some other unknown substance might explain why metals have more in common. If so, the explanation of why metals are similar may well be different from the explanation of why burnt substances appear smaller than their unburnt predecessors.

Lavoisier postulated that everyday burning was the addition of a gaseous substance, oxygen, to more elementary substances. He also postulated that what we now call chemical reduction was the removal of the oxygen from an oxide. On this basis, he predicted that mercury after burning would weigh more than before burning. This fact was already known and his theory had been constructed to explain it, so it provided no support for his theory by the probabilist account. However, he also predicted that when he heated what we now know to be mercury oxide in a reducing environment, he would end up with a metal of lower weight plus a gas weighing the equivalent of the lost weight. This surprising prediction turned out to be true. On the probabilist account, the evidence produced by Lavoisier's experimental result supports his theory strongly because what he predicted is very unlikely to happen unless his theory is approximately true. No one would expect the weight of mercury produced by reduction to be less than that of the mercury oxide, and the gas produced to weigh the equivalent of the lost weight, unless the oxygen theory is approximately true.

Some phlogiston theorists proceeded to argue that the surprising results discovered by Lavoisier could be plausibly explained if one assumed that phlogiston had negative weight. They also argued that this assumption was not absurd, as observation of fires seems to show that something in fires rises upwards. (Aristotle had argued in antiquity that fire was a basic element with a natural tendency to rise upwards.) So, phlogiston theorists were acting in accordance with observation by modifying their theories to counter Lavoisier's claims. Nevertheless, probabilists would argue that observations were not used by phlogistonists as independent evidence for their hypothesis, but interpreted so as to fit it. Whatever seems to rise up might have nothing to do with phlogiston. Independent evidence that it is phlogiston would need to be provided. Probabilists distinguish between merely adding further theories to make a theory fit observed facts and providing independent evidence for the additional theory. According to their view, only Lavoisier had provided evidence for his theory.[10]

My example is a little oversimplified, for Whewell and others who have seriously defended inference patterns like schema x have held that for a theory to be very likely to be true, it must predict or explain *a range of facts* which the theory was not concocted to explain. This is reasonable for, after all, a theory may make a few startling predictions which turn out to be right by a fluke. Predicting or explaining a range of facts is saying that a class of things behaves in a particular way. By Whewell's account, Lavoisier's theory is justified by the evidence because it correctly predicts or explains previously unknown facts about all metals and about all of what we now call their oxides.

Probabilists hold, then, we cannot justify a theory merely by appealing to facts which seem to confirm it because we can, all too easily, 'cook the books' in a theory's favour by constructing it around confirming facts. The range of facts which justifies a theory must, in some sense, be very improbable given what we know, but not very improbable if the theory in question is true. Probabilists say, further, that for a range of facts to provide strong support for a theory, that range of facts must be highly unlikely to occur unless the theory is true. That something seems to rise in fires does not make it likely that phlogiston is rising, for it might well be that some other gas is rising or that no gas is rising.

If we accept the account of probabilists, we can explain why simple enumerative induction is problematic. The statement 'it is highly improbable that the next 500 ravens we come across will be black unless all ravens are black', is false. If we are in a limited geographical area, it is reasonably likely that all of a genus of birds will be of the same colour even if many members of that genus are not of that colour. We know this from past experience of animal colours. Thus, seeing whether the next 500 ravens we discover are black does not justify the theory that all ravens are black, although it may provide *some* support for it.

There have been some recent influential attempts to understand schema x in terms of the calculus of probability. They are partly motivated by the idea that if we actually work with something like schema x, we should be able to capture the key part of schema x in terms of the calculus of probability, which is a deductive formalism.

The calculus of probability gives us formal methods for calculating the precise probability of certain statements given the truth of other statements. In the calculus of probability, the calculation of the probability from the information given is deductive. If the premises are true, the conclusion must be true. Suppose we are trying to test the hypothesis that all of the balls in a jar are red. We examine a sample of balls from the jar, noting the colour of the ball each time we choose. The calculus of probability will allow us to know whether our hypothesis is very likely to be true on the basis of the colour of the balls in our sample, provided a number of conditions are met. The most important of these conditions is that our sample must be random or representative, and that the sample must be of a particular size in relation to the total number of balls in the jar. By a random sample, I mean one in which each of the balls in the jar has an equal chance of being chosen in every choice. By a representative sample, I mean one which retains the relevant features of all the balls in the jar. For instance, if there are 700 red balls and 300 non-red balls in the jar, a sample which had 7 red balls and 3 non-red balls would be representative.

An important problem appears to arise if we assume schema x (implicitly) uses a version of the calculus of probability. Legitimately to use the calculus of probability, we need to know that we have a random or representative sample of the total population of the things we are dealing with. If we do not know that we have a random or representative sample, we cannot know that our hypothesis is probable on the basis of the evidence that we acquire. But it seems that it would be impossible to tell whether we had a random or representative sample when we are testing scientific theories unless we have already used induction to get the information we need.

Let me explain this point through an example. Suppose we are testing the hypothesis that all the adults in Metropolis read the *Daily Rag*. We choose a sample of adults to test our hypothesis. In our sample, it turns out that 98 per cent read the *Rag*. As the sample is of sufficient size, we assume that it is very likely that at least 98 per cent of adults in Metropolis read the *Rag*. We then go to a number of streets scattered all over Metropolis to interview *Rag* readers and find, to our surprise, that virtually no one reads it. This is due to our sample being problematic because we picked it at random from a list of university graduates. It turns out that while 98 per cent of university graduates read the *Rag*, only 40 per cent of all adults read the *Rag*. The *Rag* is a strong defender of universities. Of course, in this case, we could have remedied the problem by picking adults for our sample at random from a recent census. But when we are testing many scientific theories we cannot really choose at random from the population of things we are dealing with because the theories deal with a vast number of things scattered all over the universe. We need to choose a sample of things which we take to be uncontaminated by irrelevant causal factors. To do this, we need to work out, on the basis of previous information, what is likely to affect our sample problematically. But it seems that the only way we could know this is through previous knowledge we have acquired through induction.

For example, if we know that physical processes are pretty much the same in various parts of the universe, we can test theories of physics by doing experiments with objects on Earth only and be confident that other objects will obey the same laws. It seems that to test such theories we choose a sample we know to be representative in order to do our experiments. But it also seems that the only way we could know that a sample is representative is by induction. We have found that throughout the Earth and in nearby areas, objects obey the same laws of physics. We extrapolated from this the claim that objects obey the same laws of physics throughout the universe. But this means that if schema x were meant to capture all warranted inductive reasoning, and the calculus of probability were meant to capture the force of schema x, we could not know we had a representative sample. But it seems that we often do know such things. So, it seems that there is something wrong either with the assumption that schema x captures all warranted inductive inferences or with the assumption that the calculus of probability captures the force of schema x.

There is, however, a possible response to the problem I have raised in the last two paragraphs. We might accept that we have no objectively justified method of telling whether P describes a random or representative sample. We could then say that what convinces us in real life cases that the truth of P would make the approximate truth of T very probable is merely that we cannot think of any better explanation of why T should successfully predict or explain P. But this response is inadequate. For as our judgement seems to be based only on our imagination, we cannot tell how likely it is that other relevant information exists which would imply that the conjunction of P and not-T is fairly probable. If there were other relevant information, the (absolute) probability of T predicting P even if T is largely false would be very high, and finding that P is true would not raise the (absolute) probability of T's being true at all. Other relevant information might be that the Swiss genius, Finkelstein, has conceived of 17 very different theories consistent with known evidence, and which all predict P. (However, she never published her paper.) Alternatively, other relevant information might be that we cannot think of another theory only because our conceptualizing capacities are poor.

It appears then that, based only on the information that the first premise in schema x seems to us to be true for a particular theory T and that P is true, we can never be justifiably confident of T's being the case if we assume that schema x implicitly uses the calculus of probability and that it captures the force of all warranted inductive reasoning. This is because if we knew more, the chances of P being predicted by theory T, even if T is largely false, might well be very high. In such a case, P does not *objectively* raise the probability of T being true even by a little. As a result, we can have no legitimate confidence in drawing the conclusion that T is approximately true unless we add further statements, and it is far from obvious how any such statements can be shown to be plausible without some other inductive procedure.

A further problem with using the calculus of probability to understand schema x is that it is unclear how we can be justified in assigning numerical probabilities to a universal theory on the basis of facts it predicts. If interpreted as a statement in probability calculus, the first premise in schema x must assign a numerical probability to T if P were to turn out to be true. There are mathematical methods available which assign probabilities to theories about a limited number of things on the basis of random samples of those things. However, Popper has argued that a theory like Newton's mechanics, which deals with the entire (infinite?) universe, makes innumerable predictions; so that even the confirmation of a very large number of predictions will be the confirmation of an infinitesimally small sample of predictions. Even if the sample is random, it will be too small to be significant. Thus, he argues the probability of the theory does not increase above zero even if a large number of its predictions are confirmed. (The above argument is a simplified interpretation of some of Popper's vague remarks.)

Popper's claim has been contested as: (a) it is far from clear that we can even tell that our sample is small in an uncountable domain; and (b) the sample may have features which make it representative, in which case its small size is not important. Still, it is difficult to see how one can confidently assign any numerical probability to Newton's theory on the basis of a confirmed prediction.

There have been many attempts to deal with the problems I have raised for understanding the key part of all warranted inductive reasoning in terms of the calculus of probability. I shall not discuss the proposed solutions here as a discussion would involve a great deal of detail, and the proffered solutions are unconvincing.[11]

It is important to understand that what I have said about the calculus of probability need not undermine arguments which roughly follow schema x. Understanding inductive arguments through schema x is illuminating because it sets up more intuitively plausible test conditions for hypotheses. Schema x also seems to resemble much of the reasoning used by actual scientists. In addition, there is a powerful circular inductive argument available for the claim that inferences which roughly follow schema x are cogent. The argument is the following. Theories which have been justified through inferences which roughly follow schema x have turned out successfully to predict many novel facts apart from the novel facts which were used to justify those theories. It would be highly unlikely that the theories which have been justified through schema x continued to be highly predictively successful if schema x were not cogent. Thus, it is highly likely that arguments which roughly follow schema x are cogent. So, arguments which roughly follow schema x are cogent.

In any case, to conclude that inferences which roughly follow schema x are problematic merely because of the difficulties we face in giving a formal account of how it works, assumes that all cogent inferences are cogent because they are really deductive or closely resemble deductive inferences. We also need to assume that deductive inferences are cogent solely because of their logical form.[12] It is far from obvious why we should believe either of these things.

Earlier in this century, some philosophers proposed that deductive inferences are valid because they have to do solely with the relations between the meanings of terms in statements. According to this view, we can give a formal account of why all deductive inferences are valid because the specific content of statements in deductive inferences is irrelevant to the validity of those inferences. If those philosophers had been right, then it might be thought that, by analogy, if there are any cogent inductive inferences they must also be purely formal. But accounts which hold deductive inferences can show that a conclusion follows necessarily from certain premises because facts about meaning have been strongly criticized in recent years. The reason is that no one has produced a widely accepted account of how such truths could be based solely on the meanings of terms. The conception of meaning underlying such accounts has proved to be elusive. In response to this problem, some philosophers have argued deductive logic does not consist of necessary truths, but of hypotheses based on empirical knowledge or on metaphysical principles. They have argued that, like Euclidean geometry which was once believed to consist of necessary truths but might well be false, standard logic may be false. Indeed, some of them have argued that some basic axioms of standard logic are false. In their view, the normal definition of deductive arguments suffers from a failure of presupposition. The definition says deductive arguments are ones in which the conclusion necessarily follows from the premises. But if there are no necessary truths, then there are no such arguments.[13] The debate surrounding this issue is too technical to pursue here. However, we have no good grounds for assuming that there is an asymmetry between deduction and induction merely on the basis of a highly contested account of the nature of deductive logic. This means that we should not take the failure to understand all inductive inference in terms of the calculus of probability, or some other formal system, to be a serious problem.

Conclusion

My discussion of inference to the best explanation has made clear that attempts to produce a formal account of why it is cogent are implausible. But, as I indicated, there is no good reason to think this poses a problem. Philosophers have had trouble explaining the cogency of many inferences which are supposedly deductive in formal terms. Further, inference to the best explanation is a type of inference which has been frequently used in science to justify theories that have continued to be highly predictively successful. This is evidence that it is a cogent type of inference. However, we have not much idea of why it is a cogent type of inference. Some of Hume's puzzle remains unresolved.[14]

I have discussed two types of inductive inference which appear to be cogent, inferences from instances to generalizations over statements which deal with natural kinds and inferences to the best explanation. I have argued that both types of inference can plausibly be regarded as cogent. However, there remain a number of important issues relating to induction which I shall discuss in the next chapter.

Further reading

Hume's argument that there is a puzzle about how inductive reasoning can be cogent is clearly set out in Hume's *Enquiry Concerning Human Understanding*, section 4 (available in various editions). My account of Hume's way of dealing with this puzzle is a contentious interpretation of Book 1 of Hume (1978). That work is not recommended to students. Hempel's and Goodman's paradoxes are clearly discussed in Brown, 1979. Brown puts the paradoxes into an historical framework in an illuminating way. Goodman's discussion of the grue paradox in Goodman, 1965: 59 ff. is accessible and interesting. Hempel's discussion of the paradox of the ravens in Hempel, 1965: 3–51 is only recommended for those with a background in formal logic. Giere, 1984: 84–115 contains a clear, non-technical account of inference to the best explanation. However, it does not discuss inference to the best explanation in the light of Hume's problem. It also does not discuss the problems involved in trying to explain the cogency of inference to the best explanation through the calculus of probability. A critical and largely non-technical discussion of recent attempts to explain the cogency of inference to the best explanation through the calculus of probability is contained in Miller, 1987: 267–347. Lipton's work (1991) is a subtle non-technical attempt to explain the force of inference to the best available explanation by tying it to the notion of 'loveliness'. An interesting criticism of Lipton is presented by Achinstein (1992).

Notes

1 Some commentators have said that Hume could not have understood enough about mathematical probability to make this point. If so, his claims about probability are obscure and had Hume known more, he would have put this point.

2 I am referring to Hume's argument in the *Treatise* here. My interpretation of that argument is contentious. It resembles that of Baier (1991). I am not concerned here with Hume scholarship and readers can interpret my remarks to be an account of what Hume ought to have said.

3 It may be thought that we cannot accept contradictions because we cannot make coherent sense of contradictions. Harman has plausibly argued that we do sometimes accept them. For example, when we commit ourselves to principles underlying the bi-conditional truth schema, even though we know that those principles imply some contradictions, because it is too useful to abandon that schema and we cannot figure out what is wrong (Harman, 1986: 15–17). The example shows there are deep puzzles involving deduction, and makes it odd that many philosophers should claim there is a *problem* of induction, but only *paradoxes* of deduction. Clever philosophers can, of course, avoid saying that we never accept contradictions, but they only do so by using *ad hoc* devices to save their theories of belief or logic.

4 It is important to realize that if we do not accept Hempel's translation of generalizations like 'all ravens are black' into formal logic, the paradox does not arise. In Aristotle's account of logic, 'all ravens are black' presupposes the existence of ravens, whereas 'all non-black things are non-ravens' does not. Aristotle thinks that in a universe in which there were no ravens, 'all ravens are black' would be false or inapplicable, and 'all non-black things are non-ravens' would be true. Thus, for Aristotle, the two statements are not logically equivalent, and there is no paradox. But Aristotle's view runs into trouble because it seems an implausible account of those scientific laws that apparently deal with objects which do not exist. An example is Newton's first law. There is no object in the universe which is not acted on by a force. This seems to mean that by Aristotle's account, Newton's first law should be inapplicable or false. But this is absurd, for it is clearly approximately true. Further, the only way in which the first law can be easily confirmed is by testing a law which is logically equivalent to it, such as the law that any object which is acted on by a force will not stay at rest or in uniform straight-line motion. (I have simplified the first law's equivalent here.) Because of these problems with Aristotle's account, some philosophers have thought that trying to deal with the paradox of the ravens by understanding the two generalizations in question to be non-equivalent is not plausible (Brown, 1979: 30–1). I think that Aristotle's account can be made to work if we understand laws like Newton's first law to be statements about the tendencies of things. But I cannot pursue the issue here.

5 Instances of the same mineral also vary widely in colour. Colour is only diagnostic for a mineral when we examine its streak. For further remarks about why colour predicates are rarely ones which we can use in cogent inductive inferences, see Kornblith, 1993: 39 ff.

6 Kornblith relies on the account in Holland et al. (1986); Kornblith's own account is set out in Kornblith, 1993: 61–107. An important difference between Kornblith and Mill is that Mill does not believe in full-blown natural kinds because he is suspicious of metaphysics. Like Kornblith, I think an argument for the existence of natural kinds by inference to the best explanation is very strong. I argue for the cogency of inference to the best explanation about unobservables in Chapter 7.

7 There is actually one other strategy, which is to claim that it is self-evident that some simple patterns of deductive reasoning are cogent. The problem with this claim is twofold. First, people have in the past claimed that all sorts of things are self-evident which may well be false (for example the axioms of Euclidean geometry). Second, as I point out later, in recent times some logicians have argued that some basic axioms of deductive logic may be false. This means that our inclination to believe that some pattern of reasoning is obviously cogent does not prove that it is cogent.

8 A number of philosophers have argued in detail that some circular defences of induction are unproblematic. See, for example, Papineau, 1993: 154–67.

9 I have adapted schema x from Giere, 1984: 84–115.

10 Kitcher has recently shown that the negative weight hypothesis was not popular with phlogistonists. This is not important here. He has also argued for an account of the acceptance of the oxygen theory which is very different from the probabilist account (Kitcher, 1993: 276 ff.). According to him, a scientific theory is to be preferred when it is the only account available which explains a large range of experiments and observations in a consistent way. Kitcher fails to explain why chemists came reasonably to believe that Lavoisier's account was roughly right and should be used as a basis for action. Nothing in his account makes unlikely the claim that a future scientist with more imaginative capacity than his or her predecessors would be able to save the phlogiston theory. That some account is the most consistent account available doesn't mean that it is likely correctly to predict what will happen in future cases or is likely to have more truth content than its rival. This means that nothing in Kitcher's account gives us a good reason for thinking that the oxygen theory is rationally to be preferred. (For further criticisms of Kitcher, see Leplin, 1994.)

11 Recently, attempts to understand warranted inductive inference in terms of probability have used Bayes's theorem. Howson and Urbach (1989) explain Bayes's theorem and apply it to warranted inductive inference in a comprehensible though technical manner. A technical and widely admired Bayesian account is found in Earman, 1992. Brown (1994) criticizes such accounts. An important strategy for dealing with some of the problems generated by some Bayesian accounts is to adopt an understanding of assignments of probabilities which treats them as purely subjective degrees of belief. An illuminating non-technical critique of this strategy is given by Miller (1987: 267–347).

12 Stove (1986: 115–44) points out, in an accessible way, that formalizing deductive inference has not been very successful. A vast literature on logic illustrates this point. For a minimally technical critique of attempts to use standard formal logic to capture the structure of deductive inferences in English see Routley et al. (1982).

13 There is a huge literature on the subject. A recent brief discussion is given by Mortensen (1989). Relevant logics, such as those produced by Routley and others, are consistent with the view that the truth of some supposedly basic laws of logic depends on metaphysical or empirical facts (Routley et al., 1982: 58 ff.).

14 Peter Lipton tries to solve the puzzle by tying together the notion of simplicity and the notion of likeliness. He also tries to reduce all cogent inductive inferences to inferences to the best available explanation (Lipton, 1991). His account contains many interesting observations. As some of my remarks in Chapter 7 will make clear, I think that preferring a theory because it is simple needs to be justified inductively. This means that I do not accept Lipton's view.

3

Popper and Mill: Fallibility, Falsification and Coherence

According to the epistemology of Descartes and of many of his successors, we should seek indubitable statements on which to found scientific knowledge. We should also seek precisely defined, reasoning procedures which allow us to use those statements to justify scientific laws or explanations. Such reasoning procedures should themselves be based on indubitable statements. As I pointed out in the introduction to this book, developments in science, philosophy and logic have led many thinkers to doubt there is such a foundation. Scientific and philosophical theories which appeared to be based on obviously true statements have turned out to be false or dubious. I mentioned in Chapter 2 that even some propositions of deductive logic once thought to be obviously true have recently been plausibly argued to be dubious.

The apparent lack of an indubitable foundation for the reasoning we believe to be cogent may seem to pose serious problems for the objectivity of science. In particular, despite my arguments in the last chapter, Hume's puzzle may seem to continue to raise a particularly serious problem for the credibility of scientific laws and generalizations. Inferences from truths about observed things to claims about unobserved things may continue to seem dubious or unjustified. It is important to understand better how key parts of scientific reasoning and knowledge need not have secure foundations in order to be credible. In this chapter, I shall be considering an insightful but ultimately implausible argument put by the influential fallibilist, Karl Popper, that we do not need to use inductive reasoning in a rational and objective science. I shall then discuss how certain types of inductive reasoning can be defended without appeal to precise and indubitable truths or rules, and describe aspects of a credible and realistic fallibilist scientific methodology.

Popper has been one of the strongest critics of an epistemology which seeks obviously true foundations. He has argued that no metaphysical assumption or scientific theory is immune to criticism and he even thinks the search for cogent forms of inductive inference is motivated by a lingering adherence to foundationalism. To overcome this lingering foundationalism, he has developed an account of science which stresses the fallibility of scientific reasoning and attempts to dispense with induction.[1] By his account, the origin of theories is unimportant and they can never be shown to be true or even probably true. In contrast, the nineteenth century philosopher John Stuart Mill developed an account of science which eschews foundationalism, but which attempts to refine induction. Mill thinks it is important to justify scientific theories and that the only way to justify them is to use inductive reasoning. However, he argues that inductive reasoning is often not cogent and that using it cannot be justified by appeal to fundamental truths. Further, while Mill believes some scientific and geometrical theories have been very nearly proved to be true, his account holds that, in the end, all of human knowledge is subject to empirical refutation. His view thus involves a fallibilism which is at least as strong as that of Popper.[2] As well as their differing views about induction, they also differ in their views about the origin of theories and in their attitudes to scientific conjectures.

I shall argue that while Popper fails to explain how science can dispense with induction, and his account of scientific progress and reasoning is often simplistic, his follower Imre Lakatos has developed a credible and realistic fallibilist account of scientific methodology. However, I shall also show that this account has some problems and needs to be supplemented by using some of Mill's insights.

1 Falsificationism

Popper's attempted solution

Karl Popper argues there is no problem or puzzle of induction as we do not discover regularities but conjecture that they exist. Science is nevertheless rational, because we can sometimes falsify conjectures by confronting them with basic statements with which they are inconsistent. If we are lucky, we will stumble on true conjectures; and, even if we do not, we will learn from the falsification of conjectures. The logical part of falsification is purely deductive so there is no need for a logic of confirmation. Further, there is no logic of confirmation. If inductive reasoning existed, it would not be logically valid and could not even be used to show that any conclusion is probable (Popper, 1972: 1–31).

Popper distinguishes two sides of Hume's problem: (a) the logical problem of induction, and (b) the psychological problem of induction. The logical problem is: are we justified in believing that unexperienced instances of certain kinds of things will be like experienced instances? And if so, how? Hume argues that we are not justified. Popper agrees and uses a number of cases to show how even the best inductively attested theories can turn out to be false. For example, he points out that it was widely believed that the sun rises once in roughly every 24 hours.

But Pytheas of Massalia, the Greek explorer, discovered that in northern Norway the sun sometimes does not rise for months.[3]

Popper claims to solve the logical problem by showing that there is no need for induction to preserve the rationality of science. If we assume that scientists conjecture there are certain regularities in the world because they are creatures who have evolved to postulate regularities, and we assume that the postulated regularities can be falsified by finding counter-instances, then this is all we need for science. The key parts of scientific reasoning can be plausibly reconstructed as being deductive.

Suppose, for example, a scientist conjectures that all swans are white. An explorer discovers a black swan. On the basis of this discovery, the scientist formulates the statement 'there is a non-white swan'. The knowledge that this statement is true is sufficient to falsify the conjecture that all swans are white. You may think that what Popper is saying is the experience of a black swan is sufficient to refute the statement that all swans are white. However, Popper is not saying this. He thinks our interpretation of certain experiences as being falsifying instances is, and must be, a matter of convention. He claims that, just as there is no logically justified inductive reasoning, so there is no logically justified way of getting from experiences to statements because all statements go beyond what we experience. (I criticized Feyerabend's arguments for this misleading claim in Chapter 1, and Popper's arguments are similar.) This means that we need to agree to certain descriptions of our experiences in order for those descriptions to be used to falsify theories. Popper calls such descriptions 'basic' statements but he takes them to be basic only in the sense that we have decided temporarily to put them beyond question to make the objective testing of theories possible. However, once we have chosen to describe certain experiences as falsifying instances, the state of the world will or will not produce those experiences. Thus, falsification will have become an objective matter in the sense that it does not rely on the wishes of scientists.

Against the view that scientific theories are typically very probable, Popper argues that good conjectures will often be highly improbable given current knowledge. (He says 'improbable' is used by him in the sense of probability theory (Popper, 1972: 17).) Inductivists have things upside down as they encourage us to produce cautious conjectures which are based on the state of current knowledge. Such conjectures are dangerous because their apparent cautiousness may have to do with the fact that they are rigged to succeed and are not very informative. If I conjecture that water is made of atoms because I see it moving and I know that the motion of groups of round balls can produce wave-like effects when seen from a distance, my hypothesis is not very testable. I have concocted it around the observed features of water so, of course, it seems to explain those features adequately. If, on the other hand, I conjecture that all things are made of atoms, this is likely to have a much larger group of unforeseen testable consequences. This is because a plausible corollary of the conjecture that all things are made of atoms is that one can pull apart and put back together any substance.

The psychological problem of induction is: why do reasonable people believe that unexperienced instances will be like experienced instances? Popper's solution to the psychological problem is that we conjecture the existence of certain regularities and then test our conjectures. When we find the conjectures are not refuted, we temporarily accept them. There is thus no need to assume the existence of an inductive procedure. Besides, Popper argues, regularities can only rarely be observed in nature, so inductivism has trouble explaining how we come to regularities which do not manifest themselves. We can only explain how we arrive at such laws by assuming that they are conjectures, as we could not arrive at them by induction from experience.

Consider Galileo's law of free fall which says that the acceleration of any freely falling body is a constant. Much everyday experience of falling bodies does not seem to fit with it as many bodies are affected by air resistance. For example, drop a feather and a cannonball at the same time, and the feather lands much later. As Galileo did not observe bodies falling in a vacuum, it seems he must have conjectured that the apparently contradictory data of experience could be explained by assuming that two separate types of forces were acting, and then proposed experiments to test it.

Popper takes his account to adopt the best ideas of empiricism and rationalism. From rationalism he gets the view that scientific laws are the product of the creative activity of our minds and so are not arrived at through experience. However, unlike many rationalists, he thinks that although particular ideas about regularities originate a priori, they are not known a priori. We sometimes discover empirically that the most intuitively appealing ideas are false. Thus, empiricism is right in thinking that we decide whether scientific theories are true by using experiences. Popper supports his argument by pointing out that many claims which Kant and others thought to be demonstrable a priori have turned out to be false. For instance, Kant thought that Newtonian physics could be shown to be true a priori. Yet it seems that Newtonian physics can be shown empirically to be false, as many predictions made on the basis of Newtonian physics are wrong.

It is important to understand how different Popper's view is from foundationalism. According to Popper's account, foundationalism has things upside down. It stresses that theories should have come from secure sources, and that we should cautiously move from the known to the unknown. But Popper argues that knowledge advances through bold conjectures which deal largely with what has not yet been observed. He also stresses that there are no secure sources as any statement is fallible.

In judging the merit of theories, Popper thinks we should use the notion of corroboration and not the notion of confirmation. The notion of corroboration is a comparative notion. Roughly speaking, a theory is more corroborated than its rival if it is more falsifiable and has undergone more severe tests, but has not yet been refuted. Consider the situation at the beginning of the twentieth century. Newtonian physics, which made highly falsifiable predictions about every body in the solar system and beyond, was far more corroborated than Aristotelian physics. Newtonian physics had been used to make many remarkable predictions which one would not have expected to be true on the basis of other knowledge. For example, it had been used successfully to predict the return of Halley's comet 76 years before that event occurred. In contrast, Aristotelian physics had repeatedly failed successfully to predict things it had not been specifically concocted to explain. For instance, Aristotelian physics predicts that when the effects of friction are removed, heavy things fall faster than light things. But this can be shown to be false.

Popper stresses, however, that corroboration is only a measure of the past performance of a theory, not of its future performance – that is, a well-corroborated theory may well fail at any moment. It is no more reliable than an unfalsified, but less corroborated theory. Let us return to the case of Newtonian physics. From near the beginning of the twentieth century onwards it was found that it failed to predict what happened to bodies travelling at high velocities. The new special theory of relativity produced by Einstein in 1905 turned out to be far more accurate in its overall predictive performance. Yet in 1905 Einstein's theory was merely an uncorroborated and unfalsified conjecture.

Popper recognizes that his remarks about corroboration seem puzzling if they are part of a solution to what he calls the 'pragmatic' problem of induction. The pragmatic problem is: what theories should we rely on or prefer for practical action from a rational point of view? He comments that, following his account, we should not rely on any theory because no general theory has been shown, or could be shown, to be true. He says, however, that we should prefer the best tested theory for action even if it may well break down at any time. But it is difficult to understand how Popper can say this, given that he means us to take seriously the possibility that a well-corroborated law may turn out to be false. In his view, not only do we never have a guarantee that unexperienced instances of some kind will be like experienced instances, but it is not even probable.

Popper's solution to the pragmatic problem of induction seems implausible as he seems to have no grounds for saying that we should act on the best corroborated theory. In an attempt to save Popper's view, David Miller has suggested that what Popper really meant to say is that we should act on the best corroborated theory not so much because there is any reason for supposing it to be true, but because there are no reasons for supposing it not to be true (Miller, 1982: 40 ff.).

Critical discussion of Popper

An objection which has been raised to Miller's proposal is that it gives us no reason for preferring the standard laws on which we rely to potential rivals, even though this would be absurd.[4] For example, we rely on something like Galileo's law of free fall, which holds that bodies falling in a vacuum constantly accelerate. But someone may propose that tests passed by Galileo's law have also been passed by a law which says that all bodies will obey Galileo's law until tomorrow afternoon at 5 p.m., when they will accelerate until they reach a velocity of one metre per second and then continue falling at this velocity. Call this Fudge's law. Fudge's law, it might be argued, is not only as well-corroborated as Galileo's but is more convenient if it is true. For, from tomorrow night, if we want to quickly leave the top of a 50 storey building in which the lift is faulty, we can jump off and gently float down. But clearly someone who decided to act on Fudge's law rather than on Galileo's would be crazy. It is necessary to assume some sort of inductive reasoning is cogent to explain why Galileo's law is superior to its rival.

Miller responds in two ways to this objection. First, hypotheses which include a reference to a specific time should be banned from consideration as they are less falsifiable. To falsify Galileo's law we need only a statement about a falling body. To falsify Fudge's law we need a similar statement, plus a statement about the time at which the body is falling. Second, laws which solve no problems which their unfalsified predecessors did not solve cannot be said to be knowledge-expanding, and are thus of no interest from a Popperian perspective.

Neither of these responses is adequate if one is interested in working out what to do. First, as he is working within a Popperian framework, Miller can give us no reason for believing that hypotheses which are less easily falsified, or which are not at this stage known to solve new problems, are less likely to be true. The extra component in Fudge's law is easily checked by using a watch, so the content of the hypothesis is just as empirical. (In any case, Popper never gives us any reason to think that hypotheses which are more empirical and whose predictions have been tested, are more likely to be true.) Second, Fudge's law may well solve problems which Galileo's fails to solve. We will not find this out until after 5 p.m. tomorrow (if we ever find it out) and, since on the Popperian account the past gives us no indication of what will happen in the future, we cannot have any confidence that Fudge's law solves fewer problems overall than Galileo's. In any case, if both laws are equally likely to be true, then if one is in a hurry and the lift is stuck, it is rational to prefer the most convenient route to the ground – that is, to attempt to float down. Theoretical concerns are of little interest in such a situation.

A further objection to Miller's responses is, even if we accept a ban on hypotheses which include a reference to time, a Popperian can give us no good reason for not preferring to act on a theory which has already been falsified many times; that is, he can give us no good reason for acting on a corroborated as opposed to a falsified theory. Take, for example, the hypothesis that all freely falling bodies accelerate to one metre per second and then retain that velocity. Call this Stupid's law. By the Popperian account, the fact that Stupid's law has been falsified in the past is no reason to believe it is false for future instances. If it is possible (as Popperians sometimes suggest) to compare the truth content of universal theories, Stupid's law might well have a greater overall truth content than Galileo's law. Perhaps from tomorrow at 5 p.m. all bodies will follow Stupid's law and more bodies will fall in the future than have ever fallen in the past. Further, if it is the case that Stupid's law does describe what will happen to bodies through future time, then it might well predict more; so it will turn out to have solved more problems by predicting the behaviour of a greater number of bodies. In any case, if one wants quickly and safely to get off a high building in which the lift is stuck, there is no reason to act on the assumption that Galileo's law will be true of bodies in the next few minutes. Jumping off to float down would be just as rational as assuming one should wait for the lift to be fixed.

One of Miller's responses to such arguments is that the advocate of crazy laws is raising groundless doubts about accepted laws and mere doubt is not criticism. Yet if we assume Popper is right, the advocate of Stupid's law would not be raising groundless doubts. He would be relying on Popper's argument that past instances do not imply anything about future instances and arguing that, if one is to be practical, one should use Popper's insight to save time. The principle that groundless doubts about accepted views should be ignored is one which can be justified only if one assumes accepted laws are more likely to be true. If one has a hypothesis which implies that the mechanisms causing acceptance may well not be reliable, then one is not entitled to rely on the fact that certain laws are accepted.[5]

So Popper's and Miller's attempts to solve the pragmatic problem of induction fail adequately to deal with the problem in a falsificationist manner. We may conclude from the above discussion that the only plausible way to deal with it within some sort of Popperian account is to assume that corroboration is somehow tied to verisimilitude; that is, to assume that a well-corroborated theory is more likely to be closer to the truth. But to do this one needs to introduce the view that some inductive inferences are cogent and such an assumption could not be justified or even be reasonable if falsificationism is correct. Note, however, that the pragmatic problem of induction is not identical with the problem as such. One important aspect of science is discovering laws which are useful, but another is expanding our theoretical knowledge. Pragmatic purposes can often be achieved by laws which are false but which are close enough to the truth to be useful. For example, Newtonian mechanics is often used in everyday engineering even though it is known to be false. On the other hand, false and well-tried laws are of little use when one wants to expand knowledge. Thus, it might be argued that one should stick to well-tried laws when one is acting but follow up bold and risky conjectures when one wants to expand knowledge quickly. Perhaps, then, falsificationism is correct about theoretical science, even if it is not correct about applied science. However, in the next section I will try to show that not even this is right.

Lakatos's modifications of Popper

Imre Lakatos criticizes falsificationist accounts and suggests some modifications of them. Ultimately, however, Lakatos thinks although a modified form of falsificationism has many merits, falsificationism is not correct even about theoretical science as we need to use some sort of induction to stop science from becoming a useless game. It is sometimes unclear whether Lakatos's target is Popper's own views or some other version of falsificationism. At any rate, Lakatos says there are three important problems with some variants of falsificationism.

First, many falsificationists have been reluctant to subject their account to any empirical test. To justify not subjecting the falsificationist account to empirical test, Popper stresses that theories of scientific method are normative and not merely descriptive. He points out that as normative sentences use words like 'should' and 'ought', one cannot logically derive them from descriptive statements. This is, of course, correct. But this is not consistent with the spirit of falsificationism which stresses the dangers of relying on intuitions and the value of independent tests of intuitions. Remember from my discussion in Chapter 1 that Popper says, to make our scientific theories falsifiable, we should choose to adhere to certain descriptions of what we experience, even though those descriptions have no logical connection with experience. The case of methodology is not fundamentally different from that of falsification through experiences, and thus Popperians could and should agree to adopt a reasonable convention for testing proposed methodologies. What would be a reasonable convention? One suggestion is it is a reasonable convention that the only good methodologies are ones which would have allowed theories that have greatly advanced scientific knowledge to survive and triumph.

Second, Lakatos has a criticism of the naive variant of falsificationism. This naive variant of falsificationism holds that we should treat a theory as refuted whenever it seems to be contradicted by experience. Lakatos argues that if we test this variant of falsificationism by using the history of science, we find it to be grossly implausible as it would have made us reject the theories which have been most successful in the history of science. Speaking in naive falsificationist terms, every good theory has been multiply refuted at an early stage, in the sense that it was inconsistent with apparently known facts. For example, naive falsificationism would have forced us to reject Copernican astronomy because, in its original form, it was inconsistent with: (a) the known paths of the planets; and (b) with the fact that the planets look about the same size when they are supposedly close as they do when they are supposedly far away.[6]

Third, falsificationists sometimes talk as if one were testing a single theory against the facts (theoretically interpreted). This is misleading in two ways:

1 Scientific communities will never abandon a theory, however bad, unless there is a better theory to replace it. Their attitude is reasonable as even a terrible theory might be modified to meet apparent refutations and good theories do not spring from people's minds in a fully developed state but take many years to develop.
2 The interpretation of the facts which are used to test a theory may be mistaken and sometimes a good way to find this out is to allow a rival theory to develop.

A danger of Popper's original account is that it does not discuss the conditions under which one should be allowed to question the conventional interpretation of certain experimental results. It is thus dogmatic in its adoption of conventions. For example, the nineteenth-century Newtonian scientist, Leverrier, noted that the orbit of Mercury seemed not to follow Newtonian laws, if one assumed that all the relevant planetary bodies were known. He interpreted this, quite reasonably, to mean that an unknown planetary body existed which was causing the anomaly. He was being reasonable because a similar anomaly had been previously discovered in the orbit of Uranus and it had only been resolved through the discovery of Neptune. Leverrier had no success in finding the body or bodies which he thought must cause the anomaly in Mercury's orbit. But this might well have been because many planets are difficult to find. It was reasonable for Leverrier not to take the predictive failure of Newtonian physics to be a refutation of it. In fact, it turns out that Einstein's general theory of relativity can be used to predict the actual path of Mercury without assuming the existence of hidden planets, so that there is good evidence for thinking that Newton's theory is wrong. But we only have good reason to think it is wrong because a remarkable prediction made by using Einstein's theory turns out to be correct.

To deal with these problems Lakatos proposes *the theory of research programs*, according to which assessment in science is not assessment of the absolute merit of a theory, or even of the relative merits of two theories, but of the relative merits of rival research programs. A research program consists of a core claim, a group of auxiliary assumptions and a number of techniques for solving problems. A research program is better than its rivals if it is progressive in relation to those rivals. It is worse than its rivals if it is degenerating in relation to those rivals.

The core of the Copernican research program is that the planets revolve around the sun. Copernicus also believed that they travel in circular orbits, that circles are perfect, and many other things. But these are merely auxiliary assumptions which can be modified in the light of the predictive failure of the theory without harming the core of the Copernican research program. While theorists may modify the auxiliary assumptions of a theory, some modifications are problematic because they do not advance knowledge. A research program degenerates if all its advocates do is add untestable auxiliary assumptions or if their modifications merely account for already known facts. In such a case, we can say that the advocates of a research program are merely adding modifications to the program *ad hoc* to save its core. (As I am using the term, an *ad hoc* modification to a theory is a statement which has been added to a theory to save it from refutation, but which: (a) is not justified through empirical evidence; and (b) does not enable the theory to be used to predict any novel facts.) However, if the advocates of a core idea modify auxiliary assumptions so as to make new predictions, their research program is theoretically progressive. If their predictions turn out to be correct, their research program is also empirically progressive. Thus, when Kepler dropped the assumption that planets travel in circular orbits and replaced it with the assumption that the planets travel in elliptical orbits of particular kinds, his move was theoretically progressive as he made a number of predictions not made by Copernicus. When those remarkable predictions were later confirmed, his modifications became empirically progressive. By contrast, Kepler's Ptolemaic rivals merely added untestable hypotheses to the core of their program to account for the discrepancies between their theories and observation.

Lakatos argues that a program which has more of its predictions of novel facts corroborated than its rival is more progressive than that rival. However, he warns that relatively new programs need breathing space to develop and so should be allowed a certain amount of predictive failure. This means that in judging the merits of a recently developed program it would be a mistake merely to say that it is not progressive in relation to its rivals. Further, it seems from his remarks in his detailed historical analyses that he wants to say that even fully developed programs which contain a number of *ad hoc* hypotheses may be superior to their rivals. Sometimes a program may be the best rotten program available.

Obviously, Lakatos takes the prediction of a novel fact as adding a great deal of weight to a research program's claim to be superior to a rival which: (a) has no or fewer novel facts to its credit; and (b) has to explain what was predicted by adding *ad hoc* hypotheses. Popper sometimes says similar things about novel facts, though he talks of theories rather than research programs. For example, Newton's theory (plus various facts about the known planetary bodies) was used to predict the return of Halley's comet long before it occurred. As Lakatos says, this was 'remarkable'. It is, however, difficult to understand why novel facts should be so important in Popper's account. Popper wants to claim that the fact that the predictions of a theory have been corroborated is not relevant to their future performance. But science is, at least in part, a quest for true universal theories and true universal theories are as much about the future as about the past.

To make science relevant to gathering knowledge about both the past and the future, Lakatos says falsificationists need to add a principle saying that well-corroborated theories are more likely to be close to the truth than theories which have no novel fact to their credit. That is, they need to assume the plausibility of *an inductive principle* to stop their account from becoming a useless game, even when they are dealing with the theoretical sciences. Lakatos suggests that there is no great problem in allowing such a principle as a metaphysical conjecture. After all, Popper allows various other metaphysical conjectures, such as the conjecture that the basic statements which we use as potential falsifiers of theories are true, even though he says we adopt those basic statements as a matter of convention. It does seem, Lakatos says, that such a principle cannot be justified or tested empirically, yet he claims that we could discuss the merits of such a principle through various kinds of philosophical arguments (Lakatos, 1978: 154 ff.).

Popper has not accepted Lakatos's inductivist modification of his account. To accept it is to accept that he has made little progress in dealing with the problem of induction, for Lakatos's modification seems to turn falsificationism into an inductivism which relies on a version of inference to the best explanation. Further, if one allows that some metaphysical inductive principle is necessary, it will be a matter of debate precisely which inductivist principle or principles best do the job. An appeal to intuitions about the viability and need for various principles would then be warranted, and it is unclear whether a principle which uses the Popperian notion of corroboration would then be the best principle to adopt. Nevertheless, Lakatos's claim that falsificationism is wrong in rejecting induction altogether is plausible and, as a consequence, falsificationism fails to solve the problem of induction in the theoretical sciences.

A peculiarity of Lakatos's account is that he refuses to state the conditions under which a research program has been falsified, or even the conditions under which it is not worth pursuing any further. This is because he claims there have been occasions in the history of science when a research program which had degenerated has eventually made a triumphant return. This sort of phenomenon is to be expected when one realizes that the basic statements used to test a theory are fallible and that, as a result, a theory may be correct when it appears to have been refuted.

He claims an example of this kind is the Copernican theory, which was postulated by the Greek philosopher Aristarchus of Samos, abandoned in the face of apparent refuting evidence, and revived by Copernicus. It eventually triumphed with the advent of seventeenth-century physics and the discovery of the telescope. The empirical objections to Aristarchus's theory seemed weighty even in Copernicus's time. His theory implied that the Earth turned on its axis which meant, given the best developed physics of the day, that a stone dropped from a tower should land many yards behind the point at which it was dropped. Yet the stone apparently fell straight to the ground. The theory implied that at certain times Mars was much closer to the Earth and so, one would think, should look larger. But it did not. And so on. In contrast, the rival Ptolemaic theory seemed to fit well with naive observation. So, Lakatos says, in the light of the history of science it is dubious to say that scientists are irrational who defend theories which are inconsistent with experience. Further, had such theories been abandoned, this might have severely retarded the progress of science.

Lakatos concludes that it is rational for scientists to play a risky game, provided they admit that things are going against them. As a consequence, he never gives guidelines as to when a scientist should abandon a program. He makes it clear he thinks it is pointless to give advice to working scientists. One reason for this is that scientists constitute a community and, given that the community has the shared goal of finding true theories about the world, it is reasonable for a part of it to pursue degenerating research programs. Provided that most of the community pursues progressive research programs, all is well. To this end, he says that funding bodies should discourage scientists who pursue degenerating research programs, journals should refuse to publish their papers, and so on – but he does not even give precise guidelines for funding bodies or journals to follow. Instead, he appeals to the common sense of those involved, and admits there are no mechanical rules available (Lakatos, 1978: 113, 117).

Critical discussion of Lakatos

Feyerabend has criticized Lakatos by arguing that Lakatos is really a methodological anarchist, who allows that scientists and funding bodies can do anything they want since he has shown that one can give good reasons for doing anything at all in science. He argues that by Lakatos's account, a scientist could justifiably work on a voodoo research program which is full of *ad hoc* hypotheses, has failed to predict any novel facts, and has a robust rival. The scientist could argue that that program needs time to develop. (Remember that Lakatos says degenerating programs have sometimes been resuscitated after many years, by their predicting many novel facts, whereas their initially progressive rivals have eventually degenerated very badly.) Further, funding bodies could be justified in providing money for such scientists and journals could be justified in publishing their papers. These days, scientific research is an expensive business involving collaborative research and the use of instruments. If one fails to fund a scientist, one is not giving him or her a chance to develop a program. Lakatos's arguments might thus be said to be merely a form of propaganda – unjustifiably raising the prestige of science by calling whatever happens in science 'rational' (Feyerabend, 1981b: 213–19).

There is a sense in which Feyerabend is right. Lakatos fails to give precise mechanical rules for when a theory has been finally falsified. Yet an appropriate question might be whether such rules are possible or necessary to make science rational. Philosophers often talk as if science can only be rational if precise mechanical rules are giveable, at least in the form of a logical reconstruction of how a theory was refuted. In our everyday life, we operate with rules and terms which are vague in important ways. For example, my pointing near a corner and saying to a friend: 'please, stand roughly here' could not be plausibly interpreted to mean I am asking her to stand in the house next door. Thus, the fact that Lakatos's account is hedged with vague remarks does not mean Lakatos is allowing anything at all to be classified as rational. For instance, the remark that a research program in its early stages needs breathing space to develop does not imply the program should be allowed to degenerate for a thousand years. Further, while the funding bodies and journals applying the guidelines suggested by Lakatos's account will not agree in some cases, this does not mean they will not agree in many other cases. Sometimes people disagree as to whether something is green or blue, but this does not mean that the vast majority of their judgements about colour differ radically.

In addition, the fact that scientists can sometimes rationally play risky games does not mean that any risk a scientist takes is rational. Just because a program *might* revive is not going to be sufficient justification for a scientist to work on it indefinitely. If we accept Lakatos's inductive principle, it would be true that as more novel facts are predicted by a rival program, a scientist becomes less rational in sticking to a degenerating program; the probability of that program being true decreases. The scientist who continues to spend his life developing that program would be like a punter with limited funds who continues to bet on an elderly nag in a yearly race while knowing some other horse has won every year, and that those betting on it have become wealthy. He would be irrational even though such outside bets occasionally pay off. Lakatos should have said he was giving advice in a vague way to individual scientists. There is no precise point at which an individual scientist should abandon a research program. Nevertheless, after a while, we could all justifiably agree that a scientist continuing to pursue a particular program was behaving irrationally.

In some of his recent work, Feyerabend seems to be more sympathetic to a modified version of Lakatos's account. Instead of saying that there is no method, he says that there is no method in the sense of a highly precise set of rules of the kind Hempel tried to formulate when discussing a logic of confirmation. There are, however, many rough and ready rules, the application of which has to be learned in practical contexts. Learning to use experience properly is more like learning to swim well than like learning to use the rules of a formal language. When we learn to swim well, we hear vague instructions about where to put our hands, etc. We intelligently adapt what we hear and gradually improve our stroke. This does not mean that precise rules cannot be used in certain contexts, but we need to use our judgement to decide when those rules are to be used.[7]

Despite the fact that Lakatos could adequately deal with Feyerabend's criticisms, Lakatos's account suffers from four other problems. First, Lakatos talks as if a research program which successfully predicts a single remarkable novel fact or a few scattered novel facts is likely to be approximately true. But as we saw in Chapter 2, Whewell grasped that it is not the successful prediction of scattered novel facts, but the successful prediction of a range of novel facts which is good evidence for the approximate truth of a research program. The reason for this is that a research program which is not even approximately true can easily produce occasionally successful predictions of novel facts by coincidence.

Second, Lakatos is wrong in suggesting that the assessment of research programs is solely comparative. To see this, consider that Lakatos admits that if scientific research is not to be a useless game we must use inductive inferences which show that a theory is approximately true. Obviously, when we use such inferences, our assessment of competing research programs cannot merely be comparative. For when we assess whether a theory is approximately true, we are assessing how well it describes the world.

Third, Lakatos wrongly says that the assessment of research programs is always partly comparative. However, there are times in the history of science in which there is only one plausible research program in a domain. By the early nineteenth century, the Newtonian research program was the only viable research program in some parts of physics. By the early twentieth century, the germ theory of infectious diseases was the only viable research program in some parts of medicine. When such a research program is being assessed, it is not plausible to construe its assessment as at all comparative; it is being assessed against experimental evidence, not against its rivals. Lakatos does not recognize that this happens quite frequently in the history of science, and this renders aspects of his account implausible.

Fourth, contrary to Lakatos, there are episodes in the history of science in which most scientists will not accept any of the existing research programs in a domain and most scientists in the field are not even interested in doing research on any of them. It is not true that scientists will work with the best rotten research program available, however bad it is. The reason is that it sometimes happens that none of the existing research programs have succeeded in predicting a range of novel facts and all of them have been extensively bolstered by many *ad hoc* hypotheses. This happened in geology from the 1930s to the 1950s. All of the research programs which explained the formation of large scale features of the Earth seemed very poor and many geologists reasonably concluded that they would be better off spending their time on careful mapping or on localized explanations of small-scale events.

Conclusion

Falsificationism has considerable merits. It makes clear that some theories cannot be arrived at through enumerative induction, and it rightly stresses the importance in theoretical science of producing bold conjectures which are to be ruthlessly tested. However, it fails to present a cogent account of why it is rational to act on well-corroborated theories, and also fails to explain why we should prefer well-corroborated theories if we want to arrive at the truth. It thus fails to show that preferring well-corroborated theories is rational. It needs to be supplemented by a hypothesis which says that the world is constructed so that well-corroborated theories are more likely to be true.

We learn a great deal from Lakatos's critique of falsificationism. Many falsificationists talk as if falsifying instances are relatively easy to identify or can be identified by adopting a simple convention. This is because they continue to work with the idea that if science is to be rational, there must be a precise methodology by which we falsify theories. Despite their critique of the Cartesian view of knowledge, Popper and some of his followers seem to have fallen victim to it by assuming that, for science to be rational, there must be available precise criteria which always lead to an unambiguous decision. By using material derived from detailed historical studies, Lakatos shows that such views are dubious and that the assessment of the relative merits of research programs is a complicated business for which precise rules cannot be specified. Precise conventions about basic statements are too blunt to be of any use in deciding when a theory can be reasonably said to have been falsified. He thus further erodes the assumptions behind the search for purely formal accounts of scientific reasoning and scientific method. Precise rules do not exist for rejecting research programs and, at a particular point in time, different scientists can differ rationally as to whether a program should be abandoned. Despite this, science is a rational enterprise in which a broad consensus can be reached over a large number of cases and in which disagreement, where it occurs, is frequently fruitful.

It is dubious to assume science should either conform to philosophical demands as to how it must work or be declared irrational. Science has enormously expanded both our knowledge and our ability to control the world. Philosophical arguments, on the other hand, have often given us little that is not open to serious challenge. On the basis of intuitions about secure methods, philosophers often demand that research conform to standards which no significant theory has met or could meet. Plato demanded that true knowledge be derived from the world of the forms and Descartes that it consist of clear and distinct ideas. Yet there are no such things as a world of the forms or clear and distinct ideas. Kant thought that Euclidean geometry and Newtonian physics were true a priori. Yet experts in modern physics say that both are false or problematic. And so on. Falsificationists are well aware of the infirmity of philosophical arguments in comparison to scientific reasoning. But their account is badly damaged by a philosophical obsession with the apparent faultlessness and precision of formal deductive reasoning.

In the nineteenth century, John Stuart Mill and others directed their efforts to improving scientific reasoning through a study of the argumentative strategies which were used in significant scientific work. With the development of modern logic, this project was largely abandoned in favour of a priori logical reconstructions of scientific reasoning. The original idea behind the attempt to reconstruct scientific reasoning logically was that its power would be explained through a formal system resembling those of formal deductive and mathematical reasoning. However, as we saw in Chapter 2, the formal models produced, although of some use in understanding scientific reasoning in certain contexts, have turned out to be quite misleading when they are applied across a range of cases. They have also turned out to be of little use in gaining a more general understanding of scientific method. On the other hand, Lakatos presents an account which is closer to scientific practice and which is potentially more useful to scientists.[8] With Lakatos we thus return to a nineteenth-century tradition which is less interested in producing logically precise reconstructions of scientific method than in giving us a rough understanding of the kind of reasoning which is useful in science. We now turn to Mill's account to further our understanding.

2 Mill and coherentism

Mill's refinement of induction

Like Popper, Mill claims that Descartes's view that we should start with what is indubitably true requires the impossible. In contrast with Popper, John Stuart Mill thinks that we start our investigations of nature by assuming all enumerative inductions with true premises prove their conclusions. In his view, there is no better place to start than with such assumptions. Any methodology which attempts to test scientific conjectures without using induction will fail to provide any justification for believing particular conjectures. However, Mill holds that our starting assumption needs to be substantially modified. We quickly realize that enumerative inductions over some sorts of cases produce many generalizations which are falsified. We then justifiably say that the premises in such inductions provide little support for their conclusions. For example, we quickly realize that when we infer from the colour of a few instances of a species that all members of that species have that colour, our premise provides little support for its conclusion. However, in other sorts of cases, enumerative induction seems to produce statements which are not falsified, so we come to understand that enumerative inductions over such cases provide stronger support for their conclusions. For instance, we find that the generalizations about the broad structural anatomy of all the members of species arrived at by enumerative induction are rarely wide of the mark so we conclude that such inductions provide strong support for their conclusions.

Just as Popper argues that we are naturally disposed to conjecture certain laws are true, Mill thinks we are naturally disposed to assume that all enumerative inductions prove their conclusions, although we quickly come to modify that assumption. Unlike Popper and like Lakatos, Mill holds we must assume that some inductive reasoning is cogent if science is to be more than a useless game. (Mill thinks the only cogent inductive reasoning is some enumerative inductive reasoning.) But he goes further than Lakatos by arguing that the assumption that enumerative inductions provide a specific degree of support for their conclusions in specific types of cases is both empirically testable and modifiable. Note, however, that in Mill's view inductive arguments are often probabilistic. This means that the conjecture that enumerative inductive arguments over some type of thing will provide strong support for their conclusions cannot be falsified by their failure in a single case. As a consequence, the assumption that such inductions have a particular degree of probative force is difficult to refute. According to Mill's view, no logically precise account can be given of when the theory that inductive arguments provide a particular degree of support for their conclusions over particular sorts of cases is refuted. Nevertheless, Mill thinks we can and do decide on the basis of large numbers of trials that enumerative inductive arguments about some sorts of cases are at least much less probative than such arguments about other sorts of cases. In effect, Mill claims we have implicitly adopted a methodological convention which at least forces us to modify our estimates of the probative strength of enumerative inductions over particular types of things in the light of experience. (Literally speaking, an argument must be either probative or not but I am adopting a nineteenth-century convention in using the term 'probative', by which probativeness comes in degrees.)

Consider Mill's discussion of examples. He says that the statement that all swans are white had been enumeratively confirmed many times, even though it is clearly false. But it was known before the discovery of black swans that it was quite likely not to be true. We know that generalizations about the colour of swans are likely to fail to be universal truths because we know, from the frequent failure of other enumerative inductions, that the colour of animals often varies in different parts of the world. However, Mill distinguishes between statements about the colour of animals and statements about broad features of structural anatomy, such as the statement that humans' heads never grow beneath their shoulders. This statement is much more certain because broad features of structural anatomy of members of particular species or genera are known to be invariant on the basis of enumerative induction across many types of animals.

Mill claims that after a period of time, we arrive at fairly stable and justified inductive practices. We use statements at a high level of generality, such as those about variability of colour or the invariance of broad features of structural anatomy, to decide which inductions at a lower level of generality are justified and what degree of support they provide for their conclusions. The high level statements themselves are justified through the success of many low level inductions over particular types of things, for example, inductions dealing with the positions of the heads of cats, pigs, etc. The inference to any particular high level generalization is supported by the success of many generalizations at the lower level. The inference to any particular lower level generalization is supported by the success of the higher level generalization. Now you may think Mill's remarks are problematic, for he appears to be arguing in a circle by using enumerative induction to support certain types of enumerative induction. It is important to point out, however, that Mill does not see himself as arguing in a problematic circle because he does not see himself as having to respond to a generalized scepticism about induction. In his view, various problem cases only show that enumerative inductions sometimes fail to justify their conclusions.[9]

Mill's argument, that we come to know when we can reliably use enumerative induction, relies on a kind of *coherence theory of justification* of our inductive practices. According to coherence theories, there are no foundational statements we can appeal to which can be proved to be certain or even proved to be likely. We come to be justified in believing some statement by testing whether that statement coheres with our other current and future beliefs. Those beliefs, in turn, are justified by the extent to which they cohere with each other and with that statement. In this case, high level claims about induction are justified through the empirical success of specific kinds of low level inductions, any one of which will have its force boosted by the high level claims. Mill's edifice is, as it were, held together by the fact that the inductions implicitly licensed through the higher level statements rarely produce statements which are empirically falsified and typically produce statements which are multiply confirmed. Mill thinks that the continuing broad empirical success of science and, in so far as we can tell, of the generalizations our inferences seem to justify, means there is no need to appeal to an absolutely secure foundation for our inferential practices. Of course, it is possible that future discoveries will show that our confidence in our inferences is unwarranted. Perhaps tomorrow we will discover many animals from known species whose heads are in unexpected places; perhaps we will also discover that all the other inductive inferences we think reliable have led to false conclusions. In that case, our confidence in science and in some inductive inferences will have turned out to be misplaced. We will have totally to revise our judgement about the cogency of inductive inferences. But while Mill does not think he can rule out this possibility, he refuses to treat it as if it poses a serious problem because he thinks that to look for a foundation for our scientific inferences in statements which cannot be doubted is fruitless. In any case, as I pointed out in Chapter 1, to establish it is possible that a statement is false is not to give us a reason to doubt it.

Mill's methods

Mill's discussion of how we refine enumerative induction is a background to his description of a more elaborate methodology which is closer to the actual practice of many scientists. He takes it that, as a result of repeated experimentation and of the repeated use and refinement of enumerative induction, we have come to some high level conclusions about the world and about the kinds of causes which operate in particular domains of investigation. An important high level conclusion he thinks we have shown to be almost certain is that all events have a cause.[10] Mill also thinks we have shown that only certain kinds of causes operate in particular domains of investigation. An example is that our previous pattern of medical successes has strongly supported the germ theory of disease, which is the theory that all infectious diseases are caused by micro-organisms. Finally, Mill claims we know a great number of other generalizations which we use to guide our experimental practice, such as generalizations about where particular kinds of causal agents are likely to be found. On the basis of all this background knowledge, and of detailed observations, we can experimentally narrow down the potential causes of an event. We are now in a position to adopt procedures which will eliminate all the candidates except one.

Consider how well Mill's account seems to fit aspects of day-to-day scientific practice. Researchers often start out with the assumption that only a certain type of causal agent could be producing an effect. They then use assumptions concerning, roughly, where that agent is likely to be found and what it is likely to look like. These assumptions are bolstered by previous enumerative inductions. By relying on such assumptions and on observation, biologists investigating flu epidemics are able to narrow down their causes to a few possible viral agents. Using further procedures, they arrive at the cause – a specific virus.

Popper objects to Mill's account by arguing that the number of potential causal agents is infinite, so that an eliminative method cannot do the work it purports to do. But he neglects the fact that most of Mill's methods are meant to be used only after enumerative induction has provided a background field of knowledge which narrows down the possibilities. In Mill's account, the refutation of hypotheses plays an important role but it is a very different role from the one it plays in Popper's epistemology.

In drawing up some canons for eliminative reasoning, Mill relies on at least three assumptions. First, the phenomenon being examined has a cause. Second, the list of potential causes being examined is exhaustive. Third, a cause is both necessary and sufficient for a particular type of phenomenon. Mill makes it clear that the second assumption is revisable in the light of new background knowledge. He is also aware that there is sometimes a plurality of causes for a phenomenon; that is, that several different types of event can bring about a phenomenon. He discusses this kind of case in a separate section of his account which I cannot deal with in detail here.

The first canon, the method of agreement, states that if two or more instances of a phenomenon have only one circumstance in common, then the first is a cause (or effect) of the second. For instance, if two crystalline substances have only a preceding liquid state in common out of all the known potential causes of the crystallinity, then the liquid state is the cause of the crystallinity.

The second canon is the method of difference. This says that if an instance of a phenomenon occurring and an instance of it not occurring have every circumstance in common except one, then the circumstance in which the two differ is an effect or cause or part of the cause of the phenomenon. For example, if man X who is in the prime of life suddenly dies and his death was preceded by a gunshot wound, we could plausibly conclude that his death was caused by the gunshot wound. We can justifiably reach this conclusion because the gunshot wound would be the only one of the potential causes present which is not present in the case of man Y, who did not die and who is also in the prime of life.

Mill's next two canons – the joint method of agreement and difference, and the method of residues – are really variations on the previous two methods, so detailed discussion of them is not called for here. His fifth canon is the method of concomitant variation which says that if two phenomena vary concomitantly, one is the cause of the other. For example, variations in the position of the moon are regularly and proportionately connected with the times and places of high tides, so the position of the moon is the cause of these tides.

Mill's account makes sense of much of the ordinary work of scientists. He does not, of course, remove the possibility of error from science; the background assumptions with which researchers work might be mistaken. When eliminative inquiry fails to come up with causal hypotheses which remain unrefuted, Mill recognizes that we need to return to our background assumptions and consider their plausibility. Yet he takes it that science has proved to be remarkably successful in using such methods, and that this is evidence in turn of the probative force of the enumerative inductions by which he claims we ultimately arrive at the list of potential causes. The idea is presumably that we turn back to our assumptions less and less as time goes on and that this strengthens the case for believing we now know when we are licensed in using assumptions justified by enumerative induction.

Critical discussion

Two objections that may be raised to Mill's account are that: (a) he does not produce an adequate logic of discovery, and (b) he presents an inadequate logic of justification because of his emphasis on enumerative induction. A logic of discovery is a method by which we can discover scientific generalizations or laws on the basis of experience. A logic of justification is a method by which we can justify scientific generalizations or laws on the basis of experience.

From our discussion in Chapter 1, it will be obvious that John Stuart Mill must be wrong when he talks as if we can simply extract relevant observations for enumerative inductions. Something must guide us into concentrating our attention on specific features of particular things. On the other hand, as we saw in the same chapter, it is by no means clear that something elaborate is required to bring some features of the world to our attention. Having been caused to pay attention to certain details, we may formulate generalizations by enumerative induction. This seems to happen in fields like structural anatomy, as Mill was well aware. Alternatively, having conjectured certain hypotheses, we may then be able to justify them by enumerative induction. Mill does allow that sometimes hypotheses are not *arrived at* by enumerative induction, although he thinks they then need to be *justified* by enumerative induction. Further, once a range of theories in a field is widely accepted, the area in which we need to look for causes may be narrowly delineated. This would explain why scientists working independently in different parts of the world often come up with the same causal explanations. Mill's claim that there is some sort of logic of discovery operating in science ties in well with what seems to happen in some fields of research, such as that into infectious diseases.

At least two sorts of cases seem to be illuminated by Mill's account. First are the cases in which there are only a few well-established research programs which are likely to be relevant. If we know, for example, that a disease is very likely to be caused either by a particular bacterium or a particular virus, and we know many other things about bacteria and viruses, we can construct an experiment which shows that the phenomenon is caused by one or the other, using Mill's methods.

The second sort are cases in which an explanation successfully used in specific cases is applied with greater and greater confidence to other types of cases. An example is the development and ratification of a general germ theory of infectious diseases from specific theories which dealt with some plant diseases.[11] The germ theory has gradually become a practical tool tied to all sorts of auxiliary knowledge which specifies roughly how and where germs causing infectious diseases of particular parts of the body are likely to be found. Both the theory and the auxiliary knowledge are justified through previous successes.

When we turn to breakthroughs at a fundamental level, however, Mill's account is less satisfactory. Background knowledge may be useful in ruling out some alternatives, but it does not provide scientists with a set of clearly delineated viable alternatives or indicate where a causal agent is likely to be found. Consider Wegener's continental drift hypothesis, which holds that a whole range of important geological features and facts about biogeography are to be explained by postulating that continents are actually moving very slowly – that is, 'drifting'. It was a bold conjecture rather than an alternative to which we are guided by existing knowledge or a theory we can arrive at or even justify through enumerative induction. The most plausible test of such hypotheses is to see whether one can get startling predictions of novel facts by adding auxiliary assumptions to them. That is, when scientists are dealing with such theories, they convert them into research programs and rely on some sort of inference to the best explanation to confirm them. Mill was aware of the view that scientists sometimes proceed by producing conjectures and testing them, but he wrongly rejected inference to the best explanation for reasons I cannot go into here.

Having said that Mill's account needs to be expanded to allow for conjectures and to allow inference to the best explanation to be a legitimate mode of argument, it is worth pointing out that inference to the best explanation might be gradually refined in a similar way to the way in which Mill suggests that simple enumerative induction can be refined. I discussed inference to the best explanation in detail in Chapter 2, so I do not need to discuss it further here.

Conclusion

Mill's coherence theory of justification shows how we can arrive at justified and successful inductive practices if we start by assuming that all inductive reasoning of a particular sort proves its conclusion from true premises, and then modify that assumption in the light of what we learn. Lakatos's view that the inductive principles we need in science must remain untestable metaphysical conjectures is thus too pessimistic. In addition, Mill shows us how we can use enumerative induction and his eliminative methods to arrive at, and justify, some hypotheses. However, Mill's account does not offer a plausible logic of discovery or of justification in the case of revolutionary research programs.

By putting together the insights of Mill with those of Lakatos and the probabilists, we can begin to formulate a plausible account of scientific method. Producing conjectures, trying to refute them and modifying them in a way which is not merely *ad hoc* are all important procedures in producing revolutionary breakthroughs. But, contrary to Popper, this does not mean that enumerative induction never plays any part in such breakthroughs. The germ theory of infectious diseases, for example, seems to have been gradually developed into a general theory of disease by extrapolation from cases where micro-organisms could be plausibly shown to be key causal agents. Further, as Lakatos emphasizes, it is often useful to test research programs by considering their merits in comparison to rival research programs, and not against refuting facts which would be available independently of the existence of a rival theory. However, such research programs also need to be tested to see whether they are likely to be true and sometimes the only way to test them is to see whether their prediction of a range of novel facts is correct. The probabilists, described in Chapter 2, rightly emphasized that the confirmation of such facts shows that a theory is probably approximately true, even if we cannot give a precise account of how it shows it. But the probabilists and Lakatos do not give us much insight into what happens when a single well-developed research program has come to be the only viable program in a field.

In Chapter 2, I showed that Hume's puzzle does not pose a serious problem for induction or for the rationality of science, even if we do not know precisely why plausible inductive reasoning is cogent and cannot present a plausible formal reconstruction of how inductive reasoning works. In this chapter, I have shown that a fallibilist theory of scientific method can be used to refine enumerative induction and develop the theory of research programs into a viable scientific methodology.

Further reading

Popper very clearly defends his position in Popper, 1972: 1–31. The first part of John Worrall's entertaining argument (1989) that Popper fails to solve the pragmatic problem of induction requires no background knowledge. Lakatos's difficult 'Falsification and the Methodology of Scientific Research Programmes' is worth grappling with, although aspects of it are too hard for students (Lakatos, 1978: 8–101). Feyerabend's critique of Lakatos should be largely comprehensible to students (Feyerabend, 1981b: 202–30). A view which has been influential primarily among historians of science and which resembles the view of

Lakatos is defended by Laudan (Laudan, 1977). Laudan differs from Lakatos. He claims that the ability of theories to solve conceptual problems is as important as their ability to solve empirical problems and he proposes a method of evaluating theories which has nothing to do with their truth. An accessible description of Laudan's view is given by Riggs, 1992: 95–123. A useful critique is Feyerabend, 1981c. I am unconvinced by Laudan's central claims and I criticize some of them in Chapter 7, but I have no space to pursue the issue in detail.

Mill's view is very clearly presented and plausibly modified in Skorupski, 1989: 167–202. David Papineau (1993: 141–70) ties Mill's account to a defence of induction in a clear and interesting way. Mill's own account is confusing and sometimes inconsistent.

Notes

1 At times, Popper seems to admit that some inductive reasoning is cogent. For an illuminating discussion of Popper's *ad hoc* manoeuvres, see Newton-Smith, 1981: 67 ff. I have taken Popper's stronger claims to represent his main position.

2 My interpretation of Mill is contentious. At a number of points, Mill talks as if one can prove various things and as if a number of scientific theories had been proved. However, other parts of his account make it clear that Mill means to be a fallibilist and that his talk of proof cannot be justified. (The word 'proof' seems to have been used in a loose way in the nineteenth century.) I rely on the account of Skorupski (1989: 192 ff.), I also rely on the insightful remarks in Papineau, 1993: 162–67. In any case, the issue here is not Mill scholarship and readers who do not accept my interpretation of Mill can take it to be an account of what Mill ought to have said.

3 Popper's use of such examples is misleading for two reasons. First, his examples use simple enumerative induction and many inductivists have not favoured simple enumerative induction. Like other logically minded thinkers he ignores the details of some sophisticated accounts, presumably because they are believed to be in some sense logically equivalent to simple enumerative induction. Yet such a procedure begs the question, as it assumes induction must work like deduction and goes against intuitions which distinguish simple enumerative induction from other procedures. Second, the examples Popper uses are ones in which the theories concerned are approximately true. On one account of the value of induction, we might not arrive at a true theory but we are likely to arrive at a theory which is approximately true. If induction were a method for arriving at theories which are at least approximately true, it might still be of great benefit both pragmatically and in helping the progress of science. (This does not mean, of course, that one will be content with a theory which is only approximately true, so after one finds out it is false, one will have to go beyond it.) It is thus not clear whether Popper's criticisms by way of discussion of examples touch key claims of real inductivists.

4 My critique of Popper's solution to the pragmatic problem of induction relies heavily on Worrall's excellent discussion (Worrall, 1989).

5 In *Science and Scepticism*, John Watkins (1982) has also proposed an interesting solution to the pragmatic problem of induction which fails for the reasons cited in Worrall, 1989. To explain the problems with Watkins's proposal properly I would need to deal with technical aspects of probability theory, which would be inappropriate in a book for students.

6 This is because (a) Copernicus's original hypothesis assumed the planets travel in circular orbits whereas they travel in elliptical orbits; and (b) the telescope had not yet been invented, so that the difference in the apparent diameter size of the planets had not been noticed.

7 Feyerabend, 1981a: 17. See also Brown (1988) for a similar view.

8 Lakatos says that he is presenting a rational reconstruction of how science works, and that he is not trying to give advice to scientists. Despite his intentions, I think he gives scientists vague but useful advice.

9 Mill does not deal with Hume's puzzle. He may have been unaware of Hume's argument. He seems to assume that all that has been shown by inductive sceptics is that inductive reasoning is sometimes not truth transmitting, and that it is not quite like deductive reasoning.

10 The development of quantum theory has cast doubt on this claim. Nevertheless, we can agree with Mill that the vast majority of macroevents have causes.

11 For a brief discussion of the early stages in the development and ratification of the germ theory, see Dubos, 1950: 258 ff.

4

Revolutionary Change and Rationality: Kuhn and his Rivals

The image of science which is often found in science textbooks, in popular accounts of the lives of great scientists, and in everyday discussions of science is one of an enormous and cumulative growth of knowledge. At any rate, this is the picture many accounts give of natural science since the time of Galileo. This image has great power. It gives science enormous prestige and makes it easier for scientists to get vast amounts of money for research projects which deal with matters very remote from everyday life, like the origins of the universe. It encourages students of human behaviour to call themselves social scientists, to imitate the methods of the natural sciences, and to be suspicious of other approaches for understanding human conduct. It makes many philosophers think that the only respectable epistemological theories are those which can explain the success of science. It induces other philosophers to reconstruct their ontologies so as to include entities like warped space-time and to reject entities like god. It is obviously very important to assess whether this image is justified.

The image underlies Karl Popper's famous essay, 'The Aim of Science' which discusses the development of modern physics from the sixteenth century to the early part of the twentieth century (Popper, 1972: 191–205). Popper describes the growth of physics as a growth in both predictive scope and detail. Galilean physics allowed us successfully to predict a vast range of events. However, in so far as it was successful, Galilean physics was explained and superseded by Newtonian physics. Galilean laws only successfully predict what happens in a narrow domain and are less accurate than Newtonian laws within that domain. In addition, Galilean laws are wildly off the mark outside that specific domain. For example, the Galilean law of free fall predicts the behaviour of a falling body in a vacuum fairly accurately, but it wrongly asserts that the rate at which a body accelerates in falling is constant. In fact, as bodies approach the centre of the earth, they accelerate faster – as predicted by Newtonian theory. Further, Galilean physics wrongly predicts that a long distance missile will follow a parabola. In fact, as Newtonian physics predicted, the path followed by the body is nothing like a parabola: it travels in an ellipse. In describing the behaviour of falling bodies, Galilean physics is roughly correct. In describing the behaviour of long distance missiles, it is quite mistaken.

According to Popper's account, Newtonian physics was in turn replaced by Einsteinian physics which corrects Newtonian physics in the domain of objects travelling at low velocities and makes accurate predictions about objects travelling at very high velocities, a domain in which Newtonian physics makes predictions which are quite wrong. A constant growth of knowledge thus occurs, in which the predictive detail and scope of theories improves. Popper says that each theory explains and corrects its predecessor, for each theory makes some similar but more accurate predictions to those of its predecessor in a particular domain and some very different, but roughly accurate, predictions outside that domain.

By this account, it is somewhat unclear what we should say about physics before Galileo. There are two plausible possibilities: the first is it was part of a constantly growing scientific knowledge; the second that it was mostly pre-scientific speculation, which was useful enough in its time but was largely replaced by theories introduced in the scientific revolution. Popper seems to favour the second option; but either way, physics after the seventeenth century was an advance.

Several important assumptions underlie such accounts. First, there are objective standards by which the relative merits of theories or research programs can be judged and we can tell there has been a growth of knowledge by reference to those standards. An example of a standard of this kind is that a theory which is better corroborated is preferable. Popper would say that knowledge grows when we change theories because a new theory is better corroborated than its predecessors. Within the mature sciences (such as physics) the old theory is typically similar to the new theory, so the old theory can be plausibly regarded as having some truth content. However, the new theory has greater truth content. A second assumption is that the standards are independent of the content of theories or of the assumptions behind theories. For instance, in much of his work Popper talks as if he can articulate the appropriate standards by which rationally to compare scientific theories that deal with the same items, no matter what the content of the theories. Although Aristotelian physics and Galilean physics are wildly different in many ways, they can be legitimately compared by appeal to the same standards. Third, the standards we should use to judge theories should be understood to be rules which are capable of coherent expression in the form of precise general statements. An example here might be that the relative merits of two scientific theories should be judged by whether one of them has been falsified.

Popper's account also contains two normative assumptions, as is clear from the title of his paper and his discussion of science elsewhere. First, science has a *proper aim* which is not to fill in details in our knowledge, to solve minor problems or to facilitate the production of technologically useful devices. The proper aim of science is to produce bold hypotheses which expand our knowledge of very general features of the world.

Second, science should be conducted so as to encourage rational criticism of assumptions, however fundamental. It is possible to create a science which is authoritarian and dogmatic, but this is not in keeping with the proper value ideals of science and of our whole civilization.[1]

Thomas Kuhn challenges Popper's image of scientific growth and the assumptions underlying it.[2] Kuhn claims that the procedures scientists and others use to extend knowledge are not precise general rules for judging the relative merits of theories. They are interconnected sets of procedures and assumptions which are so subtle and complex that they can be properly learnt only by thoroughly understanding particular instances of scientific achievements and through doing scientific research in which we apply what we have learnt from those instances. If we attempt to articulate what guides research as precise general rules, we produce simplistic rules which would not lead scientists to advance knowledge. Further, the underlying assumptions and procedures which scientists learn through understanding instances of scientific achievements cannot be adequately defended on the basis of shared and more fundamental standards. They shape reasoning and perceptions in a scientific discipline, so that there is nothing more fundamental to which to appeal.

As a consequence of his account of the nature of scientific reasoning and of some descriptions of how science has developed, Kuhn also argues that in scientific revolutions progress in science does not, and cannot, occur on the basis of shared standards. Further, fundamental aspects of older theories have to be given up, which means that older theories cannot be correctly said to be approximately true. The metaphysical picture underlying the new theories is completely different from that underlying older theories.

If Kuhn is correct, it seems science cannot be an enterprise which has led to a growth of knowledge on the basis of objective standards that can be plausibly articulated as precise general rules. Indeed, his argument seems to imply that science is not even a rational enterprise. If this is correct, the place of scientific method as a paradigmatic example of how to acquire knowledge is undeserved. There is little reason to trust any of the reports of scientists about any aspect of the world. Further, if Kuhn is right about the nature of procedures for acquiring knowledge, it is hard to see how any one procedure for gathering knowledge can claim to be better than any other, except among researchers who have been trained in using the specified procedure. It is no wonder that Popper and his followers have accused Kuhn of encouraging irrationalism.

However, as I shall show, things are not as simple as they may seem. Kuhn argues that there can be good reasons for thinking a scientific research program is suffering from serious problems. He also says that when a science such as physics develops to a stage in which important assumptions and methodological standards become the accepted ones, scientists do research which leads to a certain kind of progress. In addition, he argues that from an outsider's perspective, science does progress because more puzzles are solved, more predictions are confirmed and predictions become more accurate. He wants to replace the older image of progress with an image of his own.

To support his case, Kuhn relies on an account of how scientific reasoning works and how some important scientific revolutions have occurred. He uses history because he thinks that by understanding how science works in practice, we will realize that none of the general methodological rules or the accounts of the growth of knowledge which have been articulated by philosophers look at all plausible. Far from discovering that a growth of knowledge has occurred on the basis of shared and objectively justifiable standards, we find deep disagreements between highly intelligent scientists, each of whom could produce plausible justifications for his or her position.

I shall argue that although we can learn much from Kuhn, he is wrong in suggesting that scientific growth has not occurred on the basis of objectively justified standards, even if those standards are imprecise.

1 Kuhn and scientific revolutions

The nature of scientific reasoning

To explain Kuhn's arguments, I need to give a brief description of how he thinks scientific reasoning works. By his account, a mature science always has a *paradigm*, and reasoning works by following the standards of the paradigm. The notion of a paradigm is vague, though Kuhn describes some of its key features. A paradigm is partly defined by an exemplary scientific achievement in which some scientific puzzles have been set and solved by using various conceptual and empirical techniques. This achievement is typically embodied in an important scientific work, such as the *Opticks*, Newton's major work on the nature of light and colour. Members of a mature scientific discipline learn key concepts, puzzle-solving techniques and what sorts of things constitute important puzzles by working through solutions to puzzles described in such works. In the course of their learning, they imbibe deep-seated assumptions about the nature of the world and about what observations and concepts are relevant for properly conducting research in that discipline. Their understanding of key scientific concepts, their perceptions and their style of reasoning will all have been shaped by the paradigm. In this way, they become a viable community of scientific researchers.

The most important way in which Kuhn thinks a paradigm functions is in making the members of a community of scientific researchers perceive similarities between what were previously perceptually disparate things. Scientists need to learn how to apply equations to solve problems in a variety of situations. For instance, they need to perceive similarities between the behaviour of conical pendulums and balls rolling down inclined planes in order to be able to apply laws which relate force, mass and acceleration to both types of behaviour. By Kuhn's account, this process does not happen by teaching people precise rules about which features of things make them relevantly similar. Rather, it happens by changing people's perceptions. Kuhn uses the example of a child learning to see the differences between ducks and geese. At first, the parent will point to a duck and a goose, saying 'duck' when pointing to a duck, and 'goose' when pointing to a goose. The child will then try using the words and be corrected by the parent. Eventually, the child's perceptions will change as the child learns to highlight certain features which were not perceptually salient before. Initially these features themselves will be perceived as varying a great deal, so the child will also need to learn to perceive the different instances as similar. For instance, a number of neck shapes and lengths will begin to look both very similar to each other and different from another group of neck shapes and lengths. The child will now have a set of exemplars of what defines 'goose' and will be able to apply the term to new cases. In this way, the child learns to see what was not perceptually salient before and is able to enter the community of English users. At no point in this procedure do precise rules defining the features possessed by ducks or geese play an important part in teaching the child (Kuhn, 1977: 308 ff.).

Note that a paradigm is not a scientific theory, or even the hard core of a research program, although a particular paradigm may contain theories or hard cores. However, it is important to stress that a part of a paradigm is some important metaphysical assumptions, which may show themselves in the ways in which scientists explain things rather than in their explicit pronouncements. For example, by Kuhn's account, the assumption that nature consisted of some sort of corpuscular material was part of the paradigm of physics in the seventeenth century in the sense that it delimited the range of explanations of phenomena which were thought to be acceptable. However, the corpuscular view was not a scientific theory at that stage as, even when it was articulated, it was treated as an untestable metaphysical assumption behind research.

Kuhn argues that it is not an accidental feature of scientific research that scientists learn how to do it by being inculcated into a paradigm. He claims that psychological and historical research show that our methods for using concepts and for judging theories are things which we extrapolate by analogy from important instances and which we only usefully extrapolate by adapting our judgements to particular contexts. They cannot be usefully articulated as precise and general rules.[3] As an argument for his claim, he points out it is a striking feature of scientific research that scientists radically disagree about the nature of the standards for judging the merits of scientific hypotheses, even though they agree in their judgements about the merits of scientific hypotheses. He argues that someone who appeals to implicit precise general rules to explain this phenomenon is proceeding to introduce an unnecessary and unsupported hypothesis. We can better understand how useful scientific work can be done without appealing to the existence of such implicit rules.[4]

A related argument Kuhn presents against the usefulness of precise general methodological rules is that even the most advanced philosophical theories of methodology, such as Popper's falsificationism, have failed to capture anything which happens in important scientific developments and would have been damaging if they had been used as norms which tell us how scientific hypotheses should be tested. Kuhn's detailed argument for this claim is similar to that of Lakatos, so I shall not go into it here.

Kuhn thinks that a paradigm is necessary to do useful research in because we need to have ways of interpreting observations, of knowing what puzzles are significant and of distinguishing what counts as a solution to a puzzle.

The nature of scientific revolutions

In Kuhn's view, a science develops in the following way. First there is what he calls a *pre-paradigm* stage in its development. The key features of the pre-paradigm stage are that there is deep disagreement about fundamental theory and a great deal of fairly random fact-gathering which does not follow any kind of accepted procedure. At some point, things change and there emerges a widespread agreement that some scientific work in an area is an exemplar and that its example should be followed. Basic assumptions underlying that work become widely accepted; and, more importantly, the ways of doing research which are used in that work are widely imitated. This is the period during which, Kuhn says, a particular paradigm dominates that area in science.

While the paradigm dominates, the basic assumptions of the exemplary work at the heart of the paradigm are largely unquestioned. Further, the kinds of procedures for gathering facts and solving puzzles which were used in the exemplary work are used throughout that discipline. Such activities are what Kuhn calls *normal science*. The most important thing that happens when the work in an area constitutes normal science is that various puzzles are solved in the manner of the exemplary work. Many other things also occur. Factual knowledge accumulates and becomes more precise. Technological innovations are produced. However, after some time, a number of unsolved puzzles occur, many of which, on the assumptions of the community of scientists themselves, are important. Kuhn calls such failures to solve puzzles *anomalies*. As anomalies multiply, and some of them are seen to be of great importance, science in that area enters a period of crisis. The crisis is resolved when a new paradigm replaces the old paradigm.

According to Kuhn's account, most of the important scientific work occurs during the period when a normal science has come into existence.

Before this time there is too much dispute over fundamentals, and a great deal of random and directionless fact-gathering. As a result, much of the work done in the pre-paradigm phase will turn out to have been useless in solving important puzzles or even in accumulating new facts. Even the revolutionary work which grounds the paradigm could solve only a few puzzles to a very broad degree of accuracy. In the period of normal science which follows, many more puzzles are solved to a much greater degree of accuracy. Within a normal science, the kind of cumulative growth of knowledge occurs which is described by Popper and others. As an example, consider what happened after the Newtonian revolution occurred in mechanics. Newton had produced a remarkable basic theory of physics which he applied to a range of problems. Yet much of the theory required detailed work to be applied to various problems. His equations were obscure and needed to be interpreted to be applied to further problems. New areas of mathematics had to be developed to come up with further predictions. Over time, the predicted paths of planets were calculated to a far greater level of accuracy. New planets were discovered by working on anomalies in the paths of known planets. And so on.

Much of this account may seem to fit reasonably well with the older image of scientific growth, if that older account were suitably modified. But Kuhn thinks it does not fit if we fully understand what is involved in a paradigm and study what happens in scientific revolutions.

First, in a scientific revolution, the leading scientists working within the old and new paradigms will not be able to reach a rationally agreed acceptance of the superiority of the new paradigm. A traditionally minded group of scientists who want to stick to the old paradigm will develop, typically made up of the older ones who have used the old paradigm for a long time. They will be able to give good reasons for their decision, as good reasons are understood under the old paradigm. There will also be a group of rebel scientists, typically comprising younger members of the profession whose thinking is not as constrained by the old paradigm, who will be able to give good reasons for their change to the new paradigm. Those reasons will relate to the fact that it is widely recognized the old paradigm has serious problems, and they will also use the criteria of the new paradigm to judge theories developed under the old paradigm as deficient. According to Kuhn, the conflict cannot be rationally resolved. It will be non-rationally resolved through the retirement or death of older members of the profession and their failure to attract new adherents to the old paradigm.

A second way in which Kuhn thinks his account differs from the older image of scientific growth is that, in his view, theories formulated under the new paradigm are often so different from older theories that the older theories cannot plausibly be thought to be approximations of the new theories. The reason why they are radically different is that the ontological assumptions which underlie the newer theories are very different from those which underlie the older ones. Indeed in some of his work, Kuhn claims they are so different as to be conceptually incommensurable. This seems to mean that when a paradigm change occurs, we cannot legitimately talk of a growth of scientific knowledge. To illustrate Kuhn's point, let me explain his claims about the relation between Newtonian mechanics and Einstein's special theory of relativity.

Many textbooks talk as if Newtonian mechanics is very similar to Einstein's special theory of relativity. Both of them appear to use similar concepts, such as mass, velocity and time. The predictions produced by the two theories are much the same when the theories are applied to objects travelling at low velocities. Only when they are applied to objects travelling at high velocities do the predictions of the two theories diverge significantly. At first sight, it seems that all of this implies that Newtonian mechanics must be an approximation of Einstein's theory. But Kuhn argues that this cannot be right. Newtonian mechanics has an implicit ontology which is radically different from that of Einstein's theory, so that it refers to different things. In Newtonian mechanics, the mass of an object is an intrinsic property – the amount of matter it contains. In Einstein's theory, the mass of an object is a relational property which varies according to the frame of reference from which it is measured. In Newtonian mechanics, the shape of an object is an intrinsic feature. In Einstein's theory, shape is frame-relative like mass. Kuhn claims that it is not isolated terms in the two theories which mean something different, every single descriptive term in the two theories means something quite different. He argues such differences mean that if Einstein's theory is true, Newtonian mechanics cannot even be approximately true because the ontology of Einstein's theory rules out the existence of the things presupposed in Newtonian mechanics. If Einstein is right, there are no intrinsic masses or shapes, or anything of that kind. Thus, if Einstein's theory is right, Newtonian mechanics fails to refer, so that it cannot be approximately true. Similarly, if the terms in Newtonian mechanics are to be taken to refer to something, it cannot be to the entities referred to by Einstein's theory.[5]

Kuhn stresses that although his view of the development of science is very different from older images, he does not intend to defend relativism – the view that the merit of a scientific theory is dependent solely on criteria which are internal to the paradigm from which it is judged.[6] There will, he claims, be some similarity and continuity between paradigms and there will be some criteria for judging theories which are shared. After all, the new paradigm does not spring out of the air and the adherents of each paradigm have an outside life in which they use other assumptions and habits. An example might be that the adherents of both paradigms judge simpler theories to be preferable to more complicated ones. However, Kuhn says that the adherents of the two paradigms will not be able to resolve their dispute by using this criterion, because they will both rank and interpret various criteria of excellence differently.

It seems that even if Kuhn is not committed to relativism, he must be committed to the claim that no growth of knowledge occurs across scientific revolutions. But, he says, he does not deny that science progresses, even when a discipline has passed through several scientific revolutions. Science does not replace theories with other theories which are closer to the truth; but it progresses because, as paradigms succeed one another, scientists solve more puzzles, produce more successful predictions and improve the accuracy of their predictions. An observer who is viewing from outside the paradigms in question can reasonably hold that there has been progress because most of the puzzles which scientists try to solve are 'directly presented by nature, and all involve nature indirectly' (Kuhn, 1970c: 263–4).

2 Critical discussion

Many critics have been unconvinced either by Kuhn's description of the development of science or by his philosophical claims. It is important to realize that Kuhn intends to use his historical arguments to bolster his philosophical claims and vice versa, so that criticisms of Kuhn's views cannot be neatly divided into the philosophical and the historical. For Kuhn, what actually happened in the development of science is an important guide to what is possible and desirable. Like Lakatos, he holds that philosophical theories about how we can best proceed in gathering knowledge need to be tested against how important developments in science have occured. Methodological principles which would have stultified the development of science are of little use. Criticisms of Kuhn's view are of two kinds: arguments that his philosophical claims are mistaken, and arguments that he has misrepresented what has happened in the history of science. I will concentrate on the first kind of criticism, but it is important to remember that there is no sharp distinction between the two as Kuhn bases many of his philosophical claims about perception and about the importance of paradigms on his historical remarks.

Kuhn on perception

I pointed out earlier in this chapter that Kuhn argues that because paradigms shape perception, they cannot be easily rationally compared by participants. It may be thought that Kuhn unjustifiably does not draw the obvious sceptical conclusion that objectively justified knowledge is impossible considering his view about perception. It is thus important to assess Kuhn's view and discuss what implications about our knowledge can legitimately be drawn from it.[7] Before I assess his view and discuss its implications, I need to spell out the claims he makes and explain the implications sceptics may draw from them. Kuhn melds four different claims in his discussion.

The first claim is that because we change our point of focus when we are trained in a paradigm so that we notice things we did not notice before, our perceptions change. For instance, as a result of the parent's pointing, the child notices that a particular goose has a longer neck than a particular duck. He or she then notices that the necks of geese resemble one another more than the necks of ducks do. As a result of this training, when the child sees a bird, he or she tends unconsciously to concentrate on certain areas of it and not others. The child can now immediately decide whether a bird is a duck or a goose.

Sceptics may say that the first claim implies that training in a paradigm biases people's perception because they will tend to fail to notice differences and similarities on which they have not been taught to focus.

The second claim is that, through being inculcated into a paradigm, we learn to automatically classify things as of particular kinds and treat them appropriately according to that classification, however they look in experience. An example here is that we learn to treat as masses both a ball on a plane and a pendulum. We then find it difficult to treat them in any other way, just as we find it difficult to change the way in which we type once we have learnt a certain way of typing.

Sceptics may argue that the second claim implies that being inculcated into a paradigm biases our perception because we may miss other ways of usefully grouping things together in fruitful theories.

The third claim is that training in a paradigm literally changes our experiences and associated concepts so that we actually see things we did not have the capacity to experience and recognize before. For example, the child did not have the capacity to experience and recognize the differences betweeen ducks and geese, although he or she did have the capacity to recognize what makes things birds.

Sceptics may maintain that the third claim implies that training in paradigm biases our experience because after training we would experience some things as falling into separate natural classes, although it may be fruitful for us to see the similarities we saw before or other similarities to which we have been blinded by training in the paradigm.

The fourth claim is that training in a paradigm causes us to be able to experience sharp differences between things which we would previously have perceived to vary gradually. For instance, the child did not have the capacity to see ducks and geese as very different kinds of birds before training in the paradigm. Instead he or she experienced them as differing birds. Having once been trained to have this capacity, the child will have difficulty in seeing the similarities he saw before. This too will make the child see ducks and geese as falling into distinct natural classes and may be thought by sceptics to prevent the child from being able to see other similarities between them.

KUHN'S FIRST CLAIM Kuhn's first claim about the influence of paradigms on perception seems plausible. If it were true, it would explain in a simple way two curious features of visual representations. First, the fact that supposedly realistic drawings produced by past painters or scientists often seem to be curiously biased. Some features we think are obvious are not represented, others which we think hardly noticeable are curiously exaggerated. Second, the fact that past scientists seem not to have noticed features we think to be obvious in the images we see in telescopes and microscopes. Since training does sometimes influence our perception in both these ways, it may be thought that we will be biased and so cannot be in a position objectively to assess theories by using experience. But drawing this conclusion would be wrong for two reasons.

First, while we will be disposed to ignore features which might be relevant to criticizing a received theory, the influence of the training can be overcome – albeit with some difficulty. Someone with a different background can point out features of the environment to us which we have never noticed before. As we are not incapable of seeing them, we can fairly quickly learn to spot them. We may even discover them without them being pointed out. Some people are particularly attentive observers of things which hardly anyone notices. Anyone who has studied art will know the truth of this. We can fairly easily be taught to focus on features of paintings we never noticed before but some people have a remarkable untaught capacity to discover such features for themselves.

Second, if we properly understand how a mature science comes into being, we will see that the selectiveness of the focus of researchers is not a form of bias because it can be objectively justified. In a mature scientific community, observers have rightly been carefully trained to concentrate only on the kinds of features which have repeatedly been found to be relevant to solving problems and making predictions. By inductive reasoning, they could justify their particular ways of making selective observations as well as their view that it is likely to be a waste of time and resources to collect observations in any other way. Having found after an enormous research effort that certain perceptually salient features have repeatedly allowed them to solve problems and make predictions in an area, it would be folly for scientists not to train their pupils to concentrate on those features on the basis of the claim that untrained or unfocused observers *occasionally* make major discoveries.

Kuhn is thus right in thinking that training observers to focus on only a narrow range of features is a part of a normal mature science but he is wrong in sometimes talking of it as merely a kind of bias which is necessary to get the job done. In fact, it is a way of proceeding which can be justified. The naive view that a selective focus in a science is a form of unjustifiable bias is the reverse of the true situation.

KUHN'S SECOND CLAIM Kuhn's second claim about perception is also correct and important. We need to learn to use scientific descriptions in a whole range of cases, as how to use them is by no means perceptually obvious. Scientific laws deal in categories, such as force and mass, which do not describe features of things that are experienced directly, and which need to be applied by learning to link them to experience in indirect ways. It may be thought this means that once we have been trained to classify things in particular ways, our perceptions will be biased by that training so that we cannot perceive potentially refuting instances of the assumptions behind our classificatory scheme.

However, the first thing to note about Kuhn's second assertion is that no change of one's experiences actually occurs in such cases – as anyone can testify who has learnt to do the sorts of things Kuhn describes. Remarks about changes in perception are misleading metaphors. The ball on the inclined plane and the pendulum look the same before and after one has realized that they are both masses. This means that if we need to, we can test various theories about what is happening in the world by producing neutral descriptions which rely on perceptually salient features. Even if the scientific language we use is pervaded by a theory, such as Newtonian physics, we can introduce a new language by pointing out, and relying on, features which are naturally perceptually salient.

A second point to note is that scientists who produce a large number of successful novel predictions, by using descriptions of perceptually disparate things which assume that they have important underlying similarities, are justified by inductive reasoning in training their pupils constantly to use those descriptions.

Kuhn's second claim thus reveals no unjustified bias in scientific practice and does not prevent us from testing theories in an objective manner.

KUHN'S THIRD AND FOURTH CLAIMS If Kuhn's third and fourth claims are right, they might be thought to pose a particularly serious problem for objectively testing theories by using experience. For it seems that, after undergoing training, we would have difficulty in appealing to perceptually salient features of things which are independent of a paradigm to test it. However, Kuhn's third and fourth claims are implausible.

Consider a child learning new categories in the manner Kuhn describes. The child cannot learn to pick out the crucial perceptual similarities between geese and their differences from ducks by ostension unless the child can already notice the crucial features which mark out geese from a mass of things which may be being pointed to. For example, to the child, the necks of different geese must already look more alike than the necks of ducks, enabling the child to connect them to the word 'goose'. So the child must already possess the perceptual categories which roughly mark geese out, and be able to identify them in the world, before being able to understand the concept 'goose'. Perhaps the child has not noticed the manifold similarities between geese, and the differences between geese and ducks. Perhaps the child does not even have the concept of a long neck until he or she follows the finger of the parent on a number of occasions and is suddenly struck by the resemblance, thereby acquiring the concept of a long neck before having the words. Perhaps the child does not yet connect together the many similarities between geese to form an independent concept 'goose'. But what *could be* perceptually salient for the child does not change when the child learns to use the word 'goose' to describe a goose. The conceptual architecture which allows the child to be able to pick out the appropriate features in experience must already be there if he or she is to be able to learn the concept 'goose' from experience, and tie it to the appropriate word. The child could learn the concept 'goose' by studying birds for him or herself and Kuhn gives no good reason for believing that the child's experience would change in any way which would pose a threat to the objectivity of theory testing when he or she learnt this concept.

In addition, after the training, the child could learn to notice similarities he or she was not focusing on by having them pointed out. Kuhn misleadingly treats ordinary learning of concepts and terms as like seeing the Müller-Lyer illusion, where we can have great difficulty in changing our perceptions once we have seen it. But ordinary learning, in which one deals with three-dimensional objects seen in good conditions, is not like this because in ordinary cases we can fairly easily come to recognize similarities between objects we did not notice before as well as the similarities we had previously noticed. The reader will know this from personal experience of having learnt to discriminate various things. (I have already dealt with the supposed problems these sorts of claims raise for objectivity in Chapter 1, so I will not restate my criticisms here.)

As Kuhn's third and fourth claims are implausible, they do not pose any problems for objectively testing theories. Thus, in so far as Kuhn's claims about the influence of paradigms on perception are plausible, they do not raise any problems for objectively testing theories.

Kuhn's account of progress

PROGRESS WITHIN A PARADIGM Kuhn's claim that his account is compatible with the view that progress and a growth of knowledge occurs in science seems unjustified. In many places, he talks as if what determines whether a puzzle exists or not, and whether it has been satisfactorily solved, is determined by the paradigm of which it is a part. This seems to be a consequence of the thesis that observation is paradigm-laden. If so, it seems there can be no test independent of the paradigms in question of whether progress has occurred. In addition, it seems that by Kuhn's own account, he is not entitled to say that the predictive success of theories can be measured across paradigms. This is because, he stresses, there is a great deal of rational disagreement across succeeding paradigms as to whether a prediction has been successful. He explains this by appealing to the fact that checking of predictions is a difficult business requiring considerable interpretative skills – due to the inaccuracy of instruments, constant interference by irrelevant causal agents, and the different standards for judging theories which prevail across paradigms (Kuhn, 1970a: 92–110; Barnes, 1982: 69–70). That is, he explains it by appealing to a variant of the view that scientific observations are theory-laden, as well as to the claim that standards are to some degree internal to paradigms.

In the light of all this, it seems that Kuhn does not adequately explain how he can defend the thesis that science progresses. However, the reader will remember that Kuhn says that someone studying both paradigms from the paradigm of neither will be able to describe the problems each has solved in a manner independent of either tradition. Such a person will be able to decide that the work done within the later paradigm has solved more problems (Kuhn, 1970c: 264). An obvious objection to this is, though it may be a description from a standpoint different from either, by Kuhn's account it cannot be independent of any paradigm. It is unclear, then, how the account given from that standpoint should be rationally preferred because it is more objectively justified.

Implicit in a number of Kuhn's remarks are some replies to such criticisms. As I mentioned earlier in this chapter, Kuhn says that most scientific problems are directly or indirectly posed by nature. This suggests that the problems which science tries to solve exist objectively and can be perceived largely independently of paradigms. If the existence of problems is largely independent of paradigms, it might be thought that what constitutes solving problems is also largely independent of paradigms. But, if we take detailed note of Kuhn's stated view, it is difficult to see how a problem can be directly posed by nature, as he clearly holds that observations are paradigm-laden and theory-laden. However, perhaps we can make sense of the claim that many of the problems in science are indirectly caused by nature. Kuhn only holds that paradigms and the theories they contain partially affect perception, not that perception is theoretical through and through. A bright object in the sky may be perceived as a star, a planet or a god by people in different paradigms, but it will be perceived as something which stands out by any observer. Given this, one can understand how its movement will pose problems to scientists whatever paradigm they are working in. For example, What direction will it travel in next? How bright will it be? How big will it look in the future? The relative merits of theories in problem solving might be objectively assessed numerically by counting how many of these things they predict. Of course, in real life science, predictions are only roughly confirmed but one can still measure whether a theory in one paradigm is more correct in its predictions than a theory in another paradigm. There are, however, two important problems faced when trying to defend Kuhn's account in this way.

First, Kuhn argues that there will be rationally irresolvable disputes between upholders of different paradigms as to which predictions and problems are more important. This means that a numerical measure of the predictive power or problem-solving capacity of different theories will be of little use in deciding their objective merits without an objectively based account of why some predictions or problems are more important than others.

Second, according to Kuhn, whether a prediction has really been successful or a problem has been really solved must crucially depend on paradigm-dependent assumptions. But this means that theories cannot be objectively compared for their problem-solving capacity. For example, Galileo's observation of what he called 'the phases of Venus' is only a major predictive triumph for the Copernican theory if we assume that what we really see through a telescope is Venus close up. If what we see is an illusion produced by the telescope or a weird star, this should not count in favour of the Copernican theory as it has nothing to do with assessing the predictions of the theory.

You may think that Kuhn could use inference to the best explanation to argue the case that the predictions of the Copernican theory and what one sees through the telescope coincide can only be plausibly explained by assuming that Galileo really sees the planet Venus. But remember that Kuhn wants to say that inferences to the real nature of what one is seeing are always contentious. Thus, for Kuhn, someone objectively measuring whether a theory has predicted something or solved certain problems has to use standards which do not assume the truth of theories about what is not observed, such as the identity between what Kuhn sees through the telescope and the bright light we observed moving through the sky. Against such standards, there is no reason to correlate what one sees in the telescope with the object Venus, whose features are predicted by Copernican theory.

The second problem arises for Kuhn's account because he thinks that whether someone is perceiving a similar object to an object seen in other circumstances is importantly determined by the paradigm in which he or she works. I have already criticized this claim; however, whether my criticisms are correct or not, Kuhn cannot plausibly hold this opinion and also defend the view that there can be an objective measure of the predictive and problem-solving successes of theories. At most, he could defend the view that paradigms which are similar to one another in many important respects can be compared if one assumes the truth of their key assumptions. For example, paradigms which contain similar views about the reliability of telescopes can be compared in their predictions by using their own standards. But it is unclear why one would call such a comparison 'objective' or the transition from one such paradigm to another 'progress.' It is no wonder then, that Kuhn's account has been taken by some theorists to defend an implausible variety of relativism, in which judgements about whether science progresses can only be coherently made according to the standards of a particular paradigm.

FEYERABEND'S CRITICISMS Kuhn talks as if the coming into being of a normal science is necessary for progress. It stops people from wasting their time on fundamental problems and allows progress to occur in solving puzzles. Yet Paul Feyerabend claims that Kuhn wrongly encourages authoritarian forms of scientific research which would retard science and create an ethically undesirable scientific community (Feyerabend, 1970). In arguing this, Feyerabend is assuming that one of the most valuable things about science is that it contains normative ideals which are anti-authoritarian. Well-grounded criticisms of theories should always be taken seriously, even if they threaten the positions of respected and established scientists and are widely viewed as having shocking social consequences. The social and professional position of a critic should be irrelevant to how seriously that critic's work is to be taken. He sees Kuhn as subverting such normative ideals by suggesting that closing down criticisms of fundamental aspects of theories and training students to have a set of common unquestionable assumptions and practices is necessary for scientific progress.

Feyerabend argues that solving minor problems is not of interest to the aim of science, which is to give us overarching theories which advance our knowledge. He says that Kuhn fails to distinguish science from activities like organized crime, in which the major objective is solving problems in order to make money. New and ever more reliable instruments and techniques are constantly developed by criminals for breaking safes, robbing banks, embezzling, and so on. Organized crime is a Kuhnian normal science which advances technology and accumulates minor facts about the world. However, it does not aim to increase our knowledge of the fundamental laws which underlie what happens – and this is the aim of science. Feyerabend argues that to advance such knowledge, one should help theories to develop which are rivals to a widely accepted theory. The existence of such theories is often helpful and sometimes necessary to discover the inadequacies in an accepted theory. Many inadequacies in a theory will not appear until a highly developed rival theory has matured. Thus, it is unreasonable to wait for a crisis to build up before we develop a new kind of theory under a different paradigm. Even a highly successful theory should be challenged by rivals in order to facilitate progress.

Let us consider an example. By the late nineteenth century, it was well known that the orbit of the planet Mercury did not follow the path predicted by Newtonian mechanics if it were added to knowledge of other bodies in the solar system. A number of nineteenth-century scientists had tried to find other planets which would explain this anomaly.

They had failed. However, Newtonian mechanics did not enter a crisis because of the anomaly. Planets and other minor bodies are often difficult to find; they can be obscured in all sorts of ways. Further, Newtonian scientists had eventually managed to resolve a major anomaly in the orbit of Uranus by discovering the planet Neptune. Thus, it was not unreasonable to assume that the anomaly would be resolved. Perhaps if the search for the explanation of the anomaly had gone on for a long time, it would eventually have become obvious that Newtonian mechanics was unlikely to be able to explain it. But the appearance of a successful rival theory made the tedious process of searching for other bodies unnecessary. The anomaly was turned into a refutation of Newtonian mechanics when it was discovered that the general theory of relativity predicts Mercury's orbit successfully. Had Einstein's theory been developed earlier, this process could have been speeded up. But Kuhn's acccount would support the view that one should discourage theories like Einstein's from developing until there was a crisis in the Newtonian paradigm. His account is thus the sort of account which is likely to retard progress.[8]

Feyerabend is right to say that the development of a rival hypothesis to an accepted one can advance a mature science a great deal. A single paradigm is not necessary for progress, contrary to Kuhn's claims. However, it is far from clear that encouraging the development of rival hypotheses will advance science in many cases. A science can be dominated by a single theory because no one can think of any rival account which has much merit. This seems to be true today of Einstein's theories of relativity and of quantum theory. To encourage the development of implausible rival hypotheses in such circumstances is to waste valuable resources. It is possible that such a rival theory could lead to important new developments, but it is very unlikely. Of course, if someone were to develop a rival theory which is fairly consistent with what is known, promises to explain a great deal and makes some startling predictions, it should be explored.

Feyerabend's argument that solving problems is not an important part of science is also mistaken. It is an important function of science to extend knowledge of minor facts and develop new technologies on the basis of general theories about the nature of the world. (That it relies on such general theories distinguishes it from organized crime.) Science is not merely a philosophical tool for achieving a fundamental understanding of the world. A legitimate reason for pursuing it is to learn things which are useful in order to improve human life. As we shall see later, it is reasonable to believe that this ought to be our primary reason for seeking scientific knowledge. If so, developing an outlandish rival hypothesis is likely to be a waste of valuable scientific resources and brainpower. It may be that our knowledge of fundamentals would not advance as quickly as it might do if we allowed many outlandish hypotheses to be tried, but it would not be legitimate to advance such fundamental knowledge at the expense of developing applications of existing fundamental theories. Feyerabend's discussion of the analogy of organized crime wrongly suggests that those who seek useful facts or technological applications for fundamental theories merely want to make money – something which has little to do with the truly glorious part of science.

Feyerabend's claim that Kuhn unjustifiably encourages the development of an authoritarian scientific community has some plausibility. Kuhn does sometimes talk as if it is necessary, in order to progress for us to ignore fundamental criticisms of accepted theories, to train students until their perceptions are thoroughly shaped by a paradigm and to structure scientific teaching so that the authority of great scientists is simply assumed. He cannot justify such claims, as my criticism of his claims about perception in the last section makes clear. However, Kuhn can justify some weaker claims which are mildly authoritarian. A well tested theory is unlikely to be seriously wrong as it will have strong inductive support. People have to learn to notice the features of experience which are evidence for the theory and they have to learn to apply it before they can understand it properly. A busy scientist can justify not spending much time on the criticisms of the theory produced by an undergraduate student. The student, typically, will know little about the theory and is unlikely to produce a cogent criticism of it until he or she knows a great deal more. In contrast, someone who has a reputation for having done significant work in the area is more likely to know what he or she is doing, and so be able to produce important criticisms.

Given that I am right in arguing that Kuhn does not offer a viable instrumentalist account of the growth of scientific knowledge and that his methodological claims are flawed, it is important to see whether his critique of cumulativism is correct since, if it is correct, it seems impossible to resist scepticism about the growth of scientific knowledge.

Kuhn on cumulativism

The reader will remember that cumulativism is the doctrine that a cumulative growth of knowledge occurs in science, in the sense that each succeeding theory contains more and more true claims. By the cumulativist account, the predictively successful parts of older theories continue to be roughly correct, so that the older theory can be said to be approximately true within a limited domain. The successful part of the older theory is also contained within the new theory as an approximation. Kuhn's principal reason for rejecting cumulativism is that when one paradigm succeeds another, the theories the paradigms contain often have radically different metaphysical assumptions – so if the newer theories are true, no part of the older theories can be approximately true. There is, thus, no growth of knowledge of truths in such paradigm transitions.

A major criticism of Kuhn's argument against cumulativism is that it assumes a problematic theory about the component of theories which enables them to refer to the world. Kuhn thinks the relevant components are the meanings of the descriptive terms, which he identifies with the fundamental metaphysical assumptions of the paradigm to which the theory belongs. But this lands him in a puzzle for, if those assumptions are radically false of this world, it seems that the theory must refer to some other world. He talks bizarrely about people who have been trained in different paradigms occupying different worlds. He feels compelled to say this because he does not want to say that theories like Newtonian mechanics do not refer at all as it is obvious that, even though they are false, they are enormously useful. However, as he has admitted, it seems that it cannot be literally true that different theories refer to different worlds.

It has been argued that the most plausible way to escape the puzzle and save cumulativism is to assume that the way in which a theory links to the world is not through its underlying metaphysical assumptions but through causal links which establish the reference of the terms directly. For example, on this account, Newton established the meaning of the term 'mass' by introducing it in connection with various events whose underlying cause he was trying to explain. He may, for instance, have seen a beam balance go downwards in a gravitational field. By using the word 'mass' in such contexts to designate one of the two key causes of these events (the other one of which he designated 'force'), he causally tied the fundamental part of the meaning of the word to a cause of these events. People who use 'mass' after Newton are causally linked to the initial situations in which he used the term through a chain of teachers, or through books written by Newton or those inspired by his work. This account of how key scientific terms acquire the central part of their meaning is sometimes called 'the causal theory of reference' because it holds that causal links to the items in the world, and not human beliefs or conceptions, importantly determine the reference of physical quantity terms like 'mass' and natural kind terms like 'water'. 'Mass' refers to the relational physical quantity in the world, despite the wrong-headed conceptions of generations of scientists about the matter. 'Water' has always referred to H_2O, no matter what anyone thought or thinks about the nature of water.

If the causal theory of reference is correct, then a cumulativist account of scientific progress can be saved from Kuhn's criticisms. The fact that Newton had a conception of mass which is radically different from the current conception is unimportant if what is relevant to deciding whether Newtonian laws contain an approximately true component is whether that component states roughly the same things as Einsteinian laws about the items designated by Einsteinian laws.

An advantage of the causal theory of reference is that it can explain a puzzling fact about the history of science in a simple manner. Historians have noted that, even before Einstein, some scientists argued that Newton's conception of the nature of mass was inadequate while thinking that Newton's laws were correct. For instance, the influential nineteenth-century German physicist, Ernst Mach, thought that we could make little sense of the idea that mass is an intrinsic property. He was already was inclined to understand Newton's theory to be one which described a property which was relational. Since Mach seemingly did not doubt the truth of Newton's laws but understood mass to be a relational property, it appears that it cannot be an essential part of believing those laws to be true to believe that the physical quantity terms in them refer to intrinsic properties. The causal theory of reference would allow us to preserve the intuition that despite fundamental changes in scientists' conceptions of the nature of physical quantities, scientists continue to refer to the same quantities. In contrast, Kuhn seems to be committed to the view that even before the triumph of Einstein's theories, some scientists had radically changed Newtonian mechanics so that it no longer referred to the same things.

However, despite its advantages, the causal theory as stated has some problems. Consider the case of the phlogiston theory, which I discussed in Chapters 1 and 2. The term 'phlogiston' was introduced in causal connection with what we now call combustion. Yet it seems that it does not refer to the approximate cause of combustion, which is oxygen. A plausible explanation of this apparent fact is that phlogiston chemists had the wrong conception of how combustion works, for they thought it was the subtraction of phlogiston. Perhaps the term 'phlogiston' had its reference fixed by their conceptions and, since their conceptions were fundamentally wrong, it does not exist. But it seems a supporter of the causal theory of reference cannot explain this puzzling fact in this way for, in his or her view, the conceptions of those who introduced the term are irrelevant. The only thing that is relevant is the fundamental cause which prompted the introduction of the term.[9] Consider further another counter-example which will undermine the causal theory as stated. We can all agree that the term 'oxygen' refers and that it refers to the element oxygen. However, the term was originally introduced by Lavoisier to designate the cause of acidity. The word comes from the Greek word 'oxus', meaning acid. Later, Lavoisier used it to refer to the cause of combustion, for he wrongly believed that the cause of acidity and the cause of combustion are the same. Now the element which comes closest to being the approximate cause of acidity is hydrogen. Thus, according to the causal theorists' account, either 'oxygen' should refer to hydrogen or it should partly refer to hydrogen and partly refer to oxygen. But it does not. In contrast, based on the theory that conceptions crucially determine the reference of key terms in a theory, we can easily explain the actual referent of 'oxygen'. By such an account, the event which causally prompted Lavoisier to introduce the term is irrelevant. Chemists believe oxygen to refer to the element which causes combustion. Since they are right in believing that some element causes combustion, their term succeeds in referring.

However, while these historical counter-examples show that the causal theory as I stated it is implausible, the causal theory can be restated. To formulate a plausible version of the causal theory, we need only to hold that what initially prompted the introduction of a term is not important. What is important is what prompted the term when it was used in the parts of a theory which were systematically predictively successful. I shall show that, in this form, the causal theory is far better than its rival.

Something which makes the causal theory particularly plausible is the criticism it makes of Kuhn's underlying assumption that the theoretical beliefs we have about the world somehow can fix reference to real items by themselves. Theoretical beliefs cannot magically fix reference to real items. They can only serve to help fix reference through being causally tied to something real, by being prompted by the real. Theoretical terms are typically used to latch on to the causes of various observed events we are trying to explain. Scientific theories are not simply invented in people's heads, acquiring referents just as a result of those beliefs. From the outset, scientific theories are used to explain and predict aspects of real events which are puzzling. Further, if our beliefs are to be systematically predictively successful so that we can manipulate the world, there need to be real causal connections between the items in the world which prompt beliefs and beliefs. Suppose Hilary believes in spirit powers and uses them to manipulate the world. For example, Hilary may attempt to injure and cure people by putting herbs that are believed to contain spirit powers in their food, without their knowledge. If such strategies are to be more than coincidentally successful, Hilary's classificatory categories must be latching on to events which have either underlying structures in common or underlying structures with similar causal powers.

To illustrate this point, turn to the previous example of the phlogiston theory. That theory was used in connection with burning substances in order to explain why they burned. While many of the beliefs of phlogiston theorists were awry, they were actually able to manipulate real processes which they were systematically misunderstanding. It is partly correct to say that the phlogiston theory was radically mistaken because its underlying assumptions were false and to say that the term 'phlogiston' did not actually refer because fundamental theoretical beliefs of supporters of phlogiston chemistry were false. On the other hand, it has been pointed out that in the parts of phlogiston chemistry which were predictively successful, 'phlogiston' was successfully and systematically used by scientists in connection with events which were all caused either by hydrogen or by oxygen (Carrier, 1991). This means that it was used to refer to a cause of a class of events which, in fact, had a couple of underlying causes. Thus, we can plausibly say that in the parts of phlogiston theory which, in fact were predictively successful, 'phlogiston' referred to either oxygen or hydrogen, and phlogiston theorists were not wildly wrong in assuming that all those instances of burning were connected to a single underlying cause which behaved in a particular way. This is why the predictively successful parts of the phlogiston theory were easily restatable using the vocabulary of modern chemistry, and the transition to the oxygen theory of Lavoisier was cumulative in an important way. Thus, in the case of theories like the phlogiston theory, it may be misleading to say that they are partly true, but it is quite misleading to say that they are wholly false or refer to something which exists in another paradigm.

In any case, the cumulative image of scientific growth can be plausibly intended to apply only to the theories or parts of theories which scientists had good reason to believe were approximately true. I have pointed out that in the case of highly speculative theories, our only way of telling whether they are approximately true is to check whether they successfully predict a range of novel facts. As my discussion in Chapter 2 made clear, phlogiston theory is a speculative theory which was largely unsuccessful in predicting a range of novel facts. However, it has been plausibly argued that a small part of phlogiston theory was successful in predicting a range of novel facts (Carrier, 1991). (I shall discuss this argument in detail in Chapter 7.) But in that part of the theory, it seems that 'phlogiston' was being systematically used to refer to what we would now call hydrogen. This means that in the part of phlogiston chemistry which was successful in predicting novel facts, the term 'phlogiston' referred to a single underlying cause. Popper's image of scientific growth may be mistaken but it is not badly mistaken.

Conclusion

We have seen that Kuhn's critique of cumulativism is deeply flawed. He fails to show that we are unjustified in thinking of science as giving us an ever improving and approximately true account of what happens in the world. He also fails to show that we cannot justify our preference for current theories by appeal to observation and to objectively plausible standards which cross paradigms. Nevertheless, we can learn from Kuhn.

It is an important insight that, in science, training procedures – in which one learns to notice things, to group quite disparate looking things together, and to apply scientific laws – play a valuable role which cannot be precisely articulated through formal accounts of scientific reasoning. Too often, science has been described in terms of precise rules which are supposed to be logical reconstructions of how scientists acquire concepts and how they apply them to specific situations. It is easy to get the impression from some of this material that one is likely to do significant research simply by being a careful observer who knows some precise rules and who has a few theories. Kuhn's account is thus valuable in further undermining formalistically minded accounts of how we acquire and test scientific knowledge.

In addition, Kuhn rightly stresses that much important work in science consists of discovering facts on the basis of fundamental theories.[10] Human and animal life is importantly influenced by such discoveries, and it is foolish to deny their importance on the basis of philosophical snobbery about the true aims of science. A theory of scientific progress which does not allow for the development of what Kuhn calls 'normal science' fails to deal with what is most valuable for many of us about science – that it can usefully guide action and lead to technological advance. Popper and the early Feyerabend describe science as if it were a game for advancing knowledge. They thus fail to tell us why taxpayers should care about it and be willing to spend vast amounts of money on scientific research and science education.

We also learn from Kuhn that sometimes the conceptions used by those who formulated a predictively successful scientific theory are radically mistaken. To confirm that a scientific theory is partly correct is not necessarily to confirm that its conception of the hidden structure of the world is correct. Both the phlogiston chemists and Newton were wrong about fundamental aspects of the world, even if their theories are partly correct. This poses an important problem for the view that science gives us knowledge of fundamental aspects of the world, for it could be argued that although science is a good instrument for predicting what happens, it provides us with no knowledge of the fundamental nature of the world. Following the path of this argument, science provides us with no knowledge of the hidden features of the world. I shall deal with this line of argument in Chapter 7.

Further reading

Kuhn's central claims are set out in a very interesting way in Kuhn, 1970a. Kuhn, 1977: 308 ff. elaborates Kuhn's account of perception. Kuhn (1970b; 1970c) also presents important replies to his critics. Lakatos and Musgrave (1970) provide a number of important critical discussions of Kuhn. Barnes (1982) tries to draw relativist implications from Kuhn's view. Donovan (1988) contains a number of articles that criticize Kuhn's historical account; Kuhn's account of the development of oxygen chemistry constitutes one of the major arguments for his view. That account is vigorously criticized in Kitcher, 1993: 276 ff. Devitt (1979) presents a very clear criticism of Kuhn which uses the causal theory of meaning/ reference. I criticize Devitt and others in Couvalis, 1989: 99 ff., though I no longer believe that those criticisms are completely successful, as the remarks in this chapter should make clear. The most thorough interpretation of Kuhn is provided by Hoyningen-Huehne (1993) however it is too detailed and too difficult for the purposes of most students.

Notes

1 See for example Popper, 1970, particularly p. 53. For the similar view of the early Feyerabend, see Feyerabend, 1961: 5–6.

2 My account of Kuhn only covers writings he published between 1962 and 1974 as it is this material which has been enormously influential. In addition, I do not discuss many of his arguments for the theory-ladenness of observation, as I have already dealt with similar arguments in Chapter 1; and I do not discuss his relativist sounding remarks about world changes, as I discuss Feyerabend's similar remarks in Chapter. 5

3 Kuhn relies heavily on arguments presented in Wittgenstein, 1968.

4 Kuhn, 1970a: 46 ff. Kuhn does not deny that such standards exist in some sense, as he makes clear elsewhere. But he thinks the vague standards scientists use need to be learned in specific contexts which teach them how to apply them to particular kinds of cases. Scientists trained in different paradigms will apply such standards differently and give different priorities to different standards. It is a misunderstanding of the nature of such standards to treat them as precise general rules (Kuhn, 1970c: 262 ff).

5 Kuhn's discussion of the conceptual differences between theories is unclear. I have relied on Feyerabend's clearer and more powerful arguments to fill out Kuhn's claims. See Couvalis, 1989 for further details.

6 In his early work, he sometimes talked as if the adherents of competing paradigms have totally different world-views and even inhabit different worlds. Yet he later withdrew this view which he admitted to be an exaggeration of the true situation.

7 It may be thought that, as I have already criticized the doctrine that experience is affected by theories in Chapter 1, I have refuted Kuhn's claims. But, as I said earlier in this chapter, Kuhn claims that training in a paradigm importantly affects perception and that paradigms are not theories, although they contain theories.

8 The example of the anomaly in Mercury's orbit is one in which the development of a rival theory is desirable, but perhaps not necessary to criticize the accepted theory. Feyerabend argues that there is also a case in which the rival theory was necessary to refute the accepted theory. For a discussion of this case, see Couvalis, 1988; 1989: 55 ff. Feyerabend also argues that the historical record does not follow the account Kuhn gives. In important periods of mature scientific development, such as the nineteenth century, there were conflicting paradigms being developed which were used to bring out each others inadequacies and develop knowledge. Feyerabend's historical claim is not very plausible. But it should be noted that careful historical work has shown many of Kuhn's historical claims to be implausible. For example, early geology seems to have developed into a scientific form without having a paradigm (Laudan, 1987).

9 My counter-argument may be thought to be something of a caricature, for few supporters of the causal theory seem to hold a variant of the causal theory which completely excludes the conceptions of the people who introduced a physical quantity term; though Michael Devitt seems to be an example (Devitt, 1981). For the implausibility of Devitt's solution to the problem raised by phlogiston, see Couvalis (1989). But causal theorists are divided about what role conceptions have in fixing the reference of a term.

10 Kuhn (1970b: 22) argues that scientists value puzzle solving in itself. But it does not follow from this that puzzle solving is an intrinsically valuable activity.

5

Relativism and the Value of Science

In Chapter 4, I discussed Thomas Kuhn's critique of the common view that science has increased our knowledge of the world enormously through using objective and shared standards for assessing theories. Like Kuhn, Paul Feyerabend has claimed that this view of scientific knowledge is deeply mistaken, as science sometimes does not lead to an accumulation of knowledge on the basis of objective and shared standards. Rather, it contains revolutionary episodes during which existing theories are completely overthrown, and our standards of theory appraisal are radically changed. He also argues that the transition from pre-science to science contains similar revolutionary episodes. Unlike Kuhn, Feyerabend sometimes argues that such changes can be so thorough that it is impossible to give a world picture independent account of why the new picture should be preferred. The standards themselves are importantly internal to the world pictures of which theories are a part, so that those theories cannot reasonably be judged to be true independently of the pictures (Feyerabend, 1981a: 162; 1978b: 70).[1]

Feyerabend's view amounts to a relativism in which the nature of the world and the proper standards for appraising theories are completely internal to world pictures. He argues that the world pictures are not only rival accounts of our world but in some sense world-yielding; that is, they are pictures of different worlds. The ontology of the pictures is constitutive of the nature of the world. A world picture which refers to gods is literally a picture of a world which contains gods. Because different world pictures make the world different, the causal relations between things and the ways in which it is appropriate to get knowledge are different in the different worlds. In a world which contains gods, relying on certain oracles is an appropriate way to gain knowledge, while much of experience is untrustworthy as it might be produced by malignant deities. Further, Feyerabend says that what constitutes knowledge depends on the world picture one is talking within. In the Homeric world-view of the early Greeks, knowledge is a kind of list of how aspects of things are experienced. In the world-view of the Greek philosophers, knowledge is an understanding of what is behind the misleading show of appearances.[2]

It is important to grasp how radical the implications of Feyerabend's account are. Feyerabend is, in effect, claiming that there is nothing special about current science as a method of gathering knowledge, except perhaps within one world picture. The assertion that current science is a more secure way of gathering knowledge than gleaning it from religious texts is merely the unjustifiable assertion of the superiority of one world picture over another. The current scientific world picture is no better than any other, except from a standpoint which already assumes the excellence of scientific standards.

Feyerabend does not merely raise philosophical problems for a view of scientific knowledge. He argues that science should have no special place in our lives: it does not give us an understanding of the world which is worthy of deep respect; its ideals and methods are not particularly worthy of emulation; and it should not have a special place in the education system, in medicine and in the legal system. Further, funding for science should be controlled by bodies that are under direct democratic control. If some citizens want voodoo taught to their children rather than physics, scientists should not be able to prevent it from being taught. If some citizens think faith healers can heal illnesses better than doctors, then faith healers should be able to practise medicine. If most citizens think that particle physics is dangerous and should not be funded, then particle physics should not be funded. If most citizens think that mystics know about distant events they have not seen, then mystics should be treated as expert witnesses in courts.

Part of Feyerabend's argument for saying that science should not have a special place in our society relies on his defence of relativism. But he also argues that even if science gives us objectively justified knowledge, this does not mean that science should have a special place in our society. It will depend on our other value commitments what position science should hold in society. We should feel perfectly free to treat scientists merely as people who sometimes produce useful gadgets for us for which they are then well paid.

In contrast to Feyerabend, Popper clearly thinks that science is a practice which should not be valued merely for its technological applications. He argues that science is a paradigmatic example of a rational practice in which an open critical discussion can occur and any intellectually interesting problem can be raised. He thinks that learning how properly to conduct scientific research is learning how to engage in a critical discussion in a manner appropriate to a free society. Conversely, he argues that when we restrict ourselves or others in the questions we ask and how we answer them, we take up authoritarian attitudes which are a threat to our democratic civilization. Popper also claims that for scientific research or other critical discussion to be properly rational, it cannot be restricted by predetermined goals. Imaginative solutions to problems may well transform science and our social life in completely unanticipated ways. The problems we started out with may well turn out to be trivial or to have false presuppositions. Channelling scientific research into predetermined areas is neither rational nor desirable.

The differences in outlook exhibited by Popper and Feyerabend can be traced back to the Enlightenment and its critics. Popper's outlook is descended from the Enlightenment idea that science should have a special place in our thinking because it is the supreme, rationally conducted enterprise. However, unlike some of his Enlightenment predecessors, Popper holds that scientific and social theories are fallible and that correct theories about values can in no way be logically derived from scientific knowledge. As a result, he thinks there is a need for constant debate about even the best tested scientific theories. He also thinks social policies should be subject to constant critical discussion. Nevertheless, Popper holds that by following the methodological ideals of science we will come to have tolerant social and scientific institutions, within which we arrive at tentative conclusions about the world and what we should do, through rational criticism and debate. Human life will improve as persecution is decreased and as improving technology is applied to alleviate human misery.

Feyerabend places great emphasis on the idea of individual freedom, which was defended by some Enlightenment philosophers. However, his main line of argument is descended from the anti-Enlightenment ideas that scientific ways of thinking are inadequate for understanding the world, and that scientistic approaches to many of the problems of human life lead to misery and the loss of rich and meaningful ways of living.

I shall argue that Feyerabend's arguments for relativism are mistaken. I shall also argue that his critique of the place science has in our society is inadequate and that Popper's arguments – that science should have an important role in our society – have some plausibility. Nevertheless, I shall be agreeing with Feyerabend's claim that it would not be irrational for someone to prefer that science have only a minimal role in our society.

1 Radical change and relativism

Feyerabend's historical argument

Feyerabend claims that no theory of method can justify what happens in scientific revolutions because what happens cannot be judged to have been rational by objective and shared standards. What is supposed to be the growth of knowledge is sometimes more like a religious conversion.

He says that an important example of such an episode is the Copernican revolution. This event has been thought by many historians and philosophers to have produced an enormous advance in knowledge. By attacking the standard view of it, Feyerabend means to challenge what he thinks is one of the central myths that have bolstered the current status of science. To give the reader enough background knowledge to understand his argument, let me start by describing some of the important theoretical changes which occurred during the Copernican revolution as Feyerabend would understand them.

From the late sixteenth century onwards, a medieval amalgam of the physics and cosmologies of Aristotle and Ptolemy, which I will call 'the Ptolemaic view', was replaced by the very different Copernican view of the nature and structure of the universe.[3] Ptolemaists thought there were a number of different kinds of matter, each having a different tendency. This idea was replaced by the Copernican idea that there was one kind of matter which obeyed the same laws. Ptolemaists conceived of earthy matter as needing an external mover to keep it moving in a horizontal line.[4] Further, in their view, earthy matter falling towards its natural place at the centre of the earth was supposed to accelerate in proportion to its weight. In the new Copernican conception, all matter has a tendency either to continue to move in straight-line motion, or to stay still. Bodies falling towards the centre of the earth accelerate in a way that has nothing to do with their weight, and their movement is not due to their inherent tendency but to the gravitational attraction of the earth.

Ptolemaists thought the moving heavenly bodies were in titanic crystalline spheres made of aether, a substance whose natural tendency is to be in circular motion. The earth was held to be at the centre of the heavens. In the Copernican conception, there are no crystalline spheres; and the planets are similar to the earth, which is one body among the many which revolve around the sun. These bodies are kept in their orbits by a combination of their natural tendency to keep moving in a straight line and the gravitational attraction of the sun.

Feyerabend claims there are many other differences between the Ptolemaic and the Copernican world pictures. The meanings of key descriptive terms in the two pictures are radically different. To understand his point, consider the use of the Ptolemaic term 'kinesis' and its Latin equivalents. 'Kinesis' is used by Ptolemaists to describe the movement of bodies towards the centre of the earth and the movement of the planets and stars. It does not mean 'motion', for it is used to denote any kind of change which involves the realization of a natural potentiality, such as the growth and development of a boy into a man. This means that everyday instances of what we, influenced by Copernican conceptions, would call 'motion', are conceived of by Ptolemaists either as kinesis or as unnatural change caused by an external mover (and explainable by separate principles). Feyerabend says that the differences between the two world pictures are such that not a single descriptive term of either theory can be defined by using the other theory's terms. This would make them conceptually incommensurable. (The notion of conceptual incommensurability was explained in Chapter 1.)

In his early work, Feyerabend recognizes that mere conceptual incommensurability raises problems which may not be serious since, as I explained in Chapter 1, theories which are merely conceptually incommensurable can be rationally compared. (Such theories make predictions of certain kinds and we can compare their predictions by checking them against what happens, described in each theory's own terms.) However, Feyerabend later argues that this procedure is flawed because there are no justifiable picture-independent standards for testing the relative merits of incommensurable theories. The revolutionary changes in science which occurred in episodes like the Copernican revolution involved changes in standards for appraising theories which are not themselves assessable by reference to a common standard, as the theories in question are too different. Galileo and his successors would have liked to argue that their new ways of acquiring knowledge and their new assumptions about the world, were more plausible than those of their Ptolemaic predecessors. But they were unable to do so. This compelled them to use trickery and propaganda to displace the Ptolemaic world picture, as they could not use rational methods. This means that 'progress' in science is sometimes neither cumulative nor rational according to picture-transcendent and objectively justifiable standards of rationality.

Feyerabend presents three key arguments for the claim that the Copernican revolution occurred through trickery rather than rational argument. First, Feyerabend says that Galileo surreptitiously, and without good arguments, got many of his opponents to accept that telescopic evidence was superior to evidence provided by the naked eye. According to Ptolemaists, the normal man under normal conditions perceives the world correctly. Instruments of various kinds are untrustworthy when they are used outside the normal man's range of perception. Feyerabend points out that, nevertheless, Galileo used the results of observations with the telescope as central evidence against the Ptolemaic picture. He did this without having an adequate theory of how telescopes work, which is what would have been required to rebut the Ptolemaic claims. For example, to the naked eye, the size and brightness of Venus hardly seem to change over time. Yet according to the Copernican account, its apparent size and brightness should vary a great deal as it is sometimes much closer to the earth. This seems to provide Ptolemaists with a refutation of Copernicanism. However, Galileo discovered that when it is seen through a telescope, Venus changes in size and brightness in conformity with Copernican predictions. Galileo used telescopic evidence to rebut the Ptolemaic argument against Copernicanism. But Galileo's argument unjustifiably assumes telescopic observations to be more reliable than naked eye observations.

Second, Feyerabend argues that Galileo could not deal with an important criticism of Copernicanism adequately without simply assuming the truth of an important part of Copernican theory. As he could not defend his view rationally, he used subterfuge to convert people to his view. Let me explain Feyerabend's second claim in detail.

According to Copernicans, the earth is spinning on its axis at great speed, so one would think a stone dropped from a tower would land many hundreds of metres behind the tower. In fact, it lands at the foot of the tower. Ptolemaists took this to be an experimental refutation of Copernicanism. Galileo's solution to this problem is that the stone and the tower are both moving in the same direction, but that we do not notice that the stone is moving in a Copernican fashion as we only observe its motion relative to the tower. By using a series of ingenious examples, Galileo shows that our everyday perception of motion is sometimes seriously mistaken. He shows that this happens when we perceive motion only relative to some observed object and assume that that motion is absolute. He postulates that this is also true for other cases. Feyerabend says, however, that this argument does not deal with the tower argument, as Galileo needs some principle of inertia to show that, in that particular case, everyday perception is mistaken. Feyerabend asserts that Galileo introduces the principle of circular inertia in order properly to deal with the tower argument. The principle of circular inertia states that an object moving with an angular velocity on a frictionless sphere around the centre of the earth will continue moving with the same angular velocity forever. If this principle is true, one of the central assumptions behind the tower argument is mistaken and the tower argument has no force as a criticism of the Copernican view. However, Feyerabend claims that Galileo introduces the principle of circular inertia without experimental justification. Thus, by Feyerabend's account, Galileo does not deal with the Ptolemaic argument by appealing to external evidence; instead, he smuggles in an assumption which is inconsistent with the Ptolemaic view without arguing for it. The assumption is an *ad hoc hypothesis*, so Galileo does not adequately deal with the tower argument.

Third, Feyerabend asserts that Copernicans replaced an important Ptolemaic standard for judging the relative merits of theories through trickery. Ptolemaists thought excellent scientific theories could be arrived at by using one's intuitions to grasp universal principles behind everyday observations. They were not concerned about whether a theory has to be modified *ad hoc* to account for observations. For example, the Ptolemaists' earth-centred astronomy cannot predict the movement of the planets or stars by using simple circular orbits but has to be modified in very complex ways, yet they did not think that this was a problem. In contrast, the later Copernicans placed great emphasis on the fact that their heliocentric astronomy had the power to predict novel facts. Feyerabend claims that in order to deal with such problems, Copernicans and their modern philosophical supporters have used various kinds of tricks to replace the Ptolemaic view with their own, without providing good arguments.

Feyerabend's argument from relativism

Apart from his historical argument, Feyerabend has another major argument for the claim that scientific revolutions cannot be judged to have been rational by objective standards. It is that incommensurable theories constitute world pictures which necessarily refer to different items, so that one cannot rationally compare them. By this he does not mean that incommensurable theories deal with different domains of explanation in our world and so refer to different items. He is not saying, for example, that theories of geology and theories of economics are incommensurable and so refer to different items. Rather he is saying that incommensurable theories deal with different items in the same domains of explanation. For example, by his account, in trying to explain the movements of planets, Ptolemaists refer to planets as features of crystalline spheres whereas Copernicans refer to planets as earthlike objects in the sky. Both the Ptolemaic and Copernican views deal with the same domain of explanation, so they exclude one another in the sense that one cannot believe both of them to be true.

To understand Feyerabend's argument in detail, consider two conceptually incommensurable theories which deal with the same domain. As we saw in Chapter 1, they will be such that: (a) not a single descriptive term of either theory can be defined by using the descriptive terms of the other, and (b) the use of either one of the theories renders inapplicable the terms of the other. Feyerabend argues that such theories must refer to different worlds because:

> we certainly cannot assume that two incommensurable theories deal with one and the same objective state of affairs (to make this assumption we would have to assume that they both at least *refer* to the same objective situation. But how can we assert that 'they both' refer to the same objective situation when 'they both' never make sense together? Besides, statements about what does and does not refer can be checked only if the things referred to are described properly, but then our problem arises again with renewed force.) Hence, unless we want to assume that they deal with nothing at all, we must admit that they deal with different worlds and that the change (from one world to the other) has been brought about by the switch from one theory to another. (Feyerabend, 1978b: 70)

His ultimate conclusion is that two incommensurable theories yield different worlds and thus cannot be objectively compared. This amounts to an ontological relativism, as it is being claimed that the adoption by a group of certain fundamental theoretical assumptions about the nature of the world sometimes is sufficient to make those assumptions true for them and to make rival fundamental assumptions false for them. As Feyerabend says, on his argument, 'our epistemic activities may have a decisive influence even upon our most solid piece of cosmological furniture – they may make gods disappear and replace them by heaps of atoms in empty space' (Feyerabend, 1978b: 70).

The argument seems flawed as it stands, for it seems we may be able to use terms which do not belong to either theory and which are neutral between them, to refer to items in the world. It seems that we could then check whether the items referred to are described properly by either of these theories by checking predictions made by the theories. For example, it might be said in common-sense English that a planet is an item in the sky and part of what it is to be a planet is normally to look a particular way, so we would have no trouble locating what was being referred to. But Feyerabend makes clear elsewhere that when he is talking about incommensurable theories, he is only speaking about incommensurable theories which constitute world pictures; that is, theories which deal with everything there is, and every feature of it (Feyerabend, 1988: 269; 1981b: 154, main text and fn 54). He claims such theories have implications for the use of any term in any context. In the case of two incompatible world pictures, no descriptive term in one can even be partially defined in terms of the descriptive terms of the other. Further, each theory rules out the other in the sense that the adoption of one theory makes it impossible for any term in the other to be construed as referring. In the Ptolemaic view, 'sky', 'look', and other terms mean something quite different from what they mean in the Copernican view. Thus, according to Feyerabend's account, a Copernican using common-sense English must be using terms in a Copernican sense, while a Ptolemaist using common-sense English must be using terms in a Ptolemaic sense. In addition, any other language whose terms could be used to refer to relevant items in the sky would be permeated by the cosmological assumptions of some world picture, so that the use of its terminology would not be neutral as to the nature and activities of stars and planets.

Critical discussion

CRITICISMS OF FEYERABEND'S HISTORICAL ARGUMENT All of Feyerabend's key historical claims can plausibly be rebutted. First, as I pointed out in Chapter 1, we do not need a complex theory to know that instruments such as telescopes are reliable. Telescopic data can be checked for accuracy in the terrestrial domain, and it is plausible to extrapolate from such knowledge. The Ptolemaic response that telescopes are unreliable in the celestial domain is implausible if one uses induction, a variety of reasoning the cogency of which can be asserted without begging the question as to which theory of physics or celestial mechanics is superior.

It is of course possible, though implausible, that telescopes are unreliable in the celestial domain, as Ptolemaists claimed. But in any case, Galileo used inference to the best explanation to show that the Copernican theory is very plausible, and inference to the best explanation is another method of reasoning whose cogency can be asserted independently of a particular theory of physics or celestial mechanics. By using Copernican assumptions, Galileo was able to predict what items would look like through telescopes in advance of those items being observed. On many occasions, supposed illusions looked like things which would be expected according to the Copernican view. Consider two examples:

1 Galileo predicted the disappearance and reappearance of the dots he believed to be Jupiter's moons. As he said, if the dots were always artefacts produced by the telescope, why was he repeatedly able successfully to calculate the period of their disappearance and return by assuming that they were satellites of Jupiter?
2 When they saw the moon through a telescope, many independent observers thought that features on the moon looked rather like mountains and seemed to cast shadows in precisely the way mountains would cast shadows.[5] As Galileo pointed out, why would these features look this way if Ptolemaists were correct?[6]

In any case, Galileo not only postulates that ordinary naked eye observations of the planets are unreliable, but *shows experimentally* that the irradiation that surrounds a light source which is small, bright and distant confounds the naked eye at night. He establishes this by experiments in which we see a distant torch at night and compare its apparent size to that perceived during the day. At night, the torch appears much larger than its true size. (This is actually using an approved Ptolemaic style of argument to argue the point, that is, taking as a standard the daytime observations of a normal observer.) Further, Galileo argues that when Venus is viewed at twilight with the naked eye – that is, when it is not an abnormally bright object against a dark background – it appears to change in size in conformity with Copernicanism. Thus, if we set up experimental conditions in which we have good reason to think that the irradiation which confounds the eye is eliminated, the planets look, as Copernicanism predicts they should look, even with the naked eye (Chalmers, 1990: 56 ff.).

Feyerabend replies to such arguments by pointing out that many telescopic illusions are inter-subjective and that many early telescopic observations were illusory. This is, of course, also true of illusions which occur when we use our eyes (and Galileo was able to show this easily). Thus, the fact that telescopes sometimes produce illusions does not indicate that they cannot function properly in many circumstances. More importantly, we are talking about reasonably precise predictions of the appearance of certain supposed illusions, which cannot be explained plausibly by assuming they are artefacts. Of course, Feyerabend rightly says telescopes are sometimes unreliable, but this only means that observations needed to be inter-subjectively checked and, if possible, predictions should be made on the basis of theories. Galileo's claims were reasonably well supported by common-sense arguments. Telescopic observations were known to be often unreliable, but Galileo plausibly argued that they are reliable in particular circumstances.[7] The fact that Galileo sometimes went wrong, and that it was known that his methods might fail, is only of importance if one wrongly assumes knowledge must be absolutely reliable.

Second, Feyerabend's claim that Galileo used circular inertia as an *ad hoc* device is wrong. Galileo had carried out detailed experiments with inclined planes to show that the existence of a kind of *horizontal* inertia could be demonstrated experimentally by using naked eye observations before he publicly defended the Copernican view (Chalmers, 1986: 12 ff.).

Having dealt with Feyerabend's first two historical claims let me turn to Feyerabend's third key historical claim, which is that there was a genuine and unresolvable difference in standards for judging theories between Ptolemaists and Copernicans.

It does indeed seem as if Ptolemaists were rather unworried about modifying hypotheses *ad hoc*. However, when we keep in mind that Ptolemaists could recognize that they had to justify the assumption that it is reasonable to modify hypotheses *ad hoc* by appealing to shared standards, Feyerabend's case can be seen to be much weaker. The Ptolemaic view was the dominant view at the time in intellectual circles, but was not the only view on offer. It had only very partially affected the common sense of late medieval society. The Ptolemaic view was seen to have had serious problems from a common-sense viewpoint as the Copernican revolution developed. Until around the time of Kepler and Galileo, no one had produced a theory which did not have to be vastly modified *ad hoc* before it could be used as an instrument for making a few meagre predictions. It would have been pointless to argue that a theory should not be *ad hoc*, and should predict many novel facts as there simply were no such theories – and it was not obvious that anyone could produce them. But from that time on, the Copernican research program began to produce a whole series of remarkable predictions of novel facts. From a common-sense perspective, this offered a new and undreamed of kind of evidence supporting the Copernican program. Scientific standards for judging theories were rationally modified when it became clear what theories could be used to do. In the light of this rational shift in scientific standards which was motivated by common sense, the Ptolemaic view was seen to be quite implausible.

In addition, as I have said above, Galileo could claim that his theories about the tendencies and nature of objects could be justified by using everyday observations, such as those he carried out by using inclined planes or by observing Venus at twilight. Many of his general claims seemed to be ones one could extract from everyday observation in a manner Ptolemaists would have had to approve of, even on their own assumptions. In this way, Galileo could use Ptolemaic methods of gaining knowledge to extend the ways in which one could get knowledge (for example by using the telescope), criticize the reliability of the approved techniques in certain circumstances (for example by showing naked eye observation at night to be unreliable), and criticize Ptolemaic theories of physics and cosmology (for example by arguing plausibly for the existence of other planets like our own). The Ptolemaic view was not a seamless web of ideas which formed a world picture, but something which one could use some parts of to criticize others. Thus, Feyerabend's third historical claim is also false.

One important problem with Feyerabend's account of the history of the Copernican revolution is that he talks as if the Ptolemaic view permeated every aspect of everyday life in a way which made all observations and arguments dependent on Ptolemaic assumptions. That is, he talks as if the theories were world pictures. Yet the Ptolemaic view had relatively recently become the more or less official doctrine and other doctrines were widely discussed. It was also well known that Ptolemaic arguments had been challenged in antiquity and Ptolemaists still had to defend their views. Further, many thinkers were inclined to accept some aspects of the Ptolemaic view but not others. The holistic picture of beliefs which is presupposed by Feyerabend is not consistent with the historical evidence.[8] Finally, common-sense standards could be used to assess both the Ptolemaic view and its rivals.

The problem which pervades Feyerabend's account of the Copernican revolution is a problem which permeates all relativistically minded accounts of historical events. For the purposes of simplicity, anthropologists often describe certain assumptions as the prevailing assumptions of a society which are interconnected and shape everything. Yet these assumptions are more of a hotchpotch of sometimes contradictory views than a conceptually unified whole. In addition, all real human societies contain dissenters who hold views that are quite different and whose views are fairly widely known.[9] In the end, even the advocates of the so-called 'prevailing view' recognize various problems with it and try to resolve them.

Another important problem with Feyerabend's account is that he assumes that the reasoning which people find cogent is determined by what is prescribed by the supposed prevailing view. Thus, he assumes that Ptolemaists could not be persuaded by reasoning which was not supposed to be plausible outside of Ptolemaic theory. But people will sometimes find certain reasoning cogent, whether it is prescribed or not. (This seems particularly true when the reasoning involves their practical interests.) I suggest that this is because, just as when we have been trained in a particular environment, our biological structure will cause things to look a certain way to us, so too the arguments which will strike us as cogent are fairly impervious to theoretical influences. I propose that many of our intuitions about plausible reasoning are not affected by our theoretical beliefs. Of course, just as we can learn to override the prima facie reports of our senses, we can learn to override the reports of our intuitions about types of arguments. But if am right, these reports will retain a certain residual power, and can be brought into play when widely accepted standards for judging the relative merits of theories are in question.[10]

I have discussed Feyerabend's most important case study and found his account implausible. However, the reader should note that Feyerabend is right to urge that it is in part an empirical issue as to whether radical changes in scientific theories occur for objectively good reasons. It is always possible that newly discovered historical material may bear out Feyerabend's analysis of scientific revolutions. It is also always possible that empirical material will come to light which undermines some of the non-historical claims I have used to criticize Feyerabend. For instance, my claim that there is an underlying common sense by which we can judge the plausibility of arguments and which transcends particular theoretical perspectives, is a testable claim about human psychology. Thus, whether Feyerabend's account is right or not depends crucially on empirical findings.

A CRITIQUE OF RELATIVISM Feyerabend's argument for relativism does not work for two reasons. First, he could not show us that there are two incommensurable world pictures which refer to items in different worlds. On his own assumptions, to show this in the world of our world picture, he would need to show this while using our concepts and fundamental assumptions. But this would be impossible, since, by his account, the reference of our concepts is determined by the fundamental assumptions of our world picture – which are radically different from the assumptions in other postulated world pictures. This means that in our world picture the concepts in the other supposed world picture cannot refer. Thus, when he relies on our fundamental assumptions to argue that the concepts in the other world picture also refer, he must fail.

Second, to establish that relativism is right while presenting arguments which used our concepts, he would need to show that some individuals in our world also have a world picture radically incommensurable to ours and so inhabit a different world. (If they only inhabit the world generated by their world picture, we cannot have evidence that they exist using the concepts of our world picture.) This means that perceiving individuals would have to inhabit both worlds at the same time since, to perceive a world you must be in it, and to be perceived in a world you must be in it. But, this implies that if Feyerabend could show there were two worlds, there must be one world – as the term we use to refer to an individual in our world must also refer to the same individual in another world.

Feyerabend cannot justify his theory that there are incommensurable world pictures which are world yielding.[11] Thus, Feyerabend cannot produce a good argument for the claim that some changes in theories are so radical that those theories cannot be assessed by a common standard. Different scientists can have radically different theories about our world and about standards for assessing the merits of such theories. But such theories can be plausibly assessed by appealing to the experiential evidence accessible to normal human beings, or by appealing to how the predictions of a theory fare in comparison with its rivals. (I described such procedures for comparing radically different theories in Chapter 1.)

Conclusion

Incommensurable world-views are an artefact of philosophers' or historians' reconstructions rather than a real feature of science. People in every society accept some parts of doctrines, have doubts about others and reject yet others. They continue to be able to use experience and some common-sense methods of reasoning to judge theories if critics point out problems to them. They are not completely taken in by widely accepted claims.

Nevertheless, Feyerabend has shown that big changes can occur in the standards for judging theories accepted in science, so that simplistic pictures of the growth of scientific knowledge on the basis of unchanging standards cannot be sustained. Deep assumptions about the nature of the world and how we should proceed in finding out things about it can change in scientific revolutions. Galileo and others were gradually able to show that our naked eyes are unreliable instruments in astronomy and that seemingly powerful arguments from everyday observation can turn out to be very thin. They thus pointed the way to an astronomy in which careful experimentation, observations through well-constructed instruments and precise predictions play a crucial role.

2 The value of science

In this book I have been arguing that, by and large, science gives us objectively justified knowledge. People often suppose that this would be enough objectively to justify scientists doing virtually any kind of scientific research. After all, to say that science gives us objectively justified knowledge is to say that science gives us truths about the world. But, to justify scientific research we would need to show far more than that scientific research gives us such truths. That science gives us truths does not tell us whether seeking those truths is worth while. To justify scientific research, we need reasons for thinking that seeking scientific knowledge is valuable. Scientific research uses up a great deal of money and time which could be spent on other things, and it is used to transform people's lives in a great variety of ways. Even if we assume that seeking scientific knowledge is typically a valuable activity, this does not tell us the kinds of scientific knowledge we should try to discover. It does not tell us whether we should be seeking only knowledge which is likely to be useful or whether it might be better not to find out certain things. As a result of all these features of scientific research, an important philosophical problem arises. The problem is: what, if any, are the proper aims of scientific research?

That this is a serious problem can be appreciated by considering that colossal amounts of money and time are spent on scientific research which might be more usefully spent elsewhere, and by considering the role scientific knowledge of all kinds has played in transforming human life for the worse. Vast amounts of money are spent on scientific research into the most abstruse matters. At least since the bombing of Hiroshima, great numbers of scientists have been employed in very expensive research which directly or indirectly helps governments to produce enormously destructive weapons. In addition, since the Industrial Revolution, people all over the world have been greatly affected by non-military scientific advances. Millions of agricultural labourers have been made redundant by the application of scientific discoveries. Many of them are forced to work long hours in awful factories in order to produce previously undreamed of commodities. They live in polluted slums which surround vast cities. Their previous social and cultural life has been shattered in a matter of a few generations.

Apologists for science reply to those who bring such facts to their attention that the misuse of scientific knowledge does not affect the value of seeking scientific knowledge. It only affects the value of *applying* scientific knowledge in an immoral manner (for example Popper, 1966: 234). But to reply in this way presupposes that scientists never bear any moral responsibility for the problematic applications of scientific knowledge because they are unintended or unanticipated. This presupposition is very implausible. If someone produces something which he or she knows is reasonably likely to be used to bring about some result, that individual bears some moral responsibility for the result. This is true even if he or she did not bring it about directly. Scientists often know the broad kinds of ways in which knowledge in an area is likely to be applied and the results which will be produced when the knowledge is applied. In the modern world, much scientific research can only be done with funding from governments or companies. Everyone knows that those governments or companies intend to use that research in ways which are likely to produce particular results. A major reason why companies spend money on certain kinds of geological research is that they will be able to find more oil. A likely result of such research is that oil will be used further to pollute the environment. Some governments fund fundamental particle research so that the knowledge which will be produced will enable them to manufacture better nuclear weapons. A likely result of such research is that other nations will be threatened by such weapons. A major reason why computer companies spend money on research in cognitive science is to produce better computers. A likely result of this research is that better computers will be applied in ways which will result in thousands of people losing their jobs.[12] Scientists are perfectly aware of such facts and bear some responsibility for the predictable consequences of their research activities.[13]

Of course, apologists for scientific research would reply that, on the whole, scientific research – including research which has been used to produce many problems – has greatly improved the lives of most people. They may argue that, for this reason, morally responsible scientists would continue to do most of the research they currently do. To feel the force of this argument consider the benefits which it might be argued that scientific research has produced. Agricultural knowledge has been used to reduce drastically the proportion of the population of the planet living on the verge of starvation. Medicine has made enormous advances in eliminating many diseases, in reducing pain and in extending people's lifespans. Contraceptives have greatly increased many women's control of their fertility. The oil which geological research allows us to discover gives many people the capacity to do things they value enormously. The computers, which research in cognitive science has allowed us to produce, have eliminated the need for a large number of mind-numbing jobs and have helped to create a large number of newer and more interesting jobs. In the light of such arguments, we might reasonably conclude that a lot of scientific research is morally and practically justified, although we could not reasonably conclude that all scientific research is so justified.

Suppose, however, that we grant that a lot of scientific research is morally and practically justified; a range of further questions arises when we consider the important role science has in most modern societies. In some important ways, science has supplanted religion. A great deal of public money is spent on teaching scientific truths and scientific methods in our schools, and the widespread acceptance of these truths has led many people to abandon or substantially modify their religious or other metaphysical views. Further, we pay great regard to the views of scientific experts on a range of issues, some of which have little to do with the areas of their supposed competence. We also help the state to increase the power of scientists by prohibiting many practices and only allowing the views of scientific experts to count as evidence in many situations. (For example, the state prohibits anyone but scientifically trained medical practitioners from practising many kinds of medicine.) Yet there is little discussion of what role scientific knowledge and scientific experts should have in our society. We can reasonably ask several important questions: What role should the supposed truths which scientists discover play in our lives? What role should a scientific education play? What role should scientific experts have in our society?

Answers to questions about the proper aims of scientific research, and about the role scientific knowledge and scientific experts should have in our lives, are not answers which can be justified in the way that answers to scientific questions can be justified. Such answers cannot be shown to be right by appealing to facts alone. As David Hume stressed in the eighteenth century, no statement about what we should do can logically be derived from a statement of fact. There is a logical gap between statements of fact and statements of value, so that the fact that some scientific theory is true does not imply that it should play a particular role in our lives. This means that it is consistent with accepting that a theory is roughly true to ban teaching it, not to allow research to be done on details of it and not to allow it to be applied to practical problems.

Consider an example. Suppose we are the leaders of a community of religious fundamentalists. Assume we believe that we should always aim to make people feel content with their lives. Let us also say that we come to learn Darwin's theory of evolution and are convinced that it is roughly true. However, we discover that acquaintance with Darwin's theory tends to make people in fundamentalist communities feel very discontented with their lives. Suppose that, consistent with our value commitments, we decide to ban anyone from mentioning Darwin's theory. If Hume is right, there would be nothing irrational about our decision. Further, if Hume is right, someone who wanted to criticize our ban could not cogently argue that we were acting wrongly without appealing to premises about values. To argue cogently that we are wrong, he or she would have to appeal to value premises. For example, the dissenter may argue that our ban is wrong because adults always have the right to know truths which may be relevant to their lives.

If there is a logical gap between statements of fact and statements about what we should do, those who think that the pursuit of scientific knowledge or the application of scientific knowledge should play an important role in our lives need to argue their case by appealing to claims about what is valuable – or at least by appealing to what people find valuable. A possible answer to some of the problems I have raised about the role of science in our lives is that most scientific knowledge is valuable because it helps people achieve a great variety of ends. Whether we want to plunder nature or save sensitive ecosystems, scientific knowledge will be useful. Further, it might be argued that scientific knowledge is more reliable than knowledge claims from non-scientific traditions because claims in these traditions have not been tested in the same rigorous manner. For these reasons, it might be said that a scientific education will be useful to most people, and most people will recognize that scientific experts are more reliable in many matters than people from other traditions. Because scientific knowledge is useful for achieving a great variety of ends and more reliable than claims from other traditions, scientific research should be pursued, scientific information and a knowledge of scientific method should have a special role in the education system, and scientific experts should be given a special role in dealing with a range of problems.

One problem with this answer to some of the problems I have raised is that it at best justifies scientific knowledge which has practical applications. It does not justify us in giving an important role to scientific education or in funding scientific research except in so far as they are likely to be useful to a large number of people. Popper has tried to present a case for the claim that a scientific education and scientific research are also valuable for other reasons. He aims to show that fundamental scientific research and a broad education in scientific method are both valuable in ways that are not captured by their obvious practical advantages. He presents three arguments.

First, the history of scientific research is one in which many valuable technological discoveries have been made as a result of pursuing quite abstruse questions. The serendipitous manner in which such discoveries were made means that even those who are solely interested in the technological applications of science should help scientists and students to pursue intellectually important problems rather than trying to confine them to predetermined goals.

Second, scientific research is the paradigmatic example of rational activity. In such research, we try to answer intellectually important problems through a critical discussion of alternative theories which are subjected to severe tests. For discussion to be truly critical, it must be conducted in a way which does not allow us to brush aside intellectually important problems. Such a critical discussion is necessary for our activities to be rational and objective. Thus, Popper argues, if we want to arrive at an understanding of the world rationally and objectively, we should allow fundamental research to be done without very specific direction and learn to do research in a scientific manner so that we can emulate the example of science.

Third, engaging in open-ended critical discussion has non-technological benefits because it also teaches us to value the ideals of a free society, for we learn to value imaginative hypotheses and well argued criticisms rather than authoritative statements or conventionally acceptable perspectives. We also learn to value tolerance, for we realize that we may be wrong in our most cherished ideas and that other rational beings may be able to produce good criticisms of them.

Popper says that his arguments for the value of scientific research which is not directed by an interest in the practical applications of scientific discoveries cannot be as strong as arguments for a scientific statement. At least his second and third arguments are arguments for an ethical position and, by his account, ethical positions are not defensible on the basis of factual evidence.[14]

Feyerabend on the role of science

Feyerabend does not believe that the role of science in modern societies can be justified either by its technological power or by arguments like those of Popper. He argues that science should not play the role which it plays in modern societies. He claims that it should be separated from the state in the way that religion was separated from the state. Scientific theories, no matter how plausible they seem to be, should have no privileged status in state-funded education. Further, scientists should have no privileged status in medical practice or in law courts. Finally, if funding is provided for scientific projects, the decision about whether and how to allocate the funds should be made more or less directly by citizens – on grounds which they decide for themselves.

Feyerabend says that we should seek to produce a free society in which science has no privileged place. Members of sub-societies in that society should be able to live in the way they want, provided they do not interfere with other sub-societies. If they do not want to give science a privileged role in their lives, they should not have to do so. All traditions in society, whether they are scientific traditions or not, should be given equal rights. In so far as general decisions have to be taken for all the society, those decisions should be taken by democratically elected committees in which debate is open, in the sense that it is not necessarily guided by scientific standards.

Many of Feyerabend's arguments for his claims rely on the relativism I have criticized in the previous section. I shall not discuss such arguments as I have criticized them in my discussion of relativism. Let me turn now to some of his other arguments.[15]

First, what is practically useful and what is not depends on decisions about how we should live. If we chose to live in some particular ways, much scientific knowledge would be useless or even a hindrance to us. Rational people could well choose to live in a way which does not rely on science. Thus, even if science gives us knowledge of the world, it should have no privileged place in a free society. To understand this point, consider a group of people who find many of the facts discovered by science bewildering and unsettling. They feel that in the world discovered by science there is no ultimate point to anything and no one really cares about us. They find very attractive the way of life of a religious fundamentalist community, in which everyone thinks that god is constantly watching them and everyone believes that the Bible provides a detailed plan of how to live. They are willing to give up a great deal of medical and other scientific knowledge to live in such a community. Feyerabend would argue that much of scientific knowledge would be of little use to such people. They would have no good reason for giving scientific knowledge and scientific experts a special place in society. As the attitude of such people would not be irrational, he thinks that society should not be so structured as to force them to accept and implement the recommendations of scientific experts or to make them have their children taught scientific method and scientific knowledge.

Feyerabend notes, in order to protect itself, society may impose limits on the degree to which anti-scientific sub-communities can ignore the recommendations of scientific experts. For example, society may interfere with such sub-communities to prevent the spread of infectious diseases to people who do not have anti-scientific values. But according to Feyerabend's account even the policy of deciding to interfere in such cases should be taken by committees of citizens and not by scientists. If such committees of citizens were to decide that they did not believe in the existence of infectious diseases, it seems that Feyerabend would be committed to the claim that interference to prevent the spread of such diseases could not be morally justified.

Second, even if what scientists say about the world is true, this is not a sufficient argument for giving the knowledge they produce a special status in education, the law or medicine. Nor is it a reason for providing a great deal of money to fund it. Many scientific research projects give few practical returns in proportion to the quantities of money which have been spent and produce little which is impressive to those who have not been brainwashed into thinking that science is intrinsically wonderful. For instance, the American moon program used vast amounts of money to get a few inarticulate men to an airless and hot stone for a short time. Some knowledge was gained, but there is no good reason to think that this achievement was worth funding. If we were not assuming the excellence of science, we might well be much more impressed by the visions of medieval mystics who claimed to have travelled through the celestial spheres to see god in all his splendour – these visions are more colourful and cost very little to produce.

Third, even if we are interested in advancing scientific knowledge, we should allow other traditions to exist and to compete with science for business. Science has often learnt important things from other traditions, and citizens have benefited from being allowed to consult those trained in these traditions because these 'alternative' practitioners have sometimes managed to handle problems which science has not been able to deal with. For example, non-scientific medical practitioners have sometimes healed diseases or relieved pain in cases in which scientific medicine has failed. In China, the revival of traditional medicine initiated by the Communists has led to the discovery of important techniques for the reduction of pain and to the discovery of a number of important drugs. Thus, individuals should be able to choose to whom to go to deal with their problems and scientists should not be able to use the law to prevent their competitors from offering their services.

Fourth, even if we think that accepted scientific theories are generally right, scientists are untrustworthy. They often make grandiose claims about things they have not investigated properly and disagree with one another about important claims. An example of the former is that many eminent scientists have signed documents condemning astrology; yet most of them can be shown to know virtually nothing about research in astrology. An example of the latter is the often passionate disagreement among medical practitioners about the treatment of certain kinds of cancers. The claims of scientists should be carefully considered by citizens, who should be free to accept or reject them. Supposed scientific experts can advise citizens but citizens should be able to reject their advice.

Fifth, the citizens of a free society should be able to decide for themselves whether they prefer to deal with a problem by consulting a scientist or someone else, even if this dramatically reduces the chances of them being successful in dealing with that problem. The reason for this is that it is morally valuable for citizens to choose how to deal with a problem which confronts them, even if this reduces the success rate in dealing with that problem. If individual citizens want their medical problems to be dealt with by faith healers rather than doctors, they should be able to put themselves in the hands of faith healers – even if this reduces the chance that their diseases will be cured. Similarly, if elected citizens' committees want to give government research funds to witchdoctors rather than to scientific researchers they should be able to do so, even if this reduces the chance of eradicating widespread diseases.

Before I begin my critical discussion, it should be noted that the claims of Popper and Feyerabend concerning the role science should have in our society, are not as opposed as they may appear. Popper argues that we should emulate scientific standards in dealing with problems in order to proceed rationally and that working through problems in a scientific manner makes us better and more rational people. But he does not argue that citizens should not be allowed to follow the advice of non-scientific practitioners. Neither does he argue that science should have a special place in society independently of the wishes of citizens. Popper's work in political philosophy makes it clear that he thinks citizens should not be coerced into doing things by supposed experts, but should let themselves be convinced by rational arguments put by those experts. Like Feyerabend, he places great value on the freedom of individuals to live as they see fit provided they do not harm others. This seems to mean that if a citizen wants to be treated for a disease by faith healers, he should be able to be treated by them. Still, there seems to be an important difference between Popper and Feyerabend. Popper thinks that, when making their decisions, citizens ought to rely on views which have been arrived at through a critical discussion which emulates scientific method. In contrast, Feyerabend thinks it is perfectly acceptable for citizens to make their decisions in a non-scientific manner.

Critical discussion

Popper's arguments for the value of fundamental research in science are all problematic. His first argument relies on the premise that fundamental scientific research and an open-ended scientific education have often turned out to be practically useful in quite unexpected ways. This premise is true but the conclusion that fundamental scientific research and an open-ended scientific education should be deeply valued does not follow from his claim. Three objections can be put to the drawing of Popper's conclusion.

1 Someone who thinks that the simple way of life of a religious fundamentalist is the best life is not going to be interested in innovative scientific discoveries which lead to our lives being transformed in unanticipated ways. To someone with such values, the serendipitous nature of scientific discovery is not a good argument for fundamental research in science or an open-ended scientific education. Popper nowhere shows that someone who holds such values is irrational or wrong. Thus, he fails to produce a universally acceptable argument for valuing fundamental scientific research.
2 Some fundamental research has turned out to produce unanticipated knowledge which produces horrific effects. Depending on our values, we might reasonably decide that fundamental research is liable to lead to unanticipated applications which are so dangerous that the research should never be carried out. For example, we may have studied the way in which research on radioactive materials in the early part of the twentieth century led to the development of nuclear weapons and nuclear power generation, and consequently may have concluded that fundamental scientific research should not be carried out.
3 Even if we think that fundamental research and an open-ended scientific education will lead us to discoveries which are likely to improve human life, it is unclear how much emphasis we should put on funding fundamental scientific research and how much should be put on applying existing knowledge to practical problems. Popper's argument for the value of fundamental research is too vague to be of much use in establishing that fundamental scientific research is of great importance.

Popper's second argument is that by conducting our investigations through open critical debates in which we allow our views to be criticized and even falsified, we are being rational. However, it is implausible to believe that people are being irrational merely because they refuse to engage in a critical discussion of their views according to scientific standards. Suppose a woman, for example, is the sort of person who is unsettled by scientific debate because she thinks it threatens her peace of mind and her preferred fundamentalist way of life. She might then be perfectly rational in refusing to enter into a critical discussion about the merits of her beliefs. Popper might argue that the fundamentalist could only be rational if she at least allowed her beliefs to be subjected to criticism. But the fundamentalist could plausibly reply that this is not necessary, as she has evidence from everyday experience of the kinds of things which unsettle her, and that she is not going to engage in further debate merely because she might be wrong.

Popper's third argument is that engaging in the kind of critical discussion which is involved in open-ended scientific research is valuable because it teaches us to value the ideals of a free society. An initial problem with this argument is that it fails to distinguish between open-ended research in science and other sorts of critical discussion. We may be totally uninterested in engaging in critical discussion of scientific theories and still learn the same lesson by engaging in a critical discussion of political theories. Further, Popper gives us no reason why we should follow the critical standards generally accepted in science. Ancient philosophers did not follow the canons of scientific method even though they engaged in a great deal of critical discussion of scientific theories. They paid relatively little attention to the success or failure of predictions in theories. Despite these problems with Popper's third argument, Popper might say that if we value a society which tolerates dissenting views and different ways of life, we will value enterprises like fundamental scientific research because we will hold the critical aspects of such enterprises to be worthy of emulation. However, there are two deeper problems with Popper's third argument:

1 If we do not already value a free society, it is unclear why we should value features of open-ended research in science.
2 As Feyerabend points out, scientific discussions restrict debate by accepting only certain critical standards for assessing theories. In this way, they encourage those who have been trained scientifically to narrow the kinds of criticisms they consider acceptable, and can create contempt for people who do not use scientific arguments to bolster or criticize theories. This means, it is arguable, that scientific training tends to create an appearance of free debate while closing the parameters of debates dramatically. For example, it may be argued that the scientifically trained tend to ignore criticisms of the use of scientific method and dismiss appeals to mystical intuitions or to religious writings as silly. Thus, even if we value a free society, we may not value training people in how to engage in a scientific debate as a way of getting people to be more tolerant.

Despite the problems I have raised regarding Popper's arguments, his first and third arguments seem to have some force if they are addressed to people who hold particular ethical views. For people who hold that a fundamentalist way of life is bad and believe that the potential technological benefits of science outweigh its potential disadvantages, Popper puts a plausible case for some funding for fundamental scientific research and for the value of an open-ended scientific education. For people who value freedom and tolerance to some degree, but think that we should discourage those who use highly dubious methods of argument to justify their claims, Popper puts a plausible case for making an open-ended education in scientific method an important component of education.

Let me now turn to a discussion of Feyerabend's arguments. The first problem is that his claim that a scientific education should not be a compulsory and important part of all children's education is implausible for three reasons.

1 Nearly all people do not find scientific knowledge to be so unsettling as to want to give up the benefits of scientific knowledge for a simpler way of life. Even most religious fundamentalists in modern Western societies use the benefits of scientific knowledge in many ways in their everyday lives. Further, whether people think that the best way to live involves the widespread application of science or not, the wider society in which they live has been so constructed that it is highly dependent on the application of science to deal with the problems of everyday life. Agricultural machinery, air conditioning, aeroplanes, cars, and so on play an enormously important part in modern life. To learn how to survive, everyone needs to know some elementary science. Even if someone only wants to know what to avoid, it helps us to have a more sophisticated knowledge of science. If a company wants to build a mobile telephone tower or a nuclear power station next to the land of a fundamentalist, the fundamentalist will need to know how this will affect him or her. All of this means that a reasonably sophisticated knowledge of science should be part of everyone's education (Munévar, 1991b: 194).
2 Children should be protected from the actions of their parents. Although some adults find that they would prefer to live a way of life in which science does not play an important part, the great majority do not. It is reasonable to believe that if a child has had the opportunity to learn about science and its applications, he or she will tend to find science valuable. Parents should not be able to deprive children of learning which they are likely to find valuable.
3 It is valuable for other members of the community to live in a community of citizens who assess factual claims according to scientific standards. Feyerabend talks as if people who think and live according to a tradition in which they pay no regard to objective standards of justification are no threat to outsiders. But the attitudes of mind which they hold are clearly a threat to outsiders. People who form their central beliefs about the world in ways that ignore scientific standards of argument are likely to be taken in by beliefs in witchcraft, religious fundamentalisms, anti-Semitism, and so on. They are likely to vote on the basis of those beliefs and to act on those beliefs in their day-to-day interaction with others (von Brentano, 1991: 200). Their attitudes of mind thus pose a serious threat to other members of the wider community. It is legitimate for the community to try to prevent such attitudes of mind from developing through education.

I should stress that none of my arguments suggest that science should be taught as a set of theories which cannot be criticized or as if it were intrinsically wonderful. In my view, students should learn that what makes claims good is the evidence and not the fact that their teacher tells them to accept them. Further, students should be encouraged to test claims for themselves where this is feasible. In addition, they should learn that science is a fallible enterprise. I should also stress that my arguments rely on widely held assumptions about what is morally right, but that such assumptions may be rejected by some people.

The second problem with Feyerabend's arguments is that his claim that practitioners of other traditions should be able to offer their services to individual members of the public (and perhaps to have an important role in education and the law) is not supported by good arguments. The reader will remember that he offers two arguments for his claim. His first argument is that other traditions have been successful in dealing with everyday problems. His second argument is that the citizens of a free society should be able to decide for themselves how to deal with a problem by consulting non-scientists, even if this reduces their chances of successfully dealing with a situation.

Feyerabend's first argument is implausible. Medicine is the sole area in which he adduces substantial evidence that problems which are not solved by scientific practitioners are sometimes solved by practitioners from other traditions. Although his remarks constitute some evidence for licensing and relying on alternative medical practitioners, he does not produce any evidence for doing this in other areas. He produces no evidence that traditional navigation, traditional house building, or a large range of other traditional practices are at all likely to be better than modern, scientifically informed practices. In areas apart from medicine, science seems to have produced knowledge which is far superior to knowledge coming from other traditions (Munévar, 1991b: 191 ff.). Further, even in the case of medicine, alternative practitioners have achieved limited successes in some areas, but this does not mean that they should be licensed for general practice or be relied upon. Many of the drugs and techniques they use are potentially dangerous and have not been tested to the same degree as scientific remedies. This means that there is a strong case for not allowing non-scientific medical practitioners to be general practitioners. They can reasonably be allowed to offer their services to the public in some matters, but not in others. (Of course, this does not mean that the claims of other traditions are never worth studying, or that science can never learn from theories in those traditions. As Feyerabend stresses, ideas from such traditions are often useful to scientists and sometimes important pieces of knowledge have been discovered in them.)

Feyerabend's second argument for the claim that practitioners of other traditions should be free to offer any of their services to individual members of the public is also implausible. There are two problems with the second argument:

1 The argument presupposes that we should greatly value the freedom of individual citizens and of citizens' committees, whether those individuals or committees tend to come up with courses of action which advance their own ends or not. But someone who did not place a high value on the free activity of citizens would disagree with this presupposition and it is difficult to see how the disagreement could be rationally resolved. Feyerabend could not argue that the consequences of allowing such freedom to exist are beneficial, for he is arguing that even if they are not beneficial people should be able to do what they want.
2 Even if we agree with Feyerabend in valuing freedom highly, there is a case for interfering with the freedom of individual citizens or groups of citizens when they are likely to kill themselves or damage themselves badly. Suppose, for example, a man who is being treated by a herbalist is imbibing herbs laced with heavy metals that are known to be highly poisonous. The danger posed by the herbs is explained to him, but he persists in trusting the herbalist. If he keeps taking the herbs, they are likely to kill him quickly so that he will never be able to act freely again. To enhance his overall freedom we could reasonably prevent him from consuming those herbs. Thus, if we are interested in protecting the long-term freedom of individuals there can sometimes be good reasons for preventing them from using non-scientific methods to deal with their problems.

I should note that while Feyerabend does not produce a good case for allowing unregulated practitioners from other traditions to offer their services, he could make a good case for constant public scrutiny of scientific practitioners. He could also very plausibly argue that the professional bodies which license scientific practitioners should be ultimately under the control of elected representatives of citizens, who should be able to change how those bodies work. As Feyerabend says, close study of the behaviour of scientific experts shows that they often make authoritative-sounding claims on matters about which they know nothing, or carry out procedures within their areas of expertise which cannot be justified by the evidence available. Like other people, scientific experts are inclined to think that their favourite ideas are the best ideas for dealing with particular problems – whether the evidence for their ideas is good or not. Like other people, they often tend to try to enhance the power and prestige of the group to which they belong because the status of that group is intimately tied to their own status (Hull, 1988). Also like other people, they are inclined to overlook cheaper procedures which are effective for dealing with problems when the use of more expensive procedures will benefit them financially. It could plausibly be argued that scientific experts need to be held in check by a social structure in which shoddy research, dangerous practices, and the use of unnecessarily expensive procedures are exposed and prevented. It could also be plausibly argued that the opinions and activities of scientific experts should be under constant public scrutiny and that the conditions under which they can practice should be regulated by bodies which are controlled by the public (rather than other scientists).

To help to spell out this point, consider that many authors – including Feyerabend – have highlighted that doctors sometimes carry out procedures which do patients a great deal of damage, on the basis of obviously shoddy evidence. It has also been frequently pointed out that doctors carry out many costly and unnecessary procedures. An important reason why these problems are worse in medicine than in some other disciplines is that the activities of doctors are not under constant scrutiny by outside experts whose interests would be served by publicly exposing poorly justified claims and activities. Whereas in some areas of science, scientists would gain professional kudos by exposing the shoddy research practices of rival scientists, medicine is a relatively closed profession in which it is thought to be bad form to criticize one's fellow professionals, particularly in a public forum (Hull, 1988: 345 ff.). The public would benefit a great deal from the break up of the power of the fairly monolithic medical profession and from restructuring the practice of medicine so as to encourage publicly aired criticisms of widely used medical treatments, as well as free and open criticism of the activities of specific doctors. The public would also benefit if its representatives could withdraw the licence to practise of medical practitioners. Doctors investigating other doctors are likely to have fellow feeling for them. They are also likely to want to cover up the mistakes of other doctors because the exposure of such mistakes damages the status of the profession. They will thus be reluctant to create a public scandal by recommending that fellow doctors have their licences withdrawn, even if those doctors are incompetent.

Conclusion

I have pointed out that we can justify giving science an important role in education, in technological practices and in the legal system if we accept some widely accepted ideas about what constitutes a good way to live. Yet I have not argued that someone who refuses to accept such ideas is irrational or mistaken. The reason is that it may be impossible to come to an objectively justified answer to the question: what role should science play in our society? Objectively to justify any answer to this question, we would need to rely on a justified theory about how we should live. But it is not obvious that theories about how we should live *can* be justified objectively. Perhaps the confidence which some philosophers of the Enlightenment had that science should play an important role in many areas of our lives cannot be justified. I cannot pursue this issue further here. There is an enormous philosophical debate about the issue in the literature on ethics. Note, however, that unless we can objectively justify some claims about how we should live, we cannot objectively justify giving science a central place in our lives.

Suppose that after having considered the issue carefully, we find that we can show that scientific knowledge and scientific experts should have a role in our lives which is similar to the one they already take. Assume we also think that we can show that science is primarily valuable because it furthers the sorts of goals most of us in modern Western societies have. We can, nevertheless, learn from various criticisms of the role scientific knowledge and scientific experts play in our society. Critics of science could plausibly argue that research, the results of which are likely to be used for immoral purposes, should not be undertaken unless the benefits of the likely applications of that research outweigh its disadvantages. Further, Feyerabend has made a good case for thinking that medical practitioners from non-scientific traditions should be able to offer their services to the public on some matters and that the claims of non-scientific traditions on medical matters are worth investigating. In addition, I have pointed out that Feyerabend could make a good case for saying that scientific professions should be under the ultimate control of elected representatives of the public and that the workings of some scientific professions should be restructured.

Further reading

Popper's arguments for the value of scientific research and an open-ended scientific education are put in scattered remarks. Particularly useful is Popper, 1966: 237 ff. Two of Feyerabend's texts (1988; 1978a) contain a number of his important historical arguments. Chalmers (1986; 1990: 50–60) are useful criticisms of Feyerabend's historical arguments. Feyerabend's arguments for relativism and his critique of the role of science in our society are well set out in Feyerabend, 1988. Feyerabend (1978b) contains a more thorough critique of the role of science in our society. Feyerabend (1993) contains some criticisms of his previous views. Couvalis (1989: 136–43) criticizes Feyerabend's argument for relativism. Munévar (1991a) contains a number of useful critiques of Feyerabend. See particularly Munévar, 1991b and von Brentano, 1991.

Notes

1 Feyerabend does not talk of world pictures but of 'comprehensive cosmological points of view' (Feyerabend, 1988: 226). I use the notion of a world picture to explain his claims since it is likely to be more familiar to the reader.

2 Feyerabend runs two different lines in his later work. One of them, which may be called anti-methodism, is the view that there is no universal method in science in the sense of precise universally applicable rules. This is not necessarily a form of relativism as it is consistent with the view that, objectively speaking, science has led to a great increase in knowledge about the world. I have no quarrel with Feyerabend's anti-methodism. A second line of argument Feyerabend runs is the form of relativism which I discuss here. In *Against Method* (Feyerabend, 1993) he claims to have given up relativism and criticizes notions such as world-views. But even in that book, he makes many relativist comments (for example in Chapter 17). The view I criticize in this chapter is one he sometimes defended from 1978 onwards.

3 Aristotle's views were rather different to Ptolemy's views and medieval thinkers also had different views from one another. What I call 'the Ptolemaic view' captures some key claims which would have been generally accepted in late medieval European cosmology. What I call 'the Copernican view' is a view some of the tenets of which were accepted by Copernicus, with all of its tenets coming to be accepted by the time of Newton.

4 This is not quite right. Some important medieval thinkers thought that straight-line motion on a horizontal plane did not require a mover for it to continue. They thus produced a 'protoinertial principle' (Chalmers, 1986: 11).

5 Galileo's prominent opponents recognized this fact. For example, to save the Ptolemaic account, which held that the heavenly bodies were perfectly spherical, the Ptolemaist Colombe maintained that the moon was contained in smooth transparent crystal. Galileo's response to this *ad hoc* hypothesis was that if such untestable hypotheses were to be allowed, anything should be allowed – including untestable *ad hoc* hypotheses which save the Copernican view (Drake, 1978: 168–9).

Feyerabend makes much of the fact that Galileo's published maps of the moon are inaccurate. He argues that this shows either that Galileo was rather indifferent to the details of what he saw through the telescope or that he saw the moon differently from us (Feyerabend, 1988: 97 ff.). In fact, Galileo was following a convention of the period in his published drawings. They were intended to be illustrations of his claims, not accurate maps. Galileo's ink washes show that he observed the moon carefully and noted its features fairly accurately (Winkler and van Helden, 1992: 208).

6 I should note that Feyerabend is right in arguing that early telescopes were often awful. For instance, a number of observers could not see the satellites of Jupiter through Galileo's first telescopes at all. However, Galileo had independent observers verify his predictions on many occasions (Drake, 1978: 235 ff.). The fact that many independent observers could verify many of his predictions constituted good evidence for his hypothesis even if other observers failed to verify those predictions, and even if some of his predictions were not verified by any observers.

7 For example, in response to the argument that the satellites of Jupiter are illusions, Galileo jokingly said that he would give 10,000 Scudi to someone who could build a telescope which would create satellites around one planet but not around others (Drake, 1978: 166). The argument behind this remark is that the apparent satellites of Jupiter are extremely unlikely to be illusions since telescopes do not produce similar illusions when other planets are observed.

8 Two examples to illustrate this point: (a) Aristotle had argued that the world had existed forever. But this was widely rejected in the medieval period as it was inconsistent with Christian doctrine, even though many of Aristotle's other doctrines were accepted. (b) The influential philosopher scientist Jean Buridan used the concept of the quantity of (prime) matter possessed by an object of a particular size in his version of Ptolemaic physics. But if Buridan had accepted all of Aristotle's theory of physics this would have been nonsensical, as Aristotle holds that prime matter has no quantity because it is formless and indeterminate (Shapere, 1974: 55–6).

9 For instance, historical searches of church court records reveal that despite the power of religion and the dominance of religious ideas, there were many upper class and 'village' sceptics who refused to believe central Christian doctrines in Europe. (For a brief discussion of the situation in England in the seventeenth century, see Thomas, 1984: 122–3. Thomas talks as if such scepticism only became at all common in about the seventeenth century. But the material in his references indicates that it was already quite common in the thirteenth century (Thomas, 1984: 348).)

10 Galileo often uses common-sense reasoning the power of which can easily be recognized by a modern reader. Drake (1978) offers many examples.

11 For a more detailed discussion of the problems with Feyerabend's arguments for relativism, see an earlier text of mine (Couvalis, 1989, particularly 136 ff.). However, in that work I wrongly accepted that there are conceptually incommensurable universal theories.

12 I am speaking of research in an area in general when I say that it is likely to produce certain results. The research of a particular oil researcher is unlikely to result in the environment being polluted because his or her research may well never lead to oil being found. But the collective enterprise of geological research on oil is very likely to produce the results I describe. An individual researcher is partly morally responsible for the results produced by the enterprise of geological research on oil because the researcher contributes to the production of knowledge which he or she knows will be applied to produce certain results. For instance, a minor Nazi rocket engineer who contributed to the expansion of knowledge of rocket engineering in Germany would be partly morally responsible for the bombing of London. (Provided, of course, that he knew that the rocket research to which he was contributing would be likely to lead to rockets being produced for use in the War.)

13 For instance, Pierre Curie's Nobel Lecture of 1905 shows that he and Marie Curie were well aware that the colossal subatomic forces they had discovered in radium could be used to produce something very dangerous (Quinn, 1995: 219 ff.). Just how dangerous was not, of course, made clear until 1945.

14 The details of Popper's view are rather unclear but the line I describe seems to underlie various statements he makes. For instance, Popper, 1966: 218 ff.; 237 ff.; 1976: 115 ff. Popper also describes the attitude of engineering students who want to stick to practically useful facts and pay no regard to intellectually interesting problems as a danger 'to our civilisation' (Popper, 1970: 53).

15 It is difficult to disentangle the arguments in Feyerabend which depend on relativism from those which do not. In some of what follows, I have tried to reconstruct what Feyerabend would have said if he were not a relativist.

6

The Sociology of Knowledge and Feminism

In the past, some histories of great scientists depicted them as lonely geniuses who were able to examine evidence and reason in an unprejudiced manner so as to arrive at important truths. This is in keeping with the Cartesian picture of knowledge, according to which those who wish to know should begin by stripping away their social and personal influences in order to examine claims in an unprejudiced manner in the natural light of reason. Recent studies seem to show that this picture of science is a caricature. The history of science seems to contain a number of great scientists who have accepted theories which were not justified on the evidence available to them. Such scientists often seem to have been influenced by external factors – that is factors which have nothing to do with the evidence in favour of a theory but rather, for instance, whether a theory would bolster the position of the social group to which they belonged. In response to the new historical material, some sociologists have argued that this means we need to study how science should be socially structured in order to prevent such external factors from having an undue influence. However, the sociologists Barry Barnes and David Bloor (1982) propose that scientists always accept theories partly because of external factors. They argue that observation, experiment and natural dispositions to reason do play some (small) part in narrowing down the range of theories a scientist will accept. However, in the end, a scientist will accept one of a number of theories because of the influence of external social factors, so that trying to rid science of the influence of such factors is ultimately useless.

Barnes and Bloor claim that their proposal is a kind of relativism. They also claim that it is well supported by historical evidence. If they are right, scientists cannot plausibly claim that accepted scientific theories are accepted because they are objectively justified. Science is merely a knowledge-producing practice which has acquired prestige in some societies. Viewed from outside the position of such societies, scientific claims are no more justified than is the claim that there are witches.

In spelling out their proposal, Barnes and Bloor stress the influence of external interests on scientific findings, such as the interests of the social class to which powerful scientists belong. However, among studies which claim to have shown the influence of external factors on science are studies of the influence of external social and personal values.

Feminist researchers have plausibly argued that the ways in which scientific data are collected and the hypotheses which scientists think are justified by the data are often affected by such values. For example, scientists who believe that women should not play a prominent role in public life often gather data badly and use poor inferences to support the claim that women are not suited for such a role by nature. From Aristotle to recent times, the shoddiness of such research has sometimes passed virtually unnoticed.[1]

Some feminists have concluded this means we need to restructure scientific research to reduce the effect of external personal and social values on scientific findings. In their view, scientific findings can be objectively justified when the influence of external value commitments on them is removed. However, Helen Longino (1990) has argued that the external values of scientists can legitimately be used to decide which inferences can be drawn from data. By this she means that there is nothing *epistemologically* wrong with scientists deciding to draw or not to draw particular inferences from data because of their external value commitments. For instance, scientists who think of humans as free agents who should be able to determine their own lives can legitimately reject the inference from data about the influence of hormones on the brain that lead to the conclusion that human sexual behaviour is determined by the influence of such hormones.

If Longino is right, scientists can properly accept or reject theories because of their external value commitments. Given that she is right, it may be thought that scientific theories cannot be objectively justified. By her account, no matter how apparently secure the evidence for a theory or the inductive inference from the evidence to the theory, scientists can legitimately reject the theory because of their value commitments. However, Longino resists the view that she is undermining objectivity by proposing that a theory which is arrived at by consensus in an ideal scientific community is arrived at objectively. In the community she believes to be ideal, individual scientists can accept or reject a theory because of their value commitments, although they cannot legitimately avoid the criticisms of other members of the community or impose their value judgements on them in an authoritarian manner. If a consensus emerges, it must be one in which members of the scientific community have come to accept external value commitments as a result of a critical discussion.

Ismay Barwell (1994) agrees with Longino that external values can legitimately influence the data gathering and drawing of inferences of scientists. However, she thinks Longino's account of objectivity is inadequate and she proposes to supplement it by adding material from the differing account of Sandra Harding (1991). According to Harding, for a community to be one which comes to an agreement about the merits of theories objectively, its members have to recognize the power of outside interests and values to distort their findings and privilege the standpoints of members of certain marginalized groups on particular scientific issues.

I shall criticize the accounts of Barnes and Bloor, Longino, and Barwell, maintaining that external interests and values need not – and should not – play the role in science that they describe. Nevertheless, I shall argue that they are right in stressing that science is importantly a social enterprise and that, if we are interested in arriving at objectively justified theories, we can learn important things from their work.

1 External interests and relativism

Barnes and Bloor's strong program

In recent years, there has been a great deal of work done in the field of the history of science which has claimed to show that scientists are caused to accept theories by external social factors rather than just by the evidence. For example, some accounts of nineteenth-century controversies about theories of evolution claim that scientists accepted particular evolutionary theories because they advanced their social interests or social interests to which they were sympathetic.[2] David Bloor and Barry Barnes have argued that social location or social interests *always* play a crucial part in determining whether scientists accept a theory and in whether a theory is justified. Observation, experiment and our natural inclinations to reason in particular ways may play an important role in delimiting the range of theories scientists find acceptable. But what makes scientists accept a particular theory will always be some social factor which is not connected with the strength of the evidence.[3]

Barnes and Bloor call their hypothesis the *strong program* in the sociology of knowledge. The strong program is a variant of relativism, for it holds that whether a theory is credible or justified is not a matter of the available experimental or observational data or the strength of the inference from that data to the theory. If the strong program is right, what makes some theory a piece of current scientific knowledge is determined by social influences which have nothing to do with the empirical data. Barnes and Bloor claim that the strong program is a relativism which is not logically problematic because it does not deny that some theories are true and others false, or that some are rational and others irrational. Further, it does not say that what makes a statement true is dependent on the standards of the group which accepts it. In contrast, various other relativisms, such as a relativism which claims that all beliefs are equally true, are paradoxical. The claim that all beliefs are equally true implies that the belief that not all beliefs are equally true is as true as the belief that all beliefs are equally true. Thus, the claim is incoherent: the belief that all beliefs are equally true, must be false if it is true.

Barnes and Bloor distinguish the strong program from a hypothesis they call the *weak program*, which holds that *sometimes* scientists will accept or reject theories merely because of social influences which have nothing to do with the data available. The weak program is not a form of relativism, for it does not hold that what makes theories credible or justified is determined by such external factors. It poses no threat to the objectivity of a great deal of scientific research. The weak program holds that the explanation of scientists' beliefs favoured by rationalists is correct. Rationalists claim that, by and large, scientists' beliefs on scientific matters can best be explained by showing that the beliefs are justified on the best evidence available. (Note that the term'rationalist' is used here with a very different meaning from its meaning in some other areas of philosophy.)

Consider an imaginary example to illustrate the differences between the strong and weak programs. A powerful group of male scientists, concerned to preserve the social status of males, infer from research findings which are open to various interpretations that it is a fact that women are innately intellectually inferior. The few women scientists, concerned to preserve their status and research funds in a male-dominated scientific community, defend the view that research shows that generally women are innately intellectually inferior. Students learn to put forward the received view in order to achieve a pass mark for their essays. Budding researchers tend to go along with the consensus about the intellectual inferiority of women in order to get their papers published. The public tends to accept the claim that women are innately inferior because society has been trained to defer to eminent scientists. And so on. In such an intellectual environment, an advocate of the weak program would hold that a deplorable use of prestige and power has resulted in the public being misled about the strength of the evidence for the hypothesis. An advocate of the strong program would hold that the claim that women are innately intellectually inferior is part of current scientific knowledge, though it may not be true.

The first argument Barnes and Bloor present for the strong program is that it has theoretical advantages over rival programs. It is, they say, simpler and more general than the weak program, for it holds that the beliefs of participants in all kinds of communities are to be explained in the same kind of way. The beliefs of members of communities which are African or European, religious or political, rationalistic or superstitious all have the same kind of explanation. They also claim that the strong program has advantages over the views of rationalist philosophers, for rationalists say that rational or true beliefs do not need to be explained causally because they are rational or true, whereas irrational beliefs need causal explanations. To sum up their first argument, Barnes and Bloor maintain that the strong program is more scientific than the weak program or the accounts of rationalists because it has four features:

1 It seeks *causal* explanations of *all* scientists' beliefs – explanations in which psychological and other components play a part but in which a social component plays the crucial part.
2 It is *impartial* with respect to the truth and falsity, rationality and irrationality, of beliefs.
3 It gives *symmetrical* explanations of beliefs in the sense that the same *types* of causal explanations are given for all beliefs.
4 It is *reflexive* because the sort of explanation which advocates of the strong program give of the credibility of scientific theories can, in principle, be applied to explaining the credibility of the strong program.

A second argument Barnes and Bloor present for the strong program is that the empirical data are always logically compatible with more than one scientific theory, so that the fact that scientists accept a particular theory cannot be the result of the data alone. Theories are underdetermined by data because any amount of data is logically compatible with a number of incompatible scientific theories. We only pick one theory rather than another because we believe certain background assumptions. This means that no particular theory which is compatible with the data is supported by the data, and we should explain why scientists accept one such theory rather than another by appealing to the social factors which cause scientists to accept certain background assumptions.

Let me explain what they mean. Suppose I am doing research on a stomach disease which frequently leads to death. I find that a great number of individuals who have bacterium x in their stomachs show the relevant symptoms and die. I also find that those who are treated with an antibiotic which kills the bacterium do not die. Further, it becomes clear that those who are not treated with the antibiotic nearly always die. I conclude that bacterium x is the cause of the disease. To validly arrive at this conclusion, I need to introduce other assumptions such as germs always cause such diseases and no relevant germs except bacterium x were present. But such assumptions might be mistaken. It may turn out that all the people who developed the stomach disease developed it due to unusual sunspot activity to which they were genetically susceptible. For Barnes and Bloor, my predilection to accept the background assumption, despite the fact that it is dubious, must have social causes. Perhaps the view of those who hand out research grants and publish papers is that all such diseases are caused by bacteria, so I will be more likely to get research grant money by conforming. Perhaps the accepted view in the field is that all such diseases are caused by germs, so I will not gain respect if I question this assumption.

Barnes and Bloor's third argument for the strong program is that a large number of studies of historical changes and historical disputes in science have supposedly shown that sociological factors played a key part in convincing scientists to accept certain theories. I have already briefly mentioned some studies of how various theories of evolution came to be accepted or rejected, which I shall be discussing briefly later. I shall not go into the details of any historical studies as other authors have discussed them very thoroughly and they are not of great relevance here.[4]

Criticisms of the strong program

THE STRONG PROGRAM IS PARADOXICAL An important problem with the strong program is that while it is not inconsistent, it is paradoxical in the sense that if it were true, it would undermine the strength of arguments which are offered in support of it. The paradoxes result from the fact that the strong program is meant to be reflexive; that is, that whatever is said by advocates of the strong program about other scientific theories also applies to the strong program.

First, Barnes and Bloor adduce a large number of empirical studies to support the strong program. But if we accept that data radically underdetermine theories, such empirical studies cannot – of themselves – provide a good reason for opponents of the strong program to change their beliefs. This means that if Barnes and Bloor are right, their empirical studies must be perfectly compatible with programs other than the strong program. For instance, according to Barnes and Bloor, if we change some relevant background assumptions then the data must be compatible with the weak program and with rationalist accounts of scientific growth. Further, by their account there is no good reason why rationalists should not change a relevant background assumption. A relevant background assumption which rationalists could change is the assumption that we can cogently reason inductively from a large number of studies to the conclusion that the strong program is likely to be true. Rationalists could replace this background assumption with the one that states that enumerative induction is not cogent when it is used to justify the strong program. In arguing for the change, rationalists might argue that the strong program clashes with central intuitions, and that if inductions over certain items lead to conclusions which are in conflict with central intuitions, those inductions cannot be cogent. (What a central intuition is, would, of course, be determined by negotiation between powerful opponents of the strong program.)

It may be thought that Barnes and Bloor could deal with the first problem by arguing that rationalists would violate various rules of rationality by replying in the way described; for instance, the rule that one should not make one's account unnecessarily complex or *ad hoc*. But a careful reader of their work will discover that they are committed to the view that all rules of rationality are subject to an indefinite number of interpretations, of which the correct one is decided by convention, negotiation or the straightforward use of professional power (for example Bloor, 1992). This means that provided an opponent of the strong program were powerful enough or relying on accepted convention, his or her reasoning would be correct and scientific. It also means that, contrary to their claim that observation and natural reasoning processes play some important part in delimiting the acceptable theories on an issue, natural reasoning processes can play no part of any significance if the strong program is correct. The reason is that a cursory glance at the accepted beliefs of some religious communities shows that *almost any* background assumption, however intuitively or observationally bizarre, can be made conventional through the use of a powerful and threatening state and clergy.

Second, if Barnes and Bloor are right, the strong program can only be part of scientific knowledge if it achieves widespread acceptance in the scientific community. If it is widely held in contempt by the scientific community, it seems it cannot be fully scientific. But from even a cursory glance at the remarks about the strong program produced by scientists, it seems that it is either held in contempt or ignored by most of them. Thus, it seems the strong program cannot be part of scientific knowledge, no matter what Barnes and Bloor claim.

Of course, Barnes and Bloor could contest the claim that their view is held in contempt or ignored by scientists. They could try to argue that the evidence that they are not scientific is subject to negotiation. At this point, however, powerful scientists and philosophers can end the negotiation by refusing to listen to Barnes and Bloor, thereby rendering them and their program, unscientific. Who will win, depends on who is more politically powerful and it seems that scientists and philosophers are more powerful.

Thus, while the strong program is not inconsistent, it is much less free of conceptual problems than Barnes and Bloor would have us believe. Still, the fact that the strong program suffers from conceptual problems does not necessarily mean that it should be abandoned. It may have other advantages which make it likely to be true. After all, the most fundamental principles of reasoning may have to be given up if a theory which implies that those principles are false turns out to predict a range of novel facts. Thus, I shall need plausibly to argue that it does not have other advantages in order to have a good argument against the strong program.

The argument from the underdetermination of theories is problematic

The reader will remember that a key argument for the strong program argues that theories are underdetermined by data, so that no theory alone is supported by the evidence because any amount of data is logically compatible with a number of incompatible scientific theories. This argument is implausible for two reasons.

First, while it is the case that any number of theories *could be* logically compatible with the data, this does not mean that there is more than one *existing* theory which is compatible with it. Scientists often find it very hard to produce even one relatively simple explanation of the data in an area. For example, for almost two hundred years Newtonian mechanics was the only theory which could relatively simply account for the relevant data in mechanics and astronomy. Einstein's theories had not yet been postulated. In these circumstances, it was reasonable for scientists to work with Newtonian mechanics. (I shall be talking about the nature and importance of simplicity in Chapter 7 so will not discuss it further here.)

Second, to say that any number of theories are logically compatible with the data is to fail to note that some theories are used to predict novel facts reasonably accurately, whereas others explain them in an *ad hoc* manner by adding further untestable or untested hypotheses. As I have argued in Chapters 2 and 3, the theories which predict a range of novel facts are more likely to be approximately true. This means that scientists are justified in believing such theories. Thus, the underdetermination of theories by data does not force us to invoke social factors in explaining scientists' beliefs.[5]

RATIONALISM IS AS SCIENTIFIC AS THE STRONG PROGRAM One of the important arguments for the strong program is that it is more scientific than rationalism. However, this argument relies on a caricature of rationalism which falsely paints it as unscientific because it uses reasons rather than causes to explain rational belief, uses different types of explanations to explain rational and irrational beliefs, and excludes sociological explanations of how scientists come to have certain beliefs.

First, while some rationalists separate the task of giving causal accounts of beliefs from the task of adducing reasons for them, many do not. A plausible and widely held view is that the reasons why scientists come to have certain beliefs also explain those beliefs. According to this view, reasons are real causes which bring about beliefs as well as sometimes justifying them. Thus, it is not correct to say that rationalists have an unscientific analysis of beliefs. Historical accounts of scientists' beliefs which concentrate on their coming to believe certain things for good reasons are as scientific as accounts which do not (Laudan, 1984).

Consider, for example, the case of continental drift. Continental drift is the theory that many of the earth's major geological features, and much of the distribution of types of flora and fauna, can be explained by assuming that the major continents were once joined and have since split off and moved – that is, drifted. Continental drift was defended by Alfred Wegener and others in the early years of the twentieth century but failed to win many adherents. Although the theory had considerable explanatory power, it had many problems. For example, Wegener proposed that the continents ploughed through the ocean floor, a process which was physically impossible; Wegener also made predictions about the movement of Greenland which were falsified; and so on. In the 1960s a new model was proposed for drift in which oceanic crust was formed at mid-ocean ridges while other bits of oceanic crust disappeared under the edges or rims of the continents, thereby explaining how continents could move without violating well-confirmed physical laws. The fact that the ocean floor is very young in comparison to the continents fitted this model and the drift account very well. Further, some scientists produced some remarkable predictions about features of magnetic stripes on the ocean floor on the basis of the new version of the drift theory. These predictions were stunningly confirmed. Rationalist historians of science have used the success of these predictions, or the fact that the new model escaped the serious problems faced by the old model, to provide plausible causal explanations for the fact that drift came to be generally accepted in the 1960s and 1970s.[6]

It may be thought that Bloor and Barnes could object that even causal rationalist accounts are at least less scientific than the strong program because the kinds of causes which rationalists use to explain justified beliefs are different from the causes they use to explain unjustified beliefs. Following this line of argument, rationalist accounts are less scientific because they are not symmetrical like the strong program. However, this objection is not cogent for two reasons. (a) Advocates of the strong program use a variety of different types of causes to explain scientists' beliefs, so their account is far from symmetrical (for example, they use interests, training in a tradition, childhood upbringing in a society, and so on). (b) It is legitimate to use different types of causal explanation if those explanations fit the facts better. For instance, geologists typically use quite different explanations of erosion and uplift. Uplift is explained through the movement of continental plates produced by convection currents in molten material deep within the earth, whereas erosion is explained though the action of abrasive and chemical agents.

Second, in any case, producing social explanations of how scientists come to have beliefs on scientific matters is not incompatible with rationalism. Some rationalists explain how scientists come to have such beliefs by arguing that the scientific community is structured so that social factors and the personal interests of scientists are likely to induce them to arrive at their beliefs on the best evidence available.[7] Taking this view, far from being impediments to the rationality of science, social influences and personal factors tend to make scientists more reasonable.

Proponents of such accounts agree that scientists often accept certain conclusions because of personal interests, the reputations of other scientists, or because they are inclined to accept assumptions which have become conventional in their field. But they argue that this is perfectly compatible with rationalist accounts of the objectivity of science because (a) scientists' personal interests tend to drive them to accept scientific claims on the basis of the best evidence available; (b) the way in which eminent scientists have achieved their reputations makes it likely that their claims are more reliable than those of unknowns; and (c) conventional assumptions have typically become conventional because the evidence for them is considerably stronger than the evidence for rival assumptions.

According to this kind of account, scientists left to themselves might be inclined to believe all sorts of poorly argued scientific hypotheses which suit their social and personal interests. However, science is so structured as to induce scientists not to believe such hypotheses because they will damage both their reputations and those of their allies, as well as the credibility of any social causes to which they are committed. Science is such that there is a great deal of kudos to be gained from exposing the faulty data collection or faulty arguments of other scientists and from having a reputation as a careful researcher. Scientists who do not collect their data carefully, or who do not justify their conclusions on the basis of good evidence, are likely to have their reputations severely damaged by other scientists who check their data or inferences. Scientists often divide into competing camps on contentious issues, with each camp trying to expose the shoddy research of the other and trying to produce better data than the other. This means that someone who has become an eminent scientific researcher is likely to have been trained to justify his or her scientific beliefs on the basis of good evidence. Such researchers will be likely to be esteemed only when their data are well collected and strongly justify their conclusions. Science is a social process in which scientists can enhance their reputations by exposing the poor research practices of other scientists or other groups of scientists. The constant repetition of experiments and the constant checking of inferences by other scientists make scientists very careful, in general, and make it fairly easy to expose shoddy research practices.

Further, because science is structured in this way, it makes good sense for many researchers to focus on and generally accept the findings of scientists with a high reputation. There is a vast amount of scientific research done, so researchers need to be selective about where they will focus their research. Factors like funds, time, limited ability and limited knowledge, only permit many researchers to check the cogency of a tiny amount of the research they rely on to build new knowledge. Eminent scientists will usually have gained their reputations by having their work constantly subjected to careful scrutiny.[8]

I should note that by such accounts, scientists will not necessarily agree in their beliefs. In the early stages of work on a new theory, there may well be a great deal of controversy about the merits of the theory. Competing camps of scientists may well have different views about its merits. After all, it will be unclear on the evidence whether the theory should be believed or not, and those who have developed the theory will have a strong incentive to defend it – if it succeeds, they will enormously enhance their reputations. However, over time it is likely that more evidence will roll in and most scientists will be either convinced by the theory or abandon it. A strong consensus will then develop because most scientists do not want to have their reputations damaged by being seen as irrational.[9]

I have pointed out that some rationalists argue that social factors are of the greatest importance in the causal processes which bring about scientists' beliefs but that by and large such social factors help to keep science objective. This means the claim that social factors indirectly influence scientists' beliefs in no way implies that rationalism is dubious. Of course this does not, by itself, show that rationalist sociological accounts are more plausible than the strong program. Whether they are more plausible or not needs to be shown by appealing to the evidence in a large number of cases. After all, a key argument for the strong program relies on the claim that a large number of historical studies support it.

THE HISTORICAL ARGUMENT FOR THE STRONG PROGRAM IS DUBIOUS Let me start by discussing whether the kinds of studies which advocates of the strong program produce could provide good evidence for it. Many of the studies claim to show that particular scientists in a particular historical setting came to have scientific beliefs because of social or personal factors. Some of them claim to show that the theories of particular scientists became widely accepted in a particular country because the acceptance of those theories suited the interests of dominant groups. The first problem is that, even if these claims are true, this is nowhere near sufficient to show that the acceptance of a theory by the scientific community can be explained by invoking such factors. Supposedly successful scientific theories, such as Newton's mechanics, have gradually come to be accepted as true or approximately true by scientists with a wide variety of religious beliefs and social interests, and who live in societies with ruling groups with a wide variety of interests. Scientists who are monarchists, buddhists, democrats, Catholics, Communists, and so on have accepted that Newtonian mechanics is true or approximately true. These scientists have lived in a bewildering variety of settings. This makes it look very implausible that scientists *in general* come to have beliefs on scientific matters because of external factors which have little to do with making scientists reason properly from the evidence (Laudan, 1990: 151 ff.).

A second problem with the historical argument for the strong program is that many of its historical claims have been found to be dubious. I do not have the space here to discuss such criticisms in detail. However, let me turn to David Hull's criticisms as an example. Hull (1988) plausibly argues that in historical accounts of the development of biology since the publication of Darwin's *The Origin of Species* in 1859, analyses of the causes of scientists' beliefs have often failed to show any general correlation between particular sorts of external interests and particular kinds of beliefs. Theories which are said by sociologists to be (implicitly) politically conservative are not particularly likely to be adhered to by conservative scientists. They may just as well be held by politically radical scientists. For example, the use of game theory models to explain the traits and behaviour of animals in terms of what is likely to advantage their genes is said by some sociologists to be conservative. But both the scientist who introduced such models and the scientist who has most developed their use are Marxists. The idea that the unit of selection in evolution is the gene rather than the group or species has been strongly developed by left wingers and also attacked by left wingers. This means that a strong program *scientific* account of the causes of belief which uses laws or law-like generalizations is not likely to be plausible. Further, Hull argues, even in the case of individual scientists, the claims of the strong program are often not clearly borne out. Whenever scientists adopt beliefs there will be some local social conditions or other which the advocate of the strong program could claim were the causes of their beliefs. But the claim that these are, in fact, the causes needs to be supported by independent evidence, which it is difficult to acquire.

The historical argument for the strong program is very dubious. However, the reader should not conclude from this that scientists are never influenced by social factors and tempted into disregarding relevant evidence or into making shoddy inferences. This does happen in science; indeed, it happens fairly often. This is why science is structured so as to punish poor work. Further, as I show later, the scientific community as a whole can sometimes be influenced into accepting theories for which there is poor evidence by social influences. External influences can cause poorly supported scientific theories to become widely accepted, at least for a time. As we will see in the second half of this chapter, this is particularly likely to happen when the scientific community is dominated by the members of one group, and the research they are doing might have important consequences for the welfare of that group. But this is only evidence for the weak program in the sociology of knowledge, not for the strong program.

Conclusion

The strong program and its relativist claims have not been adequately justified and it suffers from many problems. It poses no serious threat to the objectivity of science. However, the claim that science is importantly a social enterprise is plausible. What tends to make scientists work well is the training and the constraint and reward structure of the scientific community. It typically limits the degree to which prejudices and social agendas can be used to interpret data and to draw inferences. In addition, good scientific work is always done in a social structure by scientists who usually defer to authorities and rely on the work of others in a systematic way. The picture of the lonely observer stripping away his or her prejudices is quite misleading. Such an observer, no matter how honest he or she tried to be, would be likely to gather very limited data in a shoddy way, to reason badly, and to fail to realize that there could well be plausible rival hypotheses to the hypotheses, he or she believes. This means that if we are interested in getting scientific knowledge, we need to study how scientific communities should best be structured in order that members of those communities will arrive at their scientific beliefs on the basis of evidence by means of good inferences.

2 External values and objectivity

Longino's feminist empiricism

Helen Longino (1990) says that the external values of researchers and of the community often deeply influence what inferences can be legitimately drawn from data. She claims that this is because justified inferences from data to the plausibility of a particular theory are only possible if one adds background assumptions to the data, and external value commitments can legitimately determine background assumptions.[10] Longino's central argument for these claims goes something like this: any number of theories are logically consistent with the same data, so that if scientists are to demonstrate a particular theory on the basis of data, they must accept background assumptions which justify the inference from data to that theory. However, scientists could legitimately accept radically different background assumptions. If scientists were legitimately to accept radically different background assumptions, a different theory would be justified. (For an example, see my discussion of bacterium x in this chapter.) In choosing among various background assumptions, scientists can and do legitimately choose on the basis of their external value commitments. Thus, external value commitments can determine whether scientists are justified in holding a particular theory.

It may seem that Longino's argument is essentially the same as the underdetermination argument presented by Barnes and Bloor. At first glance, the only significant difference is that, unlike Longino, they stress the influence of interests rather than values in determining whether inferences from data to theory are accepted. However, an important difference is that Longino does *not* hold that scientists must use background assumptions which are justified by their external value commitments, because she acknowledges that they could instead use induction or some other procedure to justify particular theories on the basis of data. She recognizes that external values or external social factors do not necessarily determine the background assumptions in good scientific reasoning. But she argues that even if scientists were to use inductive reasoning, they would need to use a general principle of induction as a background assumption and such a principle might be false. (Indeed, Longino stresses that Popperians have raised serious doubts about all inductive principles.) So, by her account, whether scientists' background assumptions are determined by their value commitments or not, their assumptions are still potentially problematic.[11]

Longino distinguishes two kinds of values which she claims play an important part in science: constitutive values and contextual values. *Constitutive* values are the norms which are generated from the goals of scientific inquiry. An important goal of science is to search for the best explanations possible of natural phenomena. In their search for such explanations, scientists have to use criteria to evaluate the relative or absolute merits of various theories, such as the criterion that a theory which produces successful novel predictions should be preferred to a rival which produces no successful novel predictions. Such criteria are constitutive values of scientific inquiry. As Longino says, no one would disagree with the claim that science is and ought to be influenced by constitutive values, although there is disagreement about precisely which constitutive values should influence it.

Longino's more radical claim is that science can be legitimately influenced by *contextual values*, which are values about what ought to be the case in society, such as the value that men and women ought to be equal. (Contextual values are the same as what I have called 'external values'.) According to her account, contextual values can legitimately affect science in two ways: they can affect the *autonomy* of science or the *integrity* of science. Science is autonomous to the extent that the direction of research proceeds undisturbed by the values and interests of its social and cultural context. Science has integrity to the extent that the internal practices of science, such as gathering data and drawing inferences, are not determined by contextual values. Longino rightly takes it to be the case that science is not, and should not be, autonomous. I have already discussed this sort of view in Chapter 5, so I shall not discuss Longino's argument for it. However, as Longino points out, accepting that science is not autonomous does not commit someone to accepting that science does not produce objectively justified theories. Whether research can be done in an area, and how it is to be done, are separate issues. Only the second issue has to do with the integrity of science. By Longino's account, scientific research would have integrity if the internal practices of science – gathering data and drawing inferences – were not influenced by contextual values. Longino's central thesis can be put by saying that scientific research need not and often does not have integrity because contextual values can legitimately determine the background assumptions which scientists use to draw inferences.

Longino spells out her account by trying to show how contextual values can determine even the most fundamental assumptions of science, which we might think are only influenced by constitutive values. She says that the reason for the triumph of mechanistic theories of phenomena, such as Newtonian mechanics, over their non-mechanistic rivals was not that they had been discovered to be closer to the truth or more empirically adequate than their rivals, but that they facilitated the exploitation of nature. (A theory is empirically adequate if all its claims about observables are true.) She accepts that Newtonian mechanics was more powerful as an instrument for manipulating the world in certain ways than its rivals. But, she argues, the fact that some mechanistic theories had more instrumental power than their rivals could not have constituted a decisive argument for their scientific superiority without adding background assumptions licensed by contextual values.

According to Longino's account, the key feature which made mechanistic theories more attractive than their rivals was that the theories presupposed that matter was an inert lifeless substance whose activity was describable in mathematical terms. This feature enabled mechanistic theories to legitimate modes of interaction with the natural world like mining. (The available rival theories did not legitimate such activities because they presupposed that nature was alive or imbued with a living force. Such theories are called *vitalist* theories.) In addition, the mathematical treatment of nature, which was part of the mechanistic picture, enabled people to control certain aspects of nature better than did rival accounts. Overall, then, the mechanistic picture of nature suited the values and needs of craftspeople and the rising capitalist class, whereas its rivals did not (Longino, 1990: 92–8).

Longino claims that the contextual values which led to the acceptance of the mechanistic picture of nature gradually transformed the constitutive values and standing assumptions of science. It came to be a constitutive value of science that an acceptable physical theory had to be instrumentally powerful. It came to be a standing assumption of science that all things consist of an inert material substrate, the properties of which are quantitatively determinate. She thinks this shows how contextual values can easily determine the constitutive values and standing assumptions of science (Longino, 1990: 93–4, 98–100).

It may be said that if Longino's arguments and central thesis are correct, scientific findings cannot be objective. For it seems that if she is right, the choice of background assumptions and, hence, the choice of theories which are justified, must depend on the prejudices of individuals or communities. However, Longino argues that her view only implies that scientists cannot produce objectively justified statements in the sense that they cannot derive statements which are true via unproblematic background assumptions. Science cannot reasonably aim to be giving us the unvarnished truth. But she urges that, in her view, scientific claims can still be objectively justified because they can be justified through assumptions which are arrived at through intersubjective agreement after following non-arbitrary procedures. Science can be objective because the effects of idiosyncratic subjective preferences on background assumptions can be reduced or eliminated.

Longino points out that her kind of objectivity requires that background assumptions be arrived at through shared procedures in a community. This means that her account of objectivity is very different from the Cartesian picture in which a lonely researcher strips away personal prejudices to examine the facts and reason from them by procedures which are obvious a priori. She specifies four conditions which a functioning scientific community should meet in order to be the sort of community which uses an objective method of inquiry:

> 1) there must be recognized avenues for the criticism of evidence, of methods, and of assumptions and reasoning; 2) there must exist shared standards that critics can invoke; 3) the community as a whole must be responsive to such criticism; 4) intellectual authority must be shared equally amongst qualified practitioners. (Longino, 1990: 76)

She argues that an important fact about science which justifies these conditions is that researchers are often oblivious of their own background assumptions, so they need other researchers to show them that data may well have a very different significance (Longino, 1990: 80). For instance, biological phenomena which today seem to be the result of natural selection were once thought to provide clear evidence for divine intervention. Without the imaginative postulation of alternatives by sceptics and evolutionists, the fact that the data did not unequivocally support the hypothesis of divine intervention would not have become clear. Sceptics and evolutionists made it clear that to use biological data to support the hypothesis of divine intervention, scientists needed the background assumption that things that were extraordinarily well adapted to survive must have been made by an intelligent agent. Sceptics and evolutionists also made it clear this background assumption was not obviously true.[12]

As a feminist, Longino is particularly concerned about contextual values which lead scientists to conclusions which might well be used to oppress women or other subordinate groups. She argues that feminist scientists and their rivals will often be influenced by different contextual values into preferring different research programs. She also argues that it is unlikely to be the case that conflicts between scientists which result from differing contextual values can be resolved by appeal to the data or to unproblematic inferences from data to a particular theory. By her account, such conflicts will eventually have to be resolved through a choice of values (Longino, 1990: 189–90). In her opinion, other things being equal, the choice should be made on the basis of the worthiness of the theories as bases for collective action to solve the common problems of a democratic and inclusive community (a community which includes women, blacks and other oppressed peoples).[13]

Longino's account might be called a *feminist empiricism*, since she recognizes that for a theory to be worth considering, it must be consistent with carefully gathered empirical data, although she argues that it is legitimate to choose between theories which seem to be equally empirically adequate on the basis of the feminist value of preferring a society in which men and women are treated as equals.[14]

The central example Longino uses to illustrate her point is the conflict between two research programs for explaining behaviour: the linear hormonal program and the selectionist program. In the linear hormonal research program, the crucial determinant of behaviour is hormones which structure the brain while the child is in the womb. Gender differences in behaviour and cognitive performance are largely ascribed to the effects of hormones in structuring the brain in foetal development. In the selectionist research program, people have a large number of neural pathways which make a variety of behaviours possible. Through their interaction with the environment, some pathways are selected and reinforced. Longino argues that the linear hormonal program's picture of human behaviour is deterministic and that it can easily be used to license hormone therapy for problematic behaviour, such as sexually aberrant behaviour. It also tends to bolster the status quo by implying that the fact that there are few women working in mathematics and some sciences is to be explained through women's natural infirmity in these areas. By contrast, the selectionist program gives an important role to people's intentions and to social factors as determinants of behaviour. It suggests that gender differences in capacities and dispositions are to be primarily explained through social factors and can be remedied by social action (Longino, 1990: 133–61).

Longino stresses that research on the linear hormonal program and its close relatives does not occur in a social vacuum. Such programs have been and will continue to be used to justify not spending money on special programs to improve women's performance in mathematics or in a range of other areas. She notes that this is not because the claim that we should not spend money on such programs is a logical consequence of such a research program. On the contrary, it is logically compatible with such a research program that we should compensate for a natural biological inability by special compensatory education or by employing people in areas to which they are not naturally suited. However, people in the United States and in similar societies are only generally committed to equal opportunity in employment in the sense of removing socially created obstacles, not naturally created ones. So, if the linear hormonal program becomes accepted, it is likely that various special programs for women will be abandoned (Longino, 1990: 166, 180–81).

Longino criticizes a number of aspects of the linear hormonal program. However, she thinks the main problem with it is not that it is poor science, but that it presents a particular picture of human beings and licenses a type of behaviour modification. She says that the research supporting the linear hormonal program cannot be said to be bad science because it has many problems, since many well-regarded research programs in many areas of science have similar problems. Without appealing to potentially problematic background assumptions, we cannot be at all sure that any program is better than any other. As she thinks that there will be no criteria that will allow us to choose between the two programs which are provided solely by the constitutive values of science, Longino argues that we should ultimately choose between the programs on the basis of our contextual values. In her view, a feminist, or someone who wants scientific results to be arrived at through a consensus which includes members of oppressed groups, should choose the selectionist program as the basis for action.

Critical discussion of Longino

LONGINO'S ARGUMENT RELIES ON SOME IMPLAUSIBLE THESES ABOUT INDUCTION

Much of Longino's argument rests on the claim that we cannot use inductive reasoning to support a particular research program without introducing potentially problematic background assumptions about the cogency of types of inductive reasoning. A crucial premise underlying her argument seems to be that as such assumptions are dubitable and are required in order to demonstrate the relevance of data to a theory, there is no strong reason for thinking science should eschew background assumptions which are licensed only by external value commitments. Inductively licensed conclusions are as potentially problematic as other conclusions because they are all derived by using dubitable background assumptions. However, Longino's premise is mistaken for three reasons.

First, as I pointed out in Chapters 2 and 3, we can, as all reasonable people do, think that particular pieces of inductive reasoning are cogent without having a general account of why they are cogent or a formal characterization of the inductive reasoning which is cogent. We need only assume that a particular piece of inductive reasoning we are using is cogent legitimately to use induction. Further, whether we have a correct account of how inductive reasoning works or not is irrelevant to whether we are justified in using inductive reasoning. Second, we do not need to *demonstrate* that data are relevant to a theory objectively to justify that theory by reasoning inductively from the data to the theory. All that is necessary is that if the data were true, the theory would be likely to be approximately true. Third, as I pointed out in Chapter 3, by acting in the manner described by John Stuart Mill we can come to have well justified inductive practices which are revisable.

Of course, our inductive practices, however well they have been tested, may be radically mistaken. But while this is true, the mere fact that they might be mistaken does not constitute a good reason for thinking that the possibility is worth taking seriously. That a practice could be radically mistaken is not a reason for thinking it is at all likely that it is radically mistaken. The sophisticated inductive reasoning we use in science is not problematic in the sense that it is likely to lead us to false conclusions from true premises.

Longino also uses the existence of Popper's inductive scepticism to bolster her claim about inductive reasoning (Longino, 1990: 58, fn 16). But as I pointed out in Chapter 3, Popper does not produce a convincing solution to the problems of induction, particularly to the pragmatic problem of induction, and his claims lead to patently absurd results. Popper's critique of induction should be taken no more seriously than Zeno's arguments that motion is impossible. Roughly speaking, the aim of science is to get at the truth about the world or, if we are using science as a tool, to get the most predictively powerful theory possible. If this is our aim, we are justified in using inductive reasoning rather than external value commitments to support or criticize a particular research program on the basis of data. Inductive reasoning is much more likely to help us achieve our aim.

Longino might, however, raise a couple of replies to my objections. First, at one point in her book, she says that it is not epistemologically justifiable to prefer a program which works well as an instrument for prediction because 'working' is not an epistemic notion (Longino, 1990: 93). She could argue that to justify preferring a theory which predicts a range of novel facts, we must use our values. If we think it is desirable to intervene in the world, we will prefer a program which is likely to predict what will happen; but if we do not, we will not. Second, she could argue that there will be many cases in which competing research programs are roughly equal on the basis of inductive evidence. (An example might be the case of the linear hormonal program and the selectionist program.) In such cases, we could legitimately appeal to our value commitments to decide which program should be used as a basis for action.[15]

The first reply to my objection is misleading for two reasons: (a) If I am right in thinking that theories which predict a range of novel facts are likely to be approximately true, then 'working' in the sense of being enormously predictively powerful is an epistemic notion. This is because such theories are both instrumentally useful and likely to be true. (b) If we want systematically to interact with the world at all, we will have good reason to prefer a program which is useful for predicting novel facts as a basis for action. We do not have to want to plunder nature in order to prefer a program which predicts a range of novel facts. Even if one of our primary aims is to preserve the natural world from damage, we will have to know what consequences our activities are likely to produce in order to avoid acting in particularly harmful ways. Thus, people with a large range of value commitments can recognize that a program which predicts a range of novel facts should be preferred. So it is misleading to talk as if *specific* value commitments lead us to prefer programs with a great deal of predictive power.

The second reply to my objection has some plausibility. In cases where two programs are roughly equally supported by the evidence, we could, consistent with the aims of science, use our values to decide which program to adopt for the purpose of interacting with the world. Given that in particular social circumstances the widespread adoption of program A may well lead to bad consequences for a particular group, we might decide to adopt its rival B instead. For example, we might decide to prefer the selectionist program to the hormonal program because, if the hormonal program were widely adopted it would lead to some criminals being treated as animals in need of hormone treatment rather than as agents. However, it is important to note two things. First, in such a situation, it is perfectly open to someone else to use different value commitments to choose between programs. For instance, there will be nothing epistemologically or pragmatically compelling about the selectionist research program. Even if the proponents of the selectionist program and the proponents of the linear hormonal program happened to belong to Longino's ideal scientific community, it is hard to see why they are rationally compelled to come to a rational consensus about which theory they prefer. The decision to choose one theory rather than another would be epistemologically and pragmatically idosyncratic and could hardly be said to be the result of an objective process. Second, even if rival programs are currently roughly equivalent in the empirical support they enjoy, further evidence might well show that one program is a lot better than its rivals. If further evidence were found which strongly favoured one research program, there would not only be pragmatic and epistemological reasons for preferring it, but also ethical reasons. It would be unjust to treat people as if they belong to a particular group for ethical purposes when there is good evidence that they do not. For instance, treating the criminals I mentioned earlier as responsible agents would be both pointless and unjust if there was enormous evidence that they are not responsible for their criminal acts.

So far, I have criticized Longino's treatment of inductive reasoning. However, it is still open for her to reply to my argument that, although criteria like ability to predict a range of novel facts might reasonably have been used to decide between research programs, the historical record shows that this does not happen. Certainly, she might say, some research programs turn out to be inadequate and can be dismissed. But, as a matter of contingent fact, there is typically still a choice between very different research programs which are equally adequate, even if we understand adequacy to include the ability to predict novel facts. Given that criteria yielded purely by the constitutive values of science do not allow us to decide between such research programs, a choice can legitimately be made on the basis of external value commitments. Longino's discussion of the rise of mechanics in the seventeenth century suggests that she has such an argument from the historical record in mind, and I shall criticize it in the next subsection.

PROBLEMS WITH LONGINO'S ARGUMENT FROM HISTORY There are two main problems with Longino's historical argument. First, it is paradoxical and, second, it is implausible. The historical argument is discussed in terms of these criticisms below.

1 Longino's argument from history is paradoxical because, like the argument from history of Barnes and Bloor, it suffers from important logical problems. If Longino is right in thinking that to demonstrate a research program from data one must always add some potentially problematic background assumptions, then this applies to her own theories about the historical data. For example, her argument that the triumph of mechanics in the seventeenth century is to be plausibly explained in terms of the interests it served must be an argument which uses potentially problematic background assumptions, as must any feminist historical account of how research in a particular area was distorted by anti-female bias. But if this is the case, it is unclear why researchers with very different metaphysical assumptions or contextual values from Longino should accept her historical claims. Her story must be merely one among a number of stories which are, as far as we know, equally empirically adequate. Even if at present it were the only account which could explain the known data (and she does not claim that it is), by her account there is no good reason to accept that it is likely to be true. Thus, if her account seems to be empirically adequate, it is hard to see why someone who does not already adhere to the position the account is intended to justify should believe it. Because it is only an account, it can provide no independent support for her position.

2 Longino's argument from history is implausible. Whether Longino's historical argument undermines itself or not, many of her important historical claims are problematic. First, it is quite misleading to claim that other research programs in the seventeenth and eighteenth centuries were as empirically adequate as Newtonian mechanics. While at the outset, other programs could claim to be equally empirically adequate, even in the sense of providing some correct surprising predictions, Newtonian mechanics very quickly provided convincing solutions to a whole range of traditional problems in mechanics, such as problems to do with the movements of the planets and the motion of projectiles. It also predicted a range of novel facts. No other existing research program could do anything of the kind (Franklin, 1992: 284).

Second, the claim that mechanical accounts were not preferred because they were thought to provide a superior account of the world, but because they were needed both to legitimate and practically to facilitate the exploitation of nature, is implausible for a number of reasons: (a) As historians like Keith Thomas have shown, traditional attitudes towards nature in Europe licensed the wholesale exploitation of nature for the benefit of humans. Widely accepted views of animals and plants would have horrified modern Europeans (Thomas, 1984). Thus, the mechanical account of nature was hardly needed to legitimate the exploitation of nature. (b) Exponents of the mechanical view of aspects of nature, like Newton himself, typically did not exclude vitalist explanations from their account of the world. Many of them used them to explain the properties of living things (Teeter Dobbs and Jacob, 1995: 27). Thus, the gap between mechanist and vitalist accounts of nature which Longino presupposes, does not seem to have been anywhere near as clear at the time of the rise of mechanist theories. (c) Vitalism is perfectly compatible with the view that women, animals and plants are inferior to civilized human males and they are used according to their proper purpose when they are used to further the ends of those males. This means that there is no good reason why vitalism should not have been used to exploit nature. (d) It does not seem as if Newtonian mechanics was particularly useful in many industries until some time after it had become generally received: thus, it is implausible to argue that it was widely accepted because it was useful in industry.[16]

Longino's central historical claims are paradoxical when they are used to defend her overall account. Even if they were not paradoxical, they are not plausible. This means she fails adequately to defend her claim that it is legitimate to use background assumptions in scientific reasoning licensed solely by external values, except perhaps in cases where rival existing research programs are all equally epistemologically and pragmatically adequate. However, the criticisms I have produced of Longino's account so far do not raise problems for her argument that a scientific community needs to be structured in the way she describes in order to be a community which arrives at a consensus objectively.

LONGINO'S ACCOUNT OF OBJECTIVITY IS INADEQUATE An important part of Longino's account is her defence of the view that scientific findings can be objective if they are arrived at in the kind of community she believes to be ideal. If she is right, the decision of the scientific community to accept a particular theory can be determined by contextual values and the community can still be objectively justified in accepting it. To say that the scientific community's decision was determined by contextual values is not to be committed to relativism. However, she fails to show that the research community she describes as ideal would arrive at theories which are objectively justified. At no point does she give an argument for the claim that the members of the community she describes are likely to agree on theories which are approximately true or even which predict novel facts. This means that Longino's ideal research community is merely a community which would come to an intersubjective agreement in a particular way. Thus, there is no good epistemological (or pragmatic) reason why someone should conform to its decisions.

Longino's defence of her ideal scientific community seems to be ultimately based on ethical rather than epistemological claims, namely the claim that an ideal community is one in which accepted views are arrived at through free critical discussion and in which authority is based on expertise in the field – not on outside sources of power, such as the superior prestige accorded to male scientists. While we may agree with her ethical view, it is a separate question as to whether the inclusive community she describes as ideal is epistemologically (or straightforwardly pragmatically) better. Longino thus leaves it open to someone who agrees with her basic epistemological position, but who does not agree with her ethical perspective, to reject her ideal community.

It might be thought that my criticism is too harsh. At one point in her account, Longino says that empirical adequacy is a condition that a scientific research program must meet, although this requirement is subject to interpretation and can be temporarily waived. This might be taken to mean that a properly scientific community must value theories in part because of their power to predict a range of observable novel facts. Yet, although Longino shows sympathy for the view that scientific theories which allow systematic interaction with the world should be preferred, she is careful not to commit herself to the view that this is a criterion which should be used to choose between theories and she treats it as a matter separate from empirical adequacy (Longino, 1990: 77). In any case, the condition that research programs should be empirically adequate does not deal with my objection. Any theory can be made empirically adequate, and even made to have predictive power, simply by adding various *ad hoc* hypotheses until a problematic fact is explained. A creation scientist with very different values from Longino could explain the problems posed by fossils for creation science theories by claiming that they have been put in rocks by God in order to test our faith. Such a 'scientist' could even do detailed empirical work on fossils to attempt to understand God's ingenuity further. This 'scientist' might even use his or her knowledge of fossils to interact with the world, for example to find useful seams of coal. That is, by co-opting elements of the theories of his or her rivals, the 'scientist' could reconstruct his or her theory to give it as much predictive power as its rivals. (It would not be as simple as some of its rivals but, as Longino indicates simplicity is not a crucial criterion for choosing between research programs, this does not matter.) Yet Longino could only say that this creation scientist was being idiosyncratic in his or her theoretical preferences, not that they were unjustified.

However, although Longino's defence of her ideal scientific community is inadequate, she could plausibly argue that it is a community which is epistemologically preferable to other communities because it is more likely to accept theories which are close to the truth and predictively powerful. Communities in which critical discussion by experts who do not agree with the dominant point of view is discouraged, or in which authority is vested in people not because of their expertise but because of other factors, are communities which are likely to be influenced by factors which have little to do with the merits of arguments. They are also communities in which individual practitioners are likely to have habits of mind which do not lead them to accept theories because of their merits – people who have become habituated to being influenced by the sex of arguers rather than by their arguments are less likely to arrive at the truth. Thus, we make it more likely that we will come to agree on true theories if we come to an agreement about the merits of theories in scientific communities which are structured in the way Longino recommends; and this is a good epistemological reason for preferring that sort of scientific community.

Barwell's modified account of objectivity

BARWELL'S CRITIQUE OF LONGINO Ismay Barwell has argued that although Longino's account of objectivity is partly correct, it needs to be supplemented. Unlike Longino, Barwell clearly connects objectivity with truth by saying it is a characteristic which enhances the probability that true theories will be produced (Barwell, 1994: 83). Like Longino, she thinks that the idea that a lonely scientist can be objective merely by claiming to put his or her biases aside and adopting a god's eye view is completely mistaken. The background assumptions of scientists are influenced by the contextual values and interests of the groups to which they belong, often in ways scientists are not aware of. However, Barwell thinks Longino's ideal community will not necessarily deal with this problem.

Barwell's central criticism of Longino's account is that the practice of a community could be objective in Longino's sense without any criticisms having being considered which challenge dubious fundamental assumptions of that community. A community of scientists who were all of the same gender and who had very similar social values and interests, might arrive at consensus concerning some theory. Yet the arguments for that theory might well be poor in ways which are unnoticed by members of that community because they are blinded by their ideological prejudices.

Consider an example to illustrate Barwell's point. Aristotle argued, using assumptions which were common among Greek males of his day, that mothers were merely there to provide matter for the foetus. Mothers did not contribute to the form of the child. While this view was challenged by some Greek thinkers, it was widely accepted in Aristotle's time. Aristotle presented what might have seemed to be good arguments against its rivals. Arguably, the Aristotelian view of the role of the mother came to be accepted through the consensus of the type of community which has an objective practice in Longino's sense. Yet we now recognize that Greek males of the time were deeply influenced by dubious assumptions concerning the inferiority of women and their inability to be the true cause of the generation of the form of living things. The consensus about who generates the form of children was not arrived at in a truly objective manner.

HARDING'S FEMINIST STANDPOINT THEORY Barwell argues that in order for a community to be truly objective, it must not only arrive at a consensus in the manner Longino describes, but must also be *strongly objective* in the way Sandra Harding (1991) describes. For Harding, a community of researchers can only be strongly objective when all background assumptions, cultural agendas and influences which determine data collection or inferences, are rendered visible and their power recognized in that community. Harding calls this the demand for 'strong reflexivity'. Researchers are being strongly reflexive when they recognize the contextual values and interests which affect their data collection and the inferences they draw. Harding thinks that these assumptions will be rendered visible only when critical perspectives from the standpoints of those who normally are not in the scientific community – such as women, blacks and the poor – are taken seriously as part of scientific debates. Harding's sort of account is sometimes called a *standpoint epistemology* because it holds that the data scientists collect, the theories they produce and the inferences they draw, are deeply influenced by the interests, values and experiences of the social groups which dominate society – that is, they are deeply influenced by particular standpoints.[17]

There are a number of arguments behind Harding's view. First, researchers who speak from standpoints outside of the white male, middle or upper class positions that have been dominant in the tradition are likely to uncover important data which have been lost to view because they are experienced predominantly by members of oppressed groups. For example, those who speak from the standpoint of women are much more likely to realize the importance of housework in the processes of economic production, and so to produce a better account of the workings of an economy. Second, people who speak from standpoints outside the mainstream have an interest in exposing slipshod arguments which may damage the social groups for whose interests they speak. For instance, people who speak from the standpoint of blacks will discover poor inferences in material which argues that blacks are intellectually inferior by nature. Third, people who speak from standpoints outside the mainstream will produce theories developed from a different set of metaphors and analogies from those which are typical in a science and so will provide valuable rival theories which allow us to understand the world in a different way. An example is the biologist Barbara McClintock, who thought of scientific research as a human and not a male enterprise, thought of nature as having integrity and immense complexity, and so was able to make important discoveries in genetics.[18]

While Harding's defence of the claim that strong objectivity is necessary for a scientific consensus on a theory to be objective may be thought to have some plausibility for the life sciences and the social sciences, the biasing effects of the standpoints of white men could be said to have little or no importance in physics and chemistry. However, Harding argues that the influence of the dominant standpoints is as important in damaging the objectivity of physics as it is elsewhere. Two of her central arguments for this claim are that a number of historical studies have shown the influence of Western middle class male thought on physics and that metaphors derived from the society in which it is developed – for example, that nature is a machine – are a crucial part of theories like Newtonian mechanics (Harding, 1991: 77–102).

It is important to understand that, if we married aspects of Longino's and Harding's accounts of objectivity in the way Barwell describes, science as we know it would be radically transformed. As things stand, few scientists feel any need to be aware of the influence of various social elements on their data gathering, their formulation of theories or their drawing of inferences. Yet Barwell implies that scientists can only practise their craft in a properly objective manner by becoming aware of many external influences on their work and by giving a great deal of authority to standpoints which are subject to different external influences. This means that if Barwell is right, scientific education and the writing of scientific papers should be transformed. Scientists should learn a great deal about the workings of societies and about how to think as an intelligent member of a marginalized group. In addition, affirmative action to raise the number of scientists from various disadvantaged groups would be useful, as such people would be more likely to speak from little-heard standpoints. Further, the uncritically accepted authority of experts who speak from the dominant standpoints would have to be challenged and removed and any consensus about the merits of a theory would have to be achieved in roughly the manner Longino describes.

CRITICAL DISCUSSION OF BARWELL AND HARDING Like Longino's account of objectivity, Harding's defence of strong objectivity has problems. The first problem is that it is far less clear than she seems to think that introducing other standpoints and giving them authority over particular issues is the way to achieve a more objective account of the world. Consider the case of the false claims of Aristotle's biology again. In the West, the importance of the role of the female in reproduction was first defended in a very plausible way by a male doctor who did careful anatomical work which enabled him to discover the ovaries and assess their true role. Even he seems to have been influenced by dominant assumptions into holding that the ovaries were testes in another form (Lloyd, 1983: 86–111); however, as far as we can tell, he got the biology partly right – not because he was influenced by female standpoints but because he carried out careful dissections and other empirical tests of Aristotle's claims. While it is true that, until modern times, theories of reproduction and anatomy were plagued by ideological assumptions about female inferiority, the cause of the persistence of these assumptions seems to have been as much the lack of a biological tradition of careful observation and experimental testing as the dominance of a male standpoint. It could be argued with some plausibility that if we want to improve the likelihood of arriving at true theories, we are better off restructuring the scientific community so that it subjects theories to more rigorous and careful tests, than including the standpoints of oppressed groups in the scientific community. Harding sometimes seems to hold the thesis that observation is theory-laden, in the sense that ideologies determine the interpretation of data unless rival points of view are given sufficient power to influence widespread perceptions. But this thesis seems to be refuted by historical examples which show that careful observers and experimenters can come to notice that the dominant ideology does not fit the empirical data.

The second problem with Harding's account is that it is also far less clear than she thinks that work in some sciences, such as in physics since the eighteenth century, has been deeply affected by the ideological prejudices of researchers. Harding argues that the metaphors used by researchers to understand their theories, such as the metaphor of nature as a machine, are a crucial part of the theories. Yet this is very implausible even for the supposed classic case of Newtonian mechanics. While some people understood Newtonian mechanics to describe the universe as God's machine, many did not. For example, while Newton thought he was describing a divinely created machine, others quickly concluded that he was merely discovering mathematical relationships between forces inherent in matter, so that his theory was best understood as showing there was no machine and no God. Later, influential Continental texts on Newtonian mechanics largely stripped the theory of ideological meaning and presented it as giving a useful account of the powers and behaviour of natural bodies. (Teeter Dobbs and Jacob, 1995: 61 ff.). While theories of physics are not merely abstract calculating devices but purport to refer to real entities such as forces and masses, the connection of such theories to ideological understandings of the world is very tenuous.

Despite these problems, the version of Harding's account defended by Barwell has some plausibility. Historical work does show that even very scrupulous observers, experimenters and theorists are sometimes unconsciously misled by dominant ideologies and their mistakes are unlikely to be pointed out in a scientific community in which a social group with common interests is dominant. Even on conservative interpretations, the history of biology contains many examples of competent researchers whose work was damaged, often unconsciously, by sexist and racist ideas. The presence of a large number of well-trained women and black researchers who spoke with considerable authority and who were aware of the potential influence of the dominant ideology, might well have helped to remedy the situation, particularly since they would have had an interest in pointing out the inadequacy of much research. In addition, a better understanding of the distorting force which dominant standpoints can have on research might well have prevented white male scientists from making serious errors, encouraged them to develop a number of alternative theories, and would have at least encouraged them to expose the shoddy research of other scientists.

As Barwell's view has some plausibility, there is a good epistemological case to be made for changing the workings and membership of scientific communities, at least in the case of the life sciences. There is also a good epistemological case to be made for changing the education of researchers in the life sciences to include the study of problematic social influences which may well damage research. Only when such changes have been made can we be reasonably confident that the community of researchers in the life sciences is accepting theories which are objectively justified. The precise way in which things should be changed, however, needs to be discussed in detail. Barwell's suggestion, that members of groups with certain kinds of experiences and with particular standpoints should be epistemologically privileged with respect to certain areas, does not seem to be warranted (Barwell, 1994: 90–1). Scientists from a subordinated group may be more likely to produce illuminating new theories and bring unnoticed facts about certain subject matters to light which do not fit the dominant ideology. They may also be more likely to uncover the influence of unconscious ideological biases in data gathering or in the drawing of inferences. However, it is also likely that they too will be influenced by their ideological prejudices, and so should not be any more epistemologically privileged than other scientists.[19]

Conclusion

Longino fails to show that external value commitments can legitimately determine background assumptions and hence the theories which are accepted by a scientific community, except perhaps in cases where the evidence is insufficient to judge the relative merits of competing research programs. Her account poses no threat to the view that for scientists to be objectively justified in accepting a theory, their decision need not and should not have been determined by their external value commitments. However, she offers some valuable suggestions about how a scientific community should function if it is to arrive at a consensus about a theory objectively. If we adapt her account by saying that such a community will be more likely to arrive at a true theory than an individual or a community structured in a different way, we can extract valuable advice from her work. Ismay Barwell, using material by Sandra Harding, also makes some insightful suggestions which might usefully be used radically to restructure some scientific communities and parts of scientific education, even if she does not give us good reasons to accept her stronger claims.

What we have learnt from our discussion of the strong program, Longino and Barwell, may seem to be of little philosophical interest because it does not deal directly with the importance of observation and experiment, and various types of inference – which are the favourite topics of discussion in the philosophy of science. Yet a careful examination of how we come to know things, both in science and everyday life, will show it to be very important if we want to acquire beliefs which are useful for action and are likely to be true. From our earliest days, we rely on the fact that various communities function well in acquiring knowledge, and it is hard to see how we could seriously do anything else. We rely on the consensus in the scientific community both to guide our actions and for reliable knowledge about the world. We do not have the skills or the time to check on the work of scientists. Even scientists in a particular area rely on specialists in various other areas to know that their instruments are working properly or that the theories their research assumes are correct.

The cognitive ideal of the tradition from which modern philosophy of science developed is the ideal of a lonely observer totally putting aside personal prejudices in order to examine reasoning practices and experiential evidence in the light of his or her intuitions.[20] Such an ideal is not useful for creatures with our natural capacities and dispositions. Although such an observer would have some natural capacities and dispositions, he or she would not know how to reason well, what instruments to rely on, what role precise experiments should play in the acquisition of knowledge, and so on. Further, without having been taught to weigh evidence and to discipline him or herself not to be uncritical about the observer's favourite ideas, the observer's habits of mind would be very sloppy. Emphasizing that reliable knowledge is arrived at by consensus in a particular kind of community which trains individual scientists, corrects their mistakes and contains disciplinary structures which punish poor reasoning and data gathering, promises to replace an irrelevant ideal of knowledge with one which is relevant to creatures like us.

Further reading

A brief and clear defence of the strong program is provided by Bloor (1992) and more thoroughly argued by Barnes and Bloor (1982). Bloor (1991) is very detailed. Two studies by Laudan (1984; 1990: 146–70) contain clear and brief critiques of the strong program. Brown (1989) produces a trenchant critique of the strong program and defends and develops an account which anticipates the account of Barwell. Chalmers presents (1990: 96–125) an interesting critical discussion of the sociology of knowledge with a very different emphasis from mine. Hull (1988: 354–96) provides an illuminating discussion of the pitfalls of accounts which invoke external interests in biology.

Longino defends her account in a clear and subtle manner in Longino, 1990, particularly 38–82. A useful critical review is that of Schmaus (1993). Barwell (1994) gives a well stated defence of both Longino's and Harding's accounts of objectivity. Harding (1991) discusses a number of feminist accounts and defends strong reflexivity (1991: 138–63). A brief and clear critique of some feminist accounts is given by Chandler (1990). Thalos (1994) presents a carefully argued critique of feminist epistemologies and of their background assumptions. However, students may find that it presupposes too much knowledge of recent epistemology. Antony (1993) presents a sophisticated analysis of recent epistemology which connects feminism to the work of the American philosopher, Quine.

Notes

1 There is a vast literature on this topic. For example, on the views of Greek scientists about the role of the female in reproduction see Lloyd (1983: 86–111); on the views of nineteenth-century biologists about the nature of women see Mosedale (1978).

2 See, for example, Desmond (1989) and Desmond and Moore (1991). Desmond and Moore are often ambiguous. I have taken their more robust claims at face value.

3 Barnes and Bloor (1982); Bloor (1991; 1992). In Bloor (1991), which is the second edition of his book, Bloor makes some odd remarks. At times he sounds like he is defending the weak program. I have ignored such remarks as they make his claims uninteresting and inconsistent.

4 A major problem with many such studies is that the claims made in them are plausibly contested by historians who are critical of the strong program. An example of such a study is Geison's study of Pasteur's debate with Pouchet about spontaneous generation (Geison, 1995: 110–42). Geison's central claims, which were originally published in papers, are plausibly contested by Roll-Hansen (1979; 1983). As Roll-Hansen points out, Geison's arguments rely on a naive falsificationism and a dubious reconstruction of the motivations of various parties in the debate.

5 Bloor seems to have considered such arguments, for in a recent account of the strong program, he says that the processes of drawing out predictions from a theory and of checking its predictions against the evidence are fraught with difficulty and can be rationally contested at every point because the criteria used are (merely?) conventional and thus always open to dispute. He cites Kuhn in support of his line of argument (Bloor, 1992). As we have seen in Chapters 1 and 4, the idea that one can reasonably interpret data according to one's favourite theory is deeply implausible, as is the related view that the meaning of data and its relation to theories is merely conventional. If Bloor does not mean that the interpretation of data is merely conventional, then he cannot justify the claim that any theory can be fitted to the data if one tries hard enough.

6 See, for example, Frankel (1979) and Le Grand (1988). For reasons I cannot go into here, I believe Le Grand misunderstands Lakatos and wrongly favours the view of Laudan. Readers should note that the rationalist explanation of this historical episode is not entirely unproblematic – for details see Le Grand's account of the rejection of expansionism.

7 For example, Hull (1988) and Kitcher (1993). The account I discuss in the text is a pedagogically useful idealization of various views. For a different kind of social rationalist account, see the critique of Kitcher put by Solomon (1995). I am not convinced by a number of the historical claims put by Solomon. In any case, even if she is right, the strong program is mistaken.

8 Of course, as a result of relying on the reputations of eminent scientists, other researchers will sometimes rely on flawed experimental work or will miss the brilliant insights of younger researchers. This is a good reason for journals to adopt practices like blind refereeing, where possible, even though such practices waste a great deal of time. Further, eminent researchers can pass off shoddy work for a time by relying on their reputations. But, on the accounts I am talking about, this is untypical of science.

9 Hull (1988: particularly 387). Hull also points out that the evidence which strikes scientists as decisive will vary to some degree. Different scientists will weigh differing criteria and pieces of evidence somewhat differently. This is why it often takes time and a variety of kinds of evidence for the consensus to move in a particular direction. Bloor seems to take the fact that different weights are assigned to different pieces of evidence to

be a problem for rationalists. But it is only a problem if they are committed to the implausible view that precise standards are required in science. Bloor's argument illustrates the point I made in earlier chapters that relativism and scepticism are wrongly made to look plausible by the philosophical passion for precise but implausible methodologies.

10 Throughout my discussion of Longino, I will be using 'determine' and 'influence' in a way which is both causal and logical. Longino is a naturalist in epistemology, so she holds that for someone to be justified in believing something, both certain logical and certain causal conditions must be met. I have no quarrel with epistemological naturalism, though other philosophers do. For a clear defence of it, see Kornblith (1994). For an interesting critique of feminist naturalism, see Thalos (1994). Many of Thalos's arguments seem to me to be ultimately unconvincing, but the issue would take too long to discuss here.

11 Longino, 1990: 40–59. Longino also defends her case by using some important arguments against inference to the best explanation, see Longino (1990: 28 ff.). As I will be criticizing such arguments in the Chapter 7, I shall not discuss them here.

12 That rival hypotheses are helpful, and even sometimes necessary, to show up the inadequacies of a dominant hypothesis was plausibly argued by Feyerabend some years ago. However, unlike Longino, Feyerabend was not concerned with how much support a hypothesis receives from evidence, but with whether we can falsify it (Couvalis, 1988; 1989: 55 ff.).

13 Longino (1990: 214). It is difficult to know what the force of 'other things being equal' is, but it seems that she means that in order to be minimally acceptable, a theory has to be able to account for known observable data. She also indicates a personal preference for theories which allow for systematic interaction with the world (although she does not make it a precondition for a theory's being acceptable that it must allow for such an interaction). She clearly indicates that she thinks the choice cannot be made on the basis of purported closeness to some reality.

14 Longino's use of the notion of empirical adequacy is puzzling. She says that normally scientific theories are required to be empirically adequate (Longino, 1990: 77). Yet a theory can only be empirically adequate if it is true of future observables and of unobserved observables. Since she talks as if inductive reasoning is highly dubious, it is difficult to see how anyone could know that a theory is empirically adequate based on her account.

15 Longino would produce a third reply, namely that as she has claimed that inductive evidence does not give us good reason to believe anything about the unobservable features of the world, and many scientific research programs deal with such features, we have no good reason for thinking that such research programs are true. Thus, we have no good purely epistemological reason for preferring many research programs to their rivals. As she relies on the arguments of van Fraassen (1980) for her scepticism about unobservables, and I deal with those arguments in Chapter 7, I have not discussed them here.

16 Warren Schmaus, stating a widely accepted historical position, argues that the Industrial Revolution of the eighteenth century occurred largely independently of the seventeenth-century scientific revolution (Schmaus, 1993). Betty Teeter Dobbs and Margaret Jacob argue that this is not correct in the light of recent research (1995: 76 ff.). However, it seems from their account that Newtonian mechanics did not become widely used for practical purposes until some time after the end of the seventeenth century, by which time it had already become widely accepted. For an account of some debates surrounding such questions, see Cohen (1994: 308–77).

17 Harding (1991: 138–63). Throughout my discussion of Harding, I have tried to concentrate on the parts of her argument which fit Barwell's illuminating account. In fact, Harding's remarks are often ambiguous, and contain a number of contentious historical and philosophical claims which are not defended in detail. In addition, she all too readily assimilates scientific and other methods of reasoning; and, despite her claims to the contrary, often presents arguments which lead to relativism.

18 This view of McClintock comes from Fox Keller (1985).

19 John Chandler (1990) has provided a good critique of some aspects of standpoint epistemologies. I do not think his criticisms affect the arguments of Barwell which I have defended.

20 Louise Antony has argued that much modern epistemology does not try to follow the ideal I describe and that Cartesian epistemology did not subscribe to this ideal (1993). She is partly right. However, much talk in modern philosophy of science discusses claims as if they were merely to be dealt with through using our a priori intuitions. Often, discussions of the social nature of science are treated as irrelevant. Further, although Descartes stressed that we have to rely on others to acquire knowledge, he used the ideal I describe in his discussions of the *foundations* of knowledge. For Descartes, once we have escaped the problems posed by scepticism, we can legitimately rely on others. But, in fact, this is an impossible way for us to proceed, for we are always relying on what we have been taught by others, even when we reason in private. If others were radically unreliable, we would be too. Of the influential epistemologists of the seventeenth and eighteenth centuries, Hume seems to me to be the only one who fully grasps the importance of this fact.

7

Realism and Instrumentalism

Scientists seem to be enormously successful in using theories about unobservables to make the world predictable and to allow us to formulate strategies for interacting with it. Their theories about entities such as bacteria, neutrons, and curved space are used to explain the behaviour of observable phenomena and to enable us to interact with them in a systematic way. For example, scientists explain a child's sore throat and high temperature by a theory about the action of particular bacteria. Their theories about the nature of these bacteria allow them to design an antibiotic which will eliminate the sore throat and high temperature.

In addition to making the world predictable and facilitating our interaction with it, scientific theories seem to tell us things about the unobservable nature and structure of the world which are of considerable philosophical interest. Ancient philosophical problems, such as problems about the ultimate constituents of the material world or about the nature of space, seem to be illuminated by scientific theories. That is, it seems science can play an important role in resolving debates in the traditional philosophical area of metaphysics, which has been riddled with inconclusive discussion for at least two thousand five hundred years. If theories which predict a range of novel facts are likely to be approximately true, what they tell us about unobservables is also likely to be approximately true. Scientific research may thus appear to provide useful knowledge which can be used to resolve some problems in metaphysics.

The view that scientific research *aims* to give us a knowledge of both observables and unobservables is 'scientific realism', abbreviated as *realism*. It is often added to the view that science *gives us* some knowledge of both observables and unobservables, which is the view that I have defended in this book. Let us call this second view 'scientific epistemic realism', which can be abbreviated as *epistemic realism*.[1] Epistemic realism implies that science can play an important role in resolving metaphysical questions.

A group of important arguments for epistemic realism is sometimes called 'the ultimate argument'. In one important version, the ultimate argument says that the success of scientific theories which purport to describe unobservables would be a cosmic coincidence if those theories were not approximately true and if the central terms in those theories did not refer. This version of the ultimate argument rests on the idea that the only plausible causal explanation of the success of theories which purport to describe unobservables is that their central terms refer. If this version of the ultimate argument is correct, we should believe that successful theories are approximately true and that the entities described by the central terms in those theories exist – whether those terms refer to observables or unobservables. The notion of success used in this version of the argument is vague but I take it the success referred to is the prediction of a range of novel facts.[2]

I shall be discussing a number of important criticisms of some influential versions of the ultimate argument later. A rival view to realism and epistemic realism which has been inspired by such criticisms is 'scientific instrumentalism', abbreviated as *instrumentalism*. Instrumentalism holds that science neither aims to give us, nor gives us, knowledge about unobservables. Theories about unobservables may be true, though we never know that they are true. Such theories are important in science because they allow adequate explanations of observable events which make them predictable and guide our practice. They are useful instruments for generating predictions about observables. However, science cannot be legitimately used to resolve ancient problems in metaphysics.[3]

Instrumentalism is not a form of relativism, for it holds that theories about unobservables are either true or false independently of human interests or beliefs, even though we do not know whether they are true or false. It also holds that we can be justifiably confident in scientific theories about observables, even about unobserved observables, such as things which have happened in the distant past. Science provides us with genuine and useful knowledge. However, instrumentalism challenges the claim of scientists to have ways of showing that claims about unobservables are likely to be true. It thus challenges the claim that we have knowledge of unobservables.

If the instrumentalist is correct, we are entitled not to believe the parts of theories which deal with unobservables, even when those theories have predicted a remarkable range of novel facts. A theory which tells us that tables consist of atoms should be accepted if it is explanatorily adequate and predictively powerful. However, when we are considering what the world is really like, we could as legitimately believe that tables consist of living pixies who are skilled at making the world appear to consist of atoms, as that they consist of atoms.[4]

In recent years, instrumentalism has been defended by Bas van Fraassen. I shall be concentrating on his arguments, although I shall also discuss some important arguments put by Larry Laudan and others which can be used to bolster instrumentalism.[5] I will argue that instrumentalism is implausible, although epistemic realism needs to be stated more precisely to avoid some instrumentalist objections.

1 Instrumentalism

Van Fraassen's case for instrumentalism

Bas van Fraassen argues for an instrumentalist account of scientific knowledge which he calls 'constructive empiricism'. Traditional empiricism holds that all our knowledge about the world is based on experience. Constructive empiricism holds that science aims to give us theories which are empirically adequate, and that to accept a theory is only to accept that it is empirically adequate, not that it is true about unobservables. A theory is empirically adequate if what it says about observables – past, present, and future – is true (van Fraassen, 1980: 12).

Van Fraassen's instrumentalism is a close relative of traditional empiricism, for it holds that experience is the only source of knowledge about the world. However, unlike traditional empiricists, van Fraassen accepts that all our descriptions of the world are theory-laden and that any item which is experienced does not wear on its face how it should be correctly described; for example someone perceiving a tennis ball for the first time would not know that it was a tennis ball. Further, van Fraassen holds that it is scientific knowledge which tells us whether something is observable or unobservable, whereas traditional empiricists thought they could draw a distinction between the observable and the unobservable merely by attending to experience. We cannot find out what is observable without referring to the most empirically adequate scientific theory about our eyes, the nature of light, and so on (van Fraassen, 1980: 56 ff.). You may think van Fraassen is claiming that what is observable is only what we can perceive with our unaided sense organs, however, he argues that we do observe some things with instruments such as telescopes because we would be able to see those things close up by travelling to them. The moons of Saturn are observable, whereas a bacterium is unobservable, even if the image of those moons seems much more distorted in a telescope than the image of the bacterium in a microscope.

Van Fraassen argues that our use of evidence about what we observe allows us to get knowledge of unobserved observables, even when those unobserved observables are in the past or in the most distant parts of space. A large number of fragments of putative dinosaur bones can give us evidence about the existence and nature of dinosaurs. However, evidence from observation about unobservables shows, at best, that some theories which describe those unobservables are empirically adequate. For example, evidence gathered from experiments with electron microscopes about viruses shows at best that theories which invoke viruses to explain empirical phenomena are empirically adequate, not that viruses exist and behave as the theories describe.

In order to decide whether to accept a theory, van Fraassen says that a scientist must appraise it to see whether it is empirically adequate, logically consistent and of significant empirical strength. He says that these are the 'epistemic virtues' of a good theory; that is, they are virtues which concern the relationship between the theory and the world. Empirical adequacy has already been explained. Logical consistency does not need explaining. However, the notion of significant empirical strength is not clearly explained by van Fraassen. His discussion suggests that it is a comparative virtue which has to do with the degree of informativeness of a theory. A theory is empirically stronger than another if it has greater informational content about observables than the other theory. For example, a theory which says that all aquatic animals except whales, dolphins and porpoises are cold blooded is empirically stronger than a theory which says that most aquatic animals are cold blooded (van Fraassen, 1980: 67).

Van Fraassen allows that, having checked whether a theory has the epistemic virtues he describes, scientists may assess theories by checking to see whether they have other virtues. However, he argues that these other virtues have to do with whether a theory provides useful explanations of phenomena, rather than with the relation between a theory and the world. Assessing a theory for whether it has such virtues is not assessing whether it is likely to be true. He calls such virtues 'pragmatic virtues'. Pragmatic virtues include being simple and unifying previously disparate accounts of phenomena (van Fraassen 1980: 87–8).

The notions of simplicity and unification may be unclear to the reader, so I shall explain them a little. While scientists often praise theories by calling them 'simple', philosophers have had great trouble explaining precisely what scientists mean. Certainly they do not mean that a theory is simple if it is easy to understand. What scientists mean by calling a theory 'simple' is roughly that it is a theory which postulates only a few entities and a few laws about the interaction of those entities, to explain a great deal. Although Einstein's theories of relativity are difficult to understand, they are simple in this sense because they explain a great variety of items by using only a few entities and postulating few relations between those entities. A theory unifies our account of hitherto disparate phenomena when it provides us with a general explanation of things which its predecessors explained by using separate principles. For example, modern thermodynamics uses standard theories of mechanics to explain heat phenomena by postulating that objects are made of molecules which obey the same kinds of laws of motion as much larger bodies. Thus, it explains heat phenomena by appealing to the same laws which are used to explain the movement of cars or aspects of the motion of planets. In contrast, a once widely accepted explanation of heat phenomena relied on the idea that they were caused by the attractive and repulsive forces of a fluid substance called 'caloric', and postulated forces and laws in addition to those of mechanics.

Van Fraassen presents many arguments against epistemic realism. I shall discuss only the more important ones. Van Fraassen's first argument against epistemic realism is that scientific practice can be explained solely by assuming that scientists believe that the best available theoretical explanation is empirically adequate, rather than that it is true (van Fraassen, 1980: 20). Scientists need only *accept* theories which deal in part with unobservables, which is to say they need only believe them to be empirically adequate. Although he does not say so, van Fraassen seems to be appealing to simplicity here; – he seems to be saying that we can explain scientists' behaviour without assuming that they have extra aims beyond empirical adequacy.

Van Fraassen supplements what seems to be an appeal to simplicity by arguing that scientists are justified in being sceptical about the truth of the parts of successful theories which refer to unobservables. The argument takes the following line. If scientists are seeking knowledge, then they need only to accept the logically weaker claim that a predictively successful theory, T, is empirically adequate to the logically stronger and untestable claim that it is true. (The claim that T is true is the claim that it is empirically adequate *plus* the claim that it is true about unobservables. This means the claim that T is true is logically stronger than the claim that it is empirically adequate.) All other things being equal, the claim that T is true has less chance of being correct, since it says more about the world. Thus, unless there is evidence for the extra claim that T is true, scientists need not believe T. Since the claims T makes about unobservables are untestable, there can be no evidence for the claim that T is true. Thus, scientists need not believe that T is true, they need only accept T (van Fraassen, 1989: 192).[6]

Van Fraassen's second argument against epistemic realism is that there is no good epistemic reason for thinking that a simpler theory is more likely to be true than a more complex theory. If he is right, it seems that epistemic realism is in trouble, the reason being that we can always concoct an indefinite number of complex rivals which are as empirically adequate as any successful simple theory. According to his account, such rivals would be as epistemically worthy as a successful theory and we would have no reason to think that the simple theory is true. For example, suppose I concoct the hypothesis that mechanical phenomena are caused by the activities of an enormous number and variety of intangible pixies (that is, stating that non-living forces and tendencies do not cause any mechanical phenomena). Let us say that my hypothesis claims that each of these pixies has a quite different reason for wanting the world to look as if Newtonian mechanics were approximately true. My hypothesis now has exactly the same observable consequences as Newtonian mechanics. On van Fraassen's account, it is epistemically no worse than Newtonian mechanics so that the realist cannot justifiably reject it on epistemic grounds. However, by using simplicity as a pragmatic criterion, scientists could legitimately refuse to accept it while remaining neutral about whether it is true.[7]

Van Fraassen's third argument against epistemic realism is that there are two versions of the ultimate argument and both versions contain untenable assumptions. According to van Fraassen, the first version of the ultimate argument says that any regularity in the world, such as the regularity that certain theories regularly and successfully predict future events, needs an explanation in terms of a regularity which talks about deeper structures.[8] It needs such an explanation because only regularities which describe such deeper structures are truly explanatory. This is because only explanations which describe such structures are properly causal explanations. As van Fraassen understands this argument, it says that it would not be a proper explanation of regular predictive success to say that theories which have been regularly predictively successful are empirically adequate, because this does not explain by appeal to a deeper structure. For instance, the limited predictive success of Ptolemaic astronomy cannot be explained simply by pointing out that the successful parts of it are a limiting case of Copernican astronomy which is more empirically adequate. Such an explanation would be merely verbal. (By Ptolemaic astronomy I mean the geocentric astronomy of the late medieval period that modified Ptolemy's astronomy. By Copernican astronomy I mean the heliocentric astronomy of Copernicus, as modified by Kepler and Galileo.) If an explanation which uses Copernican astronomy is to be adequate, it must be a deeper explanation. This deeper explanation is that Copernican astronomy is roughly true and the entities it describes exist – it is the behaviour of these entities which makes Ptolemaic astronomy, in part, predictively successful.

Van Fraassen claims that the first version of the argument contains the hidden assumption that every regularity needs an explanation which involves a deeper regularity. The deeper regularity refers to the structures which make the first regularity partly true. But he argues that this hidden assumption is absurd. We must at some point stop with a basic regularity which is unexplained and which provides a satisfactory explanation of other regularities. However, if it is the case that we must stop at a basic regularity, we need not believe that something about unobservables is true in order to explain observable regularities. If some cosmic coincidences must remain unexplained, then the constructive empiricist can hold that we need believe only that the part of a very general theory which describes observable regularities is true adequately to explain other less general observable regularities. The empirical adequacy of Copernican astronomy must be sufficient to explain the empirically adequate part of Ptolemaic astronomy. Ultimately, very general observable regularities will remain unexplained. An example of such an unexplained regularity might be the regularity that some very general theories are regularly predictively successful. Thus, van Fraassen argues, we do not need to believe that any regularities which involve unobservables are true.[9]

Van Fraassen allows that epistemic realists need not commit themselves to the hidden assumption of the first version of the ultimate argument. He says that there is a second version of the ultimate argument which claims that the success of some theories can only be plausibly explained scientifically by assuming that theories describe their objects correctly. This version of the ultimate argument assumes that the only plausible causal explanation of the fact that some theories are successful is that those theories correctly describe the unobservable items they purport to describe. However, van Fraassen thinks this assumption is false as there is another plausible explanation of the fact that some theories are successful.

Van Fraassen argues that there is another plausible explanation by using an analogy. He claims that the problem with the assumption behind the second version of the ultimate argument becomes obvious when we realize that medieval philosophers wrongly used similar assumptions to explain the behaviour of individual animals. Medieval philosophers explained the mouse running away from a cat, which was thought to be its natural enemy, by saying that the mouse perceives the cat is its enemy and so runs away. The only plausible explanation of the extraordinary ability of a mouse to run away at the mere sight of a cat was assumed to be that the mouse's perception is adequate to the order of nature. However, van Fraassen says that we would not now say that it was something about the adequacy of a mouse's perception to the order of nature which explains its behaviour, but the fact that species which did not cope with nature no longer exist. That is, since we have come to accept Darwin's theory of evolution by means of natural selection, we do not say that the mouse perceives that the cat is its enemy. We say that the species the mouse belongs to has survived. Species which did not deal with their natural enemies have been wiped out. Similarly, he argues that the constructive empiricist can plausibly say that the fact that some theory is successful does not require explanation; that our scientific theories are regularly predictively successful is to be explained by reference to the jungle of competition of theories (which is 'red in tooth and claw'). The only theories which have survived in this jungle are those which latch on to observable regularities. There is no miracle in the fact that they have survived, even though they may well be completely false (van Fraassen, 1980: 39–40).

It may be thought from the arguments I have discussed so far that van Fraassen means to say that, unlike inference to the best explanation about unobservables, inference to the best explanation about observables is cogent. But van Fraassen makes it clear he believes that inference to the best explanation does not exist. His general critique of inference to the best explanation, to which I shall now turn, constitutes his fourth important argument against epistemic realism.

Epistemic realism holds that inference to the best explanation (or some other type of inductive inference) can be used to justify our beliefs about unobservables. Even the ultimate argument seems to use inference to the best explanation. However, by van Fraassen's account, while it is true that we form expectations about the future which are reasonable without going beyond the empirical evidence, it is false that there is a type of inference or rule we use to form those expectations (van Fraassen, 1985: 280). For him, true inference involves at least three elements: (a) it uses a rule; (b) it is rationally compelling; and (c) it is objective in the sense that it is a relation solely between theory and a total body of evidence, and independent of the historical or psychological context in which the evidence appears (van Fraassen, 1985: 277 ff.; 1989: 132 ff.). He argues that there is no mode of inductive inference which has any of these elements, so there is no inference to the best explanation.

His reasons for this claim are not clearly stated and involve discussion of complex formal material, but you may guess some of them if you consider the arguments I put in earlier chapters. As we saw in Chapters 2 and 3, the search for a formal account of inductive inference seems to have been fruitless. In addition, when we describe many types of inductive inference as 'rules', we describe them only as vague rules of thumb which sometimes allow reasonable people to disagree over whether the evidence for scientific generalization is sufficient to show that it is likely to be true. Further, as my discussion of John Stuart Mill made clear, all types of inductive reasoning could be radically mistaken and are subject to correction by experience. This means that it is implausible to believe there is an inductive relation between theory and evidence which is totally independent of other features of the world – it depends on what the world is like whether a particular type of inductive reasoning is likely to allow us to justify generalizations on the basis of true statements. In the light of all these features of inductive inferences, it is easy to see why a formally minded thinker like van Fraassen would think that such inferences can hardly be rationally compelling, that they cannot deserve the name of rules, and that the very idea such rules exist is a dubious psychological hypothesis.

On top of his fourth argument, however, van Fraassen presents a fifth argument, which is that there is no such thing as inference to the *best* explanation because we only choose between available explanations and we have no good grounds for thinking that any of the available explanations is the best one in the sense that it is true. The explanations which have been thought up may merely be the best of a bad lot, and thus may not include a true explanation or even an approximately true explanation. Thus, we are not entitled to believe that any of those explanations is true (van Fraassen, 1989: 143).

Van Fraassen bolsters this argument by reference to Darwinism. He claims that according to Darwinism, which is the best available theory about the origins of our mental capacities (and might be true), there is no good reason why we should be able to think up the one true theory about the unobserved structure of the world. Natural selection has winnowed out theorizers whose theories are not adequate to their local observed environment, but it does not select for the capacity to get the unobservable environment right.

So far, I have discussed only philosophical criticisms of epistemic realism. I shall now turn to some empirical criticisms of it.

Laudan and Carrier's arguments

Larry Laudan presents an argument against epistemic realism which attacks the ultimate argument for epistemic realism. The reader will remember that the ultimate argument says that the success of scientific theories which predict a large range of novel facts would be a miracle or cosmic coincidence if those theories were not approximately true and the terms used in those theories did not refer. The underlying assumption of this argument is that non-referring or largely false theories are extremely unlikely to be successful. Laudan takes this underlying assumption to be an empirical claim which can be plausibly tested by using the history of science. If the history of science shows that theories which we now take to be non-referring were often highly successful, then we can plausibly take the underlying assumption of the ultimate argument to be refuted. The reason is that theories whose terms do not refer cannot be approximately true (Laudan, 1981).

Laudan's strategy is to treat the underlying assumption of the ultimate argument as a scientific theory. He believes that the only sound way to test philosophies of scientific method is by using empirical tests. Philosophers produce defences and critiques of methodological theories which are largely based on intuitions. But Laudan says that the method of argument in which we rely on intuitions has been discredited in the sciences, where it has been found to produce wildly inaccurate, even downright wrong, results. For instance, many of the intuitions behind Aristotelian physics, such as the intuition that there cannot be movement without a mover, have been shown experimentally to be very implausible.

When we examine the history of science, Laudan claims that we find it is littered with examples of theories which were highly successful in explaining various things but whose central terms we now take not to refer. This poses serious difficulties for realist views about the aims of science and its success in telling us about the underlying structure of the world.

Laudan lists many examples of scientific theories he thinks were very successful but whose central terms did not refer; I shall discuss a few. One example is the crystalline spheres used in Ptolemaic astronomy. The reader will remember that Ptolemaists postulated titanic crystalline spheres in the heavens to explain the movement of stars and planets. Laudan points out that Ptolemaic astronomy was very successful in explaining and predicting the movements of stars and planets, though there are no crystalline spheres, so that one of the central terms in Ptolemaic astronomy fails to refer. Another example Laudan uses comes from geology and is the Noachian deluge theory. This theory held that many facts about the earth, such as mountain ranges being littered with marine fossils, are to be explained by postulating a series of great floods which covered the entire earth with water. The Noachian deluge theory was fairly successful in explaining a range of geological phenomena but we now think that there were no Noachian deluges. A third example Laudan uses is Fresnel's ether theory of light, which assumes that there is a substance called the ether through which light propagates in otherwise empty space. Fresnel's theory was used successfully to predict a bright spot cast in the centre of a shadow of a circular disc – a prediction which was so novel it startled both Fresnel and the scientific community. But since Einstein's Special Theory of Relativity has become widely accepted, we think there is no such thing as the ether.

An important objection to Laudan's argument is that Laudan does not really deal with the ultimate argument, for it says only that terms in theories which are successful at predicting a range of novel facts refer. It is reasonable to claim that it is a cosmic coincidence if a theory predicts a range of novel facts, but its key terms do not refer. However, it is hardly surprising that theories like the Noachian deluge theory which are concocted around the known facts, are successful in explaining those facts. It is also hardly surprising that theories like Ptolemaic astronomy, which have been continually modified to fit astronomical facts, are to some extent predictively successful.

A further objection to Laudan's argument is that the ultimate argument need not say that all of the central terms of a theory which has been successfully used to predict a range of novel facts refer. Theories contain many terms referring to things which are irrelevant to their prediction of novel facts. The ultimate argument need only say that the terms in the parts of a theory which have been used to predict a range of novel facts refer. This is how the claim that the 'central' terms in a theory refer is to be most plausibly interpreted. The aspect of Fresnel's theory which was used to predict the presence of a bright spot has nothing to do with the ether, it is that light is a kind of wave (Carrier, 1991: 25–9). Thus, on the most charitable reading of the ultimate argument, the fact that Fresnel's theory was used to predict a novel fact does not pose any problems for epistemic realism.

Martin Carrier has presented an argument from the history of science which is stronger than Laudan's argument. He thinks he can give at least two examples of theories whose parts were used to predict novel facts, but whose relevant terms are non-referring. I shall explain his argument by discussing one of his examples. By Carrier's account, the phlogiston theory of chemistry was clearly used to predict novel facts. Further, the predictions relied on using the concept of phlogiston and assumptions about the nature of phlogiston. According to the phlogiston theory, phlogiston is the 'principle' which explains burning. It is what the Ancients had thought was the element, fire. It is a light and combustible element. Advocates of the phlogiston theory used phlogiston to explain the common properties of metals – shininess, malleability, etc. Phlogiston escapes from them when they are heated to form a calx (which is what we would now call an oxide), and this explains why, unlike metals, the calxes of metals are very different from one another. Burning is decomposition into phlogiston and a residue. In 1766 Cavendish dissolved some metals in acids and found that a gas was formed which was highly combustible and left no recognizable residue after burning. The outcome of the experiments did not seem to depend on the type of acid or its strength. Cavendish concluded that the gas did not originate in the acid. It was very plausible for him to believe that the gas was phlogiston. In 1782 Priestley predicted a series of novel facts on the basis of key assumptions in the phlogiston theory and some plausible auxiliary hypotheses. He reasoned that if the gas Cavendish produced was phlogiston, it could be used to transform a calx into a metal. Experiments in which he heated a number of calxes in the presence of the gas showed that the gas almost completely disappeared and the relevant metals were produced.

It may be thought that perhaps phlogiston might be approximately identified with hydrogen, at least in the parts of phlogiston chemistry which were predictively successful. To discuss the merits of this proposal, we must turn to modern chemistry. According to modern chemistry, Cavendish had isolated hydrogen, and the reductive properties of hydrogen are due to the fact that hydrogen easily gives off electrons and combines with the oxygen in the 'calx' to produce water. (Priestley noticed that water was appearing in the experiment, but he attributed it to moisture which was mixed with the phlogiston – to him it appeared to be an irrelevant by-product of the central processes.) This is not at all similar to the idea that the phlogiston is being put into the calx to produce the metal. In modern chemical theory, hydrogen is not the principle of all combustibility that is also contained in all metals. Thus, no approximate identification of phlogiston with hydrogen is possible. This means that we now think the phlogiston theory is quite false and that the success of Priestley's predictions is to be explained in a completely different way. However, it seems that the realist is committed to the claim that Priestley had objectively justified the phlogiston theory (Carrier, 1991: 29–30).

Carrier argues on the basis of this and a similar example that the assumption behind the ultimate argument is not plausible. The terms used by a theory which predicts a series of novel facts need not refer. However, he thinks that realists rightly stress that predicting a range of novel facts requires an explanation. How is it that some theories are able to predict a range of novel facts? His explanation is that all such theories bind together types of events as having a common underlying factor, and we can be sure that they have such a common factor although we can have no real confidence in what it is. The phlogiston theory postulated that what we now call combustion is the release of phlogiston and that what we now call reduction is the binding of a calx with phlogiston. It thus held that what we now call combustion and reduction are to be explained by appeal to something which was being given off or taken up respectively. This is also true of modern chemistry. If another theory replaces the modern chemical theory, we can be sure it will preserve this feature (Carrier, 1991: 32–3).

Carrier's critique of epistemic realism is not as vigorous as that of van Fraassen, for he thinks that inference to the best explanation can show us something important about how unobservables are linked to observables. However, he does not think we can learn about the real nature and causal powers of unobservables. If he is right, epistemic realists have little reason for thinking that science can tell us much of interest about unobservables.

2 Critical discussion

Criticisms of van Fraassen

CONSTRUCTIVE EMPIRICISM IS UNREASONABLE Van Fraassen argues for constructive empiricism by saying that it is as empirically adequate as realism and it does not require us to believe unnecessary and untestable extra things about unobservables. However, there are a number of problems with van Fraassen's case for constructive empiricism.

First, as scientists, we would like to believe as many true statements as possible; for we want to expand our knowledge. (Of course, we would also like not to believe false statements, so we will choose statements to believe which seem to be warranted through common sense and scientific reasoning procedures.) This means, at least, that we will be willing to believe many statements which *may* be wrong. For example, we will believe statements about unobserved observables in the distant past which we will never see. If we did not want to expand our knowledge, but to be secure, we would have the fewest beliefs that we need to have. But if this were our policy, we would not be constructive empiricists, and would refuse to believe theories about distant parts of space, as well as statements about the distant past and far into the future. After all, we will not live to test the truth of such theories, so there is no reason to believe them. We need only believe that such theories provide accounts which allow us to make predictions about objects we are likely to observe. Thus, constructive empiricism does not capture what we want in science and van Fraassen's attempt to defend it actually supports a more ontologically Spartan doctrine if it supports anything.

A second problem arises from the fact that constructive empiricism is in part a psychological or social theory which involves assumptions about the mental states of scientists or about the aims to which the enterprise of science is directed.[10] The mental states of scientists are unobservable to others, and the claim that there are ends to which science as a social system is directed is metaphysical. Since constructive empiricism says that we are agnostic about unobservables when we are being scientific, it follows that we are agnostic about constructive empiricism itself when we are being scientific. We will believe in the empirical adequacy of constructive empiricism, but not its truth. Further, we will regard it as dubitable as other theories which are empirically adequate, such as realism. But this means that as long as van Fraassen is being scientific, he cannot consistently advocate constructive empiricism as opposed to realism. Van Fraassen should tell us to believe only that realism and constructive empiricism are both empirically adequate (O'Leary-Hawthorne, 1994).

Van Fraassen tries to deal with the second problem by claiming that he is not defending constructive empiricism as a scientific hypothesis but as a metaphysical thesis (van Fraassen, 1994). But, since his general philosophical position is the empiricist one that it is best not to have beliefs about unobservables, he would be more consistent if he merely said that one should not believe constructive empiricism. After all, one does not need to have beliefs about the true aims of science to do science, and constructive empiricism might be considered by a philosopher to be merely an interesting thesis.

So far, I have argued that van Fraassen's defence of constructive empiricism is inadequate. However, I have not yet criticized van Fraassen's arguments against epistemic realism. It would be consistent for someone to say that he accepted my criticisms of constructive empiricism, but was agnostic about the merits of epistemic realism because of the force of van Fraassen's criticisms. I shall now show that his criticisms of epistemic realism are inadequate.

SIMPLICITY IS NOT MERELY A PRAGMATIC VIRTUE Van Fraassen's argument that simplicity and unification are merely pragmatic virtues presupposes that to hold that the world ultimately consists of only a few kinds of things, and that there are few laws governing these things, is merely to speculate idly about the unknown. However, he neglects the fact that many scientists have preferred theories which are simpler or more unifying not merely for pragmatic reasons, but because they think that such theories are more likely to be empirically adequate and true. The preference of such scientists can be justified through an analysis of the history of science.

In past science, many scientists have chosen the simplest and most unifying of theories which have seemed to be equally empirically adequate. They have then produced further predictions using such simple and unifying theories. It has turned out that when they followed this procedure, they were highly successful in predicting a range of novel facts. Thus, choosing between theories which have seemed to be equally empirically adequate on the basis of simplicity and unifying power is a good way to pick theories which are more likely to be empirically adequate overall. Consider the following example. The Copernican theory in the days when Galileo was doing his early work with telescopes was, as far as anyone could tell, as empirically adequate as the Ptolemaic theory. But it was simpler and more unifying because it postulated that the nature of heavenly bodies was much the same as that of things on earth and that the laws they obeyed were also much the same. Some scientists chose the Copernican theory on the basis of its simplicity and unifying power. Their choice was repaid handsomely. The heavenly bodies of the solar system are much like the earth and do obey the same kinds of laws. This pattern has been repeated many times in the history of science, and it is reasonable to extrapolate from such cases to the case of simple theories which only differ from their rivals in their claims about unobservables. Just as the simpler of two theories which are equally empirically adequate is more likely to be empirically adequate overall, so the simpler of two empirically adequate theories is more likely to be true.[11]

Van Fraassen is thus mistaken in saying that preferring simpler and more unifying theories is using a pragmatic consideration in theory choice. We have good reasons for thinking that, all other things being equal, simpler theories are more likely to be empirically adequate and true; so that choosing them is choosing on epistemic grounds. But van Fraassen could respond by saying that, although he concedes we should prefer simple and more unifying theories for epistemic reasons, this does not show that the world is likely to be simple, but only that the assumption that the world is simple is useful for allowing us to choose the theory which is most likely to be empirically adequate. After all, if van Fraassen is right in thinking that the expectations about unobservables which we form are more dubitable than those about observables, then our expectations about whether the world is simple are also more dubitable – since many parts of the world are unobservable. To deal with this problem, I will have to deal with his claim that reasonable expectations about unobservables are more dubitable than reasonable expectations about observables. But, before I turn to criticizing that claim, I shall discuss his critique of the ultimate argument.

VAN FRAASSEN'S CRITIQUE OF THE ULTIMATE ARGUMENT FAILS Van Fraassen claims that the first version of the ultimate argument contains the hidden assumption that all regularities need explanation in terms of deeper regularities if those regularities are not to be highly improbable cosmic coincidences. His criticism of this version of the argument is that this assumption is absurd. However, it is far from clear that such an assumption is absurd or that science could not continue the process of explaining indefinitely by using deeper and deeper regularities. Van Fraassen seems to assume the claim that an explanation of a regularity must move to a deeper level in order to be adequate, implies that there must be an explanation which describes the essential behaviour of things. But it implies no such thing. The fact that there may be an ever continuing series of explanations does not mean that the explanation of a particular regularity by a deeper regularity is inadequate or incomplete. Chemical theories which use the regular behaviour of carbon molecules to explain the properties of diamonds explain the properties of diamonds perfectly well, even if the regular behaviour of carbon molecules needs an explanation at a deeper level.

Nevertheless, despite the fact that van Fraassen's criticism is mistaken, we should accept a weaker criticism of what he claims to be the hidden assumption of the first version. The weaker criticism is that there need not be a deeper explanation for a regularity. It is conceivable that there are some regularities which have no deeper explanation. Van Fraassen might add to this the claim that some of the best minds in modern physics think they are getting close to such fundamental regularities. However, having accepted this criticism, I note that the prima facie *inductive* evidence is enormous that regularities nearly always have explanations in terms of deeper regularities. In many areas of science, proposed explanations in terms of deeper regularities have produced predictions of a range of novel facts indicating that those deeper regularities are true explanations. In some cases, such as in the case of the explanation of the partial predictive successes of Ptolemaic astronomy by the truth of Copernican astronomy, the explaining theory deals largely with observables and its claims can be checked directly. These facts constitute good evidence that, by and large, regularities can be plausibly explained in terms of deeper regularities. This means that the realist is justified in thinking that it is *very likely* that the fact that some scientific theories regularly predict novel facts has a deeper explanation, even if that deeper explanation cannot itself be used to predict observable novel facts. Of course, if van Fraassen is right in thinking inference to the best explanation is not cogent, this prima facie evidence will have turned out to show nothing. But he needs his fourth and fifth arguments against inference to the best explanation in order to show this, and I shall argue later that those arguments fail.

In any case, whether I am right in my criticism of van Fraassen's argument or not is ultimately irrelevant, for if we understand the first version of the ultimate argument properly it does not have to contain a hidden general assumption about regularities. Properly to understand the first version of the ultimate argument, we need to distinguish two claims. Claim (a) is that it is very likely that the regular predictive success of a theory which does not predict novel facts is to be explained by a deeper theory which is approximately true and whose terms refer. Claim (b) is that it is very likely that the prediction of a range of novel facts by a theory is to be explained by its approximate truth and by the fact that its central theoretical terms refer. A different explanation is warranted by mere regular predictive success than by the prediction of a range of novel facts. In this form, the argument is not particularly about regularities, for it only says that items that would otherwise be cosmic coincidences are likely to have deeper explanations. From this it does not follow that all regularities are likely to have a deeper explanation. The regularity that theories which predict a range of novel facts are all approximately true, and have central terms that refer, is not particularly likely to have a further explanation – it would not be a cosmic coincidence that such a regularity exists without further explanation.

Let me explain the real first version of the argument by a further discussion of astronomy. According to the first version of the argument, the regular predictive success of Ptolemaic astronomy is very likely to have a deeper explanation. The predictive success of a theory, even if it had to be constantly modified *ad hoc* to achieve it, is very unlikely to be a cosmic coincidence. After all, very few theories which are modified *ad hoc* achieve regular predictive success. However, the deeper explanation of its success will not be that its explanation of the workings of the heavens is approximately true, for part of the way in which it achieved its success is by being constantly changed *ad hoc*. The deeper explanation will be provided by another theory which is roughly true. Compare Ptolemaic astronomy with Copernican astronomy. Copernican astronomy predicted a range of novel facts – for instance that Venus would appear to have predictable phases when seen through a telescope, that Mars would look much smaller through a telescope at particular times rather than at others, and so on. By the first version of the argument, the deeper explanation of the success of Copernican astronomy is simply that it is approximately true, and that its central terms refer.

I can sum up my discussion of the first version of the ultimate argument by saying that it is plausible to reconstruct it as being two arguments which both escape van Fraassen's criticisms:

(a) Any item which would otherwise be a cosmic coincidence is likely to have an explanation. The regular predictive success of certain theories (which do not predict novel facts) would be a cosmic coincidence unless deeper theories were true. Therefore, it is very likely that the regular predictive success of those theories is to be explained by the approximate truth of deeper theories whose central theoretical terms refer.

(b) Any item which would otherwise be a cosmic coincidence is likely to have an explanation. The success of certain theories in predicting a range of novel facts is a cosmic coincidence unless those theories are approximately true and their central terms refer. Therefore, it is very likely that the prediction of a range of novel facts by those theories is to be explained by their approximate truth and by their central theoretical terms referring. (Argument (b) is very similar to the second version of the ultimate argument.)[12]

Van Fraassen's critique of the second version of the ultimate argument is that it wrongly assumes that the only plausible explanation of the regular predictive success of some theories is that those theories are approximately true and their central terms refer. The reader will remember that van Fraassen claimed that the epistemic realist's explanation of the success of some theories was analogous to an erroneous medieval explanation of the behaviour of a mouse in the presence of cats. But his claims are neither true about the medieval explanation nor about the ultimate argument.

The medieval explanation is a roughly correct explanation of the behaviour of many animals in the presence of other animals. Individual animals often do run away because their cognitive systems are so wired as to pick out members of other species which are likely to be threats to their survival. Where the medievals go wrong is in saying that this wired-in capacity was put there directly by God. But their failure properly to explain why the cognitive system of individual animals is so finely adapted to reacting to their natural enemies does not invalidate their explanation of the behaviour of individual animals. Similarly, a Darwinian explanation of why theories which predict a range of novel facts survive does not make redundant the explanation offered by epistemic realists of why theories do predict a range of novel facts. Perhaps, as van Fraassen seems to suggest, theories which predict a range of novel facts survive because we have evolved to prefer theories which allow us to predict the behaviour of observables as far as is possible. But this does not explain why some theories predict a range of novel facts. It also does not render the problem of why some theories predict a range of novel facts redundant (Musgrave, 1985: 209–10).

Van Fraassen's direct criticisms of both versions of the ultimate argument fail. However, this does not mean that the ultimate argument succeeds. The argument uses a variety of inference to the best explanation, so if van Fraassen's criticisms of inference to the best explanation succeed, all versions of the ultimate argument will not be cogent.

Van Fraassen's critique of inference to the best explanation fails

Van Fraassen's fourth and fifth arguments purport to criticize epistemic realism by criticizing inference to the best explanation. The fourth argument says that inference to the best explanation does not exist. A way of reasoning in which one draws a conclusion without using a precise rule which is warranted independently of other facts is not a mode of inference. The fifth argument says that there is no such thing as inference to the *best* explanation because one is always choosing among available explanations and there is no reason to believe that any of them is a roughly true explanation for some regularity in the world.

The first problem with these arguments is that they are an irrelevant diversion in criticizing epistemic realism. Van Fraassen accepts that we form reasonable expectations about unobserved observables by using observations. He has no serious doubt that such expectations can be so reasonable that we can say we have knowledge of unobserved observables. For instance, the careful study of apparent dinosaur bones, plus our other knowledge, warrants our believing all sorts of things about dinosaurs. This means that, while he says he does not believe in the existence of inference to the best explanation, he accepts that we somehow arrive at warranted beliefs about unobserved observables. In many cases, these are beliefs which we will never be able to test directly through observation. Now the crucial problem with van Fraassen's view is that he produces no good reason for drawing an epistemic distinction between our knowledge of some unobserved observables and our knowledge of unobservables. In much of his discussion, for example in his remarks about inference to the best explanation, he talks as if there were a problem about unobservables which is a different problem from Hume's puzzle about how we can have knowledge of the unobserved. But he does not produce a good reason for thinking that there is a problem about unobservables which is different from Hume's puzzle. Since he recognizes, like all reasonable people, that one can have knowledge of the unobserved, he is not entitled to distinguish the class of beliefs about unobservables as especially problematic without giving us reasons which show that remarks about unobservables are especially problematic.

Let me spell out this point. There are many unobserved observables which we will never observe directly, such as those in the distant past, those far into the future, and those which are too far away for us to travel to them. There are also many observables which are currently unobserved but will be observed, such as the number on the front of the bus on which I will go to work tomorrow. There are also other unobservables, such as very small objects, objects which give off the wrong kinds of radiation, and so on. These objects have nothing in particular in common. It is only because of our infirmities that we cannot observe them with our naked eyes. Some animals can observe some of them. Had we evolved with quite different sense organs, we would have been able to observe others of them. Van Fraassen holds that we form reasonable beliefs about unobserved observables by relying on what we know about other observables. He does not think that we form such beliefs by using something which merits being called a type of inference, but how we do it is not particularly relevant. Although he holds that we can have reasonable beliefs about unobservables, he clearly thinks any such beliefs are less reasonable than our beliefs about unobserved observables. He also thinks that we would be better off if we did not have them. But he gives us no reason for thinking that they are any less likely to be true than our beliefs about unobserved observables. His view is irrational; it is as if someone were to say that he or she will not believe in the truth of statements about countries to which he or she never intends to travel – such as Mongolia – but only in their empirical adequacy. Such a person may be taking fewer epistemological risks by believing less, but has no epistemically principled reason for his or her policy (Churchland, 1989: 140–5).

The second problem with van Fraassen's fourth and fifth arguments is that if they really were cogent, they would undermine constructive empiricism. The constructive empiricist holds that we know things about unobserved observables. But if there is nothing deserving the name of inference to the best explanation we can use to warrant our beliefs about unobserved observables, then we cannot know things about many unobserved observables. For example, we cannot know that purported dinosaur bones are really the bones of dinosaurs. We have never seen dinosaurs. Even if we are able to create dinosaurs from the DNA in supposed dinosaur bones, we can only warrant our belief that the bones were once parts of dinosaurs by using some sort of inference to the best explanation, for our belief is about the past of the bones not about what can be made from them. Furthermore, if we can only choose between dubitable available explanations for a phenomenon, this is true of hypotheses which invoke unobserved observables as well as hypotheses which invoke unobservables. We must take seriously the possibility that there is an unknown but true explanation of the existence of supposed dinosaur bones which is not remotely like current hypotheses – perhaps, for instance, the hypothesis that dinosaur bones were brought into existence recently by a process which has nothing to do with living things.

In adhering to constructive empiricism as opposed to a complete scepticism about the unobserved, van Fraassen implies that his fourth and fifth arguments are not cogent. But there is no alternative for reasonable people but to assume that inference to the best explanation is cogent.[13] Inference to the best explanation uses vague rules which cannot be stated in simple formal terms, and it involves substantive assumptions about the world which could be mistaken. We do not yet have any real understanding of why it works. But these are not reasons to think that there is a serious problem in using it, as I showed in Chapters 2 and 3. Further, the fact that there *might be* other simple hypotheses which predict a range of novel facts and which are not remotely like accepted theories is uninteresting. In real science, part of the reason why some theory becomes accepted is because many intelligent scientists try to find empirically equivalent alternative theories which are similarly simple, and fail. The failure of attempts of this kind, added to the power of an accepted theory to predict novel facts, give us good evidence that an accepted theory is approximately true. For instance, the fact that many intelligent people looked unsuccessfully for empirically equivalent alternatives to the germ theory is evidence that such alternatives do not exist. We have the same kind of reason for thinking that plausible alternatives to the germ theory as we have for thinking that unicorns do not exist.[14]

So far, I have dealt with van Fraassen's major arguments against epistemic realism. However, I have not dealt with Carrier's objections which are empirical rather than philosophical. I shall now turn to those.

Criticisms of Carrier

Carrier argues that the history of science shows that there is a problem with the ultimate argument because there are at least two cases of theories whose central terms were used to predict novel facts, but whose central terms would now be thought to be non-referring. In effect, he is saying that it cannot be said to be a cosmic coincidence that a theory should be successful in predicting novel facts, but that the terms which were used to predict those facts are non-referring.

The first problem with Carrier's argument is that, if it is correct, it undermines a great deal more of our knowledge than just our knowledge of unobservables. The ultimate argument is not substantially different from other arguments which use inference to the best explanation to give us our most basic knowledge of the world, such as knowledge of the fact that material objects continue to exist when we do not observe them or knowledge of the fact that we typically observe material objects rather than hallucinate. Thus, unless there is some alternative way we can know such things, we could not have this knowledge if the ultimate argument were not plausible. But Carrier and all reasonable people agree that we know such facts, and there is no other way we could know such facts except by using inference to the best explanation.[15] Therefore, Carrier's critique of the ultimate argument is mistaken.

I shall explain my argument by using an example. We know that material objects continue to exist when we do not observe them. If someone were to ask us how we know this, the only plausible argument we could offer would appeal to the fact that cosmic coincidences are unlikely. The argument would go something like this: we typically re-encounter material objects in roughly the same places we left them and they look as they would look had they continued to exist unobserved. For instance, a candle we leave burning and see again a few hours later will look pretty much like other candles we have lit and watched as they gradually melt. Further, when we do not re-encounter material objects in the same place we left them, the places where we re-encounter them are generally predictable on the assumption that they have continued to exist and have moved through space to those places – a moving ball which disappears to the left of my visual field can often be found to the left of me if I turn my head. If material objects vanished from existence when we did not observe them, it would be a cosmic coincidence that many observations of material objects can be simply explained and predicted on the assumption that they continue to exist unobserved. Now this argument would not be available to us if arguments like the ultimate argument were not cogent. According to Carrier's account, the best we could say is that the facts we currently explain by saying that material objects continue to exist unobserved will be explained in the future by an explanation which is importantly analogous to this explanation. Thus, Carrier's critique of the ultimate argument is mistaken, even if we do not know quite how it is mistaken.

The second problem with Carrier's critique of the ultimate argument is that it is not a strong critique as it stands. One response to Carrier's argument is that the ultimate argument in its modern form is only intended to be a probabilistic argument. After all, it is clearly not a logically valid argument since it uses inference to the best explanation. According to this response, the fact that there exists a false theory which predicted a range of novel facts does not pose a serious problem for the ultimate argument. Perhaps the argument should not say something quite as strong as it would be a cosmic coincidence that a theory should predict a range of novel facts and not refer. But it could still plausibly say it is very unlikely a theory should predict a range of novel facts and not refer.

A second response to Carrier's critique – which is not incompatible with the first one – is that while the prediction of one kind of novel fact is evidence for the approximate truth of a theory, the prediction of more than one kind of novel fact makes it more likely that a theory is approximately true. The phlogiston theory predicts only one kind of novel fact. It predicts that when calxes are heated in the presence of 'phlogiston', metals are formed and the phlogiston disappears. But it fails to predict the action of phlogiston in other cases which phlogiston theory was not concocted to explain. I should note here that the nineteenth-century scientist/philosopher William Whewell, who put one of the strongest versions of the ultimate argument, is ambivalent about how many kinds of novel facts are required to show that a theory is true. He usually talks as if only one kind of novel fact is required. But when he uses the wave theory of light as an example, he points out that it predicted a number of different kinds of novel facts, and talks of the degree of evidence in its favour going to a 'higher order' as it predicted more and more kinds of novel facts (Whewell, 1968: 158). As the ultimate argument is logically invalid and cannot really prove that its conclusion is true, Whewell's ambivalence is justified.

A third and more minor problem with Carrier's critique of the ultimate argument is that it does not show as much as it seems to show. Carrier thinks it shows that a theory, the key terms of which did not refer, might well predict novel facts. But it does not show this for, as far as we can tell, when the theory was successful in predicting novel facts the term 'phlogiston' was being constantly used to refer to hydrogen. What we can say is that a lot of what phlogiston theorists thought about hydrogen was quite wrong. But they were not wrong in thinking that the gas to which they were constantly referring could be used to produce a metal from a calx. Neither were they wrong in thinking that that gas could be produced by using acids in circumstances they could carefully describe. Their conception of the nature of that gas was wrong, but this does not mean that they failed to refer to anything at all. Part of what the ultimate argument claimed is that unless the terms in a scientific theory which are used to predict a range of novel facts refer, the success of that theory would be a cosmic coincidence. This claim escapes unscathed from Carrier's critique. However, the ultimate argument also claimed that a theory which predicts a range of novel facts is approximately true. In the case of the phlogiston theory, this is not really the case. The truths which phlogiston theorists knew about the mysterious gas they had isolated had nothing to do with the central conceptions of phlogiston theory. It was only by falsely describing hydrogen as phlogiston that they latched on to some true claims about the gas that any outside observer could have described in a neutral language which did not use the term 'phlogiston'. Thus, the claims of the phlogiston theory cannot plausibly be said to be approximately true.

Conclusion

Van Fraassen's and Carrier's arguments against epistemic realism fail. It is just as well that they fail for, as I have pointed out, the evidence we have for the existence and nature of unobservables is not significantly different from the evidence for some important claims about observables. If van Fraassen's and Carrier's criticisms were to succeed, we would have no plausible and principled way of knowing things about distant observables or even of knowing that they continue to exist when we do not observe them. Thus, we have objectively justified knowledge of unobservables given to us by science.

Having said this, however, it is important to remember that Carrier's critique of the ultimate argument has some force. It at least shows us that it is perfectly possible for theories to predict a range of novel facts but for them not to be approximately true. Further, the future development of science or further historical study might show that there have been theories which have predicted many kinds of novel facts, but which were not approximately true. This would indicate that the ultimate argument was not cogent. It would also indicate that many arguments which use inference to the best explanation are problematic and raise serious doubts about many of our important beliefs about observables. But we can say that, on the evidence currently available, the ultimate argument is cogent and our important beliefs about observables are secure.

Since we can take it that science does teach us things about the existence and nature of both observables and unobservables, science does have a useful role to play in practical life and in debates on metaphysics. The view of some philosophers of the Enlightenment, that science provides us with knowledge which is secure from failure for all time, is mistaken. However, their view that it provides us with an enormous amount of practically useful knowledge and with a deep insight into the nature of the world is not mistaken. On the best evidence available, science provides us with practical knowledge on a scale undreamt of by our ancestors and with a way to resolve some problems in metaphysics which was not previously available to philosophers. Whether we will use our knowledge wisely remains to be seen for, as I have pointed out, science does not tell us anything about how we should use knowledge – even though the powers it places in our hands have the potential to produce enormous destruction.

Further reading

Smart (1963: 39) presents a clear version of the ultimate argument which is aimed at a stronger doctrine than instrumentalism. Some of van Fraassen's critique of epistemic realism is set out in detail by van Fraassen (1980). Much of that book is difficult, but Chapters 1, 2 and 4 are largely intelligible to an audience with no knowledge of formal material. Van Fraassen (1985) presents a largely non-technical reply to his critics. Van Fraassen (1989) presents important arguments but is too technical and difficult for most people, even people with some formal knowledge. Musgrave (1985) and Churchland (1989: 139–51) offer useful and clear criticisms of van Fraassen. Laudan (1981) and Carrier (1991) present the historical argument against epistemic realism in a very clear form. Meehl (1992) is an important and clear critique of the historical argument.

Notes

1 I have distinguished scientific realism from scientific epistemic realism because falsificationists hold that science aims to give knowledge of both observables and unobservables, and describe themselves as scientific realists but are committed to the view that we have no way of telling whether science is successful in this aim. Note, however, that what I call 'epistemic realism' many authors call 'scientific realism'.

2 This version of the ultimate argument dates back at least to the nineteenth-century scientist, William Whewell (1968: 153 ff.). It is used in many forms by many authors.

3 'Instrumentalism' has a number of meanings in the philosophy of science. It is often used to refer to a variety of positivism in which terms which seem to refer to unobservables are held really to be about observables. This is not how I use the term here.

4 This may sound extreme, but the main instrumentalist I will be discussing, Bas van Fraassen, makes clear that he believes that simplicity is a pragmatic and not an epistemic virtue, so that it has to do with acceptance of a theory and not with belief in its truth (van Fraassen, 1980: 87 ff.). He also commits himself to the claim that 'what it is rational to believe includes anything that one is not rationally compelled to disbelieve' (van Fraassen, 1989: 172–3). Given his other claims, this means we could rationally believe that tables consist of living but unobservable pixies.

5 I will not be discussing van Fraassen's account of the semantics of theories as my objections to instrumentalism have nothing to do with the semantics of theories. Laudan and Carrier are not instrumentalists, but their arguments can be used to bolster instrumentalism.

6 Van Fraassen sometimes talks as if epistemic realism and constructive empiricism are both quite reasonable (for example van Fraassen, 1985: 253). However, many of his

arguments only make much sense if we assume he is arguing that epistemic realism is *less* reasonable in capturing the aims of science because it involves an extra and untestable leap of faith (van Fraassen, 1985: 255). This seems to be why he thinks his account of the aims of science is superior. He leaves it open, however, for a philosopher (or a scientist musing philosophically) reasonably to be a realist.

7 Van Fraassen (1980: 90). I take it that in Chapter 3 of the same work, van Fraassen is putting this argument with real examples.

8 Van Fraassen attributes the first version of the argument to Smart (1968: 141 ff., particularly 151–2). As I shall show later, Smart's argument can be plausibly understood in another way.

9 I have adapted the argument in van Fraassen, 1980: 23–5 to make it more coherent.

10 Van Fraassen (1980: 20) indicates constructive empiricism is a psychological theory. Later, Van Fraassen (1994) construes it as a thesis about the aims of science as an enterprise.

11 I adapt the argument of Musgrave (1985: 203).

12 Contrary to van Fraassen, these seem to be the underlying arguments of Smart (1968). The argument or arguments are similar to those of Whewell (1968: 149 ff.).

13 Van Fraassen thinks that there may be an alternative to be found in Bayesian theory with subjective assignments of probability. See van Fraassen, 1989, and elsewhere. But Armstrong rightly points out that that alternative would commit van Fraassen to scepticism about knowledge, no matter how much van Fraassen protests that he is not a sceptic (Armstrong, 1988: section 4).

14 Van Fraassen argues that there are a number of empirically equivalent alternative theories to successful theories in physics (1980: 40 ff.). Musgrave (1985: 200 ff.) criticizes van Fraassen's claims and points out arguments from simplicity can be used to deal with such claims. In any case, Miller (1987: 423ff). points out that it is far from clear that examples from physics can be generalized to all the sciences. In other sciences, it is extraordinarily hard to think up an empirically equivalent theory to an accepted one which is detailed enough to generate the same predictions about observables.

15 There is, of course, a tradition of philosophy emanating from Kant according to which our basic knowledge of the material world consists of some sorts of necessary truths. I take it that the style of argument used by this tradition was shown not to be cogent by its failure in physics. Kant and his followers argued that Newton's mechanics and Euclidean geometry were true a priori. But Newtonian mechanics is only approximately true and Euclidean geometry might well be false. Further, it is now fairly easy to describe worlds in which they would be quite false by using advanced formal techniques.

References

Achinstein, P. (1992) 'Inference to the best explanation: or who won the Mill–Whewell debate?', *Studies in History and Philosophy of Science*, 23: 349–64.

Antony, L. (1993) 'Quine as feminist: the radical import of naturalized epistemology', in L. Antony and C. Witt (eds), *A Mind of One's Own*. Boulder: Westview Press. pp. 185–225.

Armstrong, D. (1988) 'Reply to van Fraassen', *Australasian Journal of Philosophy*, 66: 224–9.

Baier, A. (1991) *A Progress of Sentiments*. Cambridge, MA: Harvard University Press.

Barnes, B. (1982) *T.S. Kuhn and Social Science*. London: Macmillan.

Barnes, B. and Bloor, D. (1982) 'Relativism, rationalism and the sociology of knowledge', in M. Hollis and S. Lukes (eds), *Rationality and Relativism*. Oxford: Oxford University Press. pp. 21–44.

Barwell, I. (1994) 'Towards a defence of objectivity', in K. Lennon and M. Whitford (eds), *Knowing the Difference*. London: Routledge. pp. 79–94.

Bloor, D. (1991) *Knowledge and Social Imagery* (2nd edn). Chicago: University of Chicago Press.

Bloor, D. (1992) 'Sociology of knowledge', in J. Dancy and E. Sosa (eds), *A Companion to Epistemology*. Oxford: Blackwell. pp. 483–6.

Brown, H. (1979) *Perception, Theory and Commitment*. Chicago: University of Chicago Press.

Brown, H. (1988) *Rationality*. London: Routledge.

Brown, H. (1994) 'Reason, judgement and Bayes's Law', *Philosophy of Science*, 61: 351–69.

Brown, J. (1989) *The Rational and the Social*. London: Routledge.

Campbell, K. (1988) 'Philosophy and common sense', *Philosophy*, 63: 161–74.

Carrier, M. (1991) 'What is wrong with the miracle argument', *Studies in History and Philosophy of Science*, 22: 23–36.

Chalmers, A. (1986) 'The Galileo that Feyerabend missed: an improved case against method' in J. Schuster and R. Yeo (eds), *The Politics and Rhetoric of Scientific Method*. Dordrecht: Reidel. pp. 1–31.

Chalmers, A. (1990) *Science and its Fabrication*. Milton Keynes: Open University Press.

Chandler, J. (1990) 'Feminism and epistemology', *Metaphilosophy*, 21: 367–81.

Churchland, P. (1979) *Scientific Realism and the Plasticity of Mind*. Cambridge: Cambridge University Press.

Churchland, P. (1988) ' Perceptual plasticity and theoretical neutrality', *Philosophy of Science*, 55: 167–87.

Churchland, P. (1989) *A Neurocomputational Perspective*. Cambridge, MA: MIT Press.

Cohen, H. (1994) *The Scientific Revolution*. Chicago: University of Chicago Press.

Cohen, M. and Nagel, E. (1939) *An Introduction to Logic and Scientific Method*. (abridged edn). London: Routledge.

Couvalis, S. (1988) 'Feyerabend and Laymon on brownian motion', *Philosophy of Science*, 55: 415–20.

Couvalis, G. (1989) *Feyerabend's Critique of Foundationalism*. Aldershot: Gower.

Dergowski, J. (1973) 'Illusion and culture', in R. Gregory and E. Gombrich (eds), *Illusion in Nature and Art*. London: Duckworth. pp. 161–191.

Descartes, R. (1969) *Philosophical Works of Descartes, Volume 1*. Trans. E. Haldane and G. Ross. Cambridge: Cambridge University Press.

Desmond, A. (1989) *The Politics of Evolution*. Chicago: University of Chicago Press.
Desmond, A. and Moore, J. (1991) *Darwin*. London: Michael Joseph.
Devitt, M. (1979) 'Against incommensurability', *Australasian Journal of Philosophy*, 57: 29–50.
Devitt, M. (1981) *Designation*. New York: Columbia University Press.
Donovan, A. (1988) *Scrutinising Science*. Dordrecht: Kluwer.
Drake, S. (1978) *Galileo at Work*. Chicago: University of Chicago Press.
Dubos, R. (1950) *Louis Pasteur*. Boston: Little Brown.
Earman, J. (1992) *Bayes or Bust? A Critical Examination of Bayesian Confirmation Theory*. Cambridge, MA: MIT Press.
Feyerabend, P. (1961) *Knowledge Without Foundations*. Oberlin: Oberlin College.
Feyerabend, P. (1970) 'Consolations for the specialist', in I. Lakatos and A. Musgrave (eds), *Criticism and the Growth of Knowledge*. Cambridge: Cambridge University Press. pp. 197–230.
Feyerabend, P. (1978a) 'In defence of Aristotle: comments on the condition of content increase', *Boston Studies in the Philosophy of Science*, 58: 143–80.
Feyerabend, P. (1978b) *Science in a Free Society*. London: New Left Books.
Feyerabend, P. (1981a) *Realism, Rationalism and Scientific Method, Philosophical Papers, Volume 1*. Cambridge University Press: Cambridge.
Feyerabend, P. (1981b) *Problems of Empiricism, Philosophical Papers, Volume 2*. Cambridge: Cambridge University Press.
Feyerabend, P. (1981c) 'More clothes from the emperor's bargain basement', *British Journal for the Philosophy of Science*, 32: 57–71.
Feyerabend, P. (1988) *Against Method* (2nd edn). London: Verso.
Feyerabend, P. (1993) *Against Method* (3rd edn). London: Verso.
Fodor, J. (1983) *The Modularity of Mind*. Cambridge, MA: MIT Press.
Fodor, J. (1984),'Observation reconsidered', *Philosophy of Science*, 51: 23–43.
Fodor, J. (1985),'Précis of the modularity of mind', *Behavioural and Brain Sciences*, 8: 1–5.
Fodor, J. (1988) 'A Reply to Churchland's "Perceptual plasticity and theoretical neutrality" ', *Philosophy of Science*, 55: 188–98.
Fodor, J. (1991),'The dogma that didn't bark', *Mind*, 100: 201–20.
Fox Keller, E. (1985) *Reflections on Gender and Science*, New Haven: Yale University Press.
Frankel, H. (1979) 'The career of continental drift theory: an application of Imre Lakatos's analysis of scientific growth to the rise of drift theory', *Studies in History and Philosophy of Science*, 10: 21–66.
Franklin, A. (1992) 'Review of Helen Longino,"Science as Social Knowledge" ', *British Journal for the Philosophy of Science*, 43: 283–5.
Geison, G. (1995) *The Private Science of Louis Pasteur*. Princeton: Princeton University Press.
Giere, R. (1984) *Understanding Scientific Reasoning* (2nd edn). New York: Holt, Reinhart and Wilson.
Gilman, D. (1991) 'The neurobiology of observation', *Philosophy of Science*, 58: 496–502.
Goldman, A. (1986) *Epistemology and Cognition*. Cambridge, MA: Harvard University Press.
Goodman, N. (1965) *Fact, Fiction and Forecast*. New York: Bobbs-Merrill.
Hacking, I. (1983) *Representing and Intervening*. Cambridge: Cambridge University Press.
Hanson, N. (1958) *Patterns of Discovery*. Cambridge: Cambridge University Press.
Hanson, N. (1962) 'Leverrier: the zenith and nadir of Newtonian mechanics', *Isis*, 53: 359–78.
Harding, S. (1991) *Whose Science? Whose Knowledge*? New York: Cornell University Press.
Harman, G. (1986) *Change in View*. Cambridge, MA: MIT Press.
Hempel, C. (1965) *Aspects of Scientific Explanation*. New York: Free Press.
Hesse M. (1974) *The Structure of Scientific Inference*. London: Macmillan.
Holland, J., Holyoak, K., Nesbitt, R. and Thagard, P. (1986) *Induction*. Cambridge, MA: MIT Press.

Howson, C. and Urbach, P. (1989) *Scientific Reasoning, The Bayesian Approach.* La Salle: Open Court.
Hoyningen-Huehne, P. (1993) *Reconstructing Scientific Revolutions.* Tr. A. Levine. Chicago: University of Chicago Press.
Hull, D. (1988) *Science as a Process.* Chicago: University of Chicago Press.
Hume, D. (1978) *A Treatise of Human Nature.* L. Selby-Bigge (ed.), revised by P. Nidditch. Oxford: Oxford University Press.
Hunt, S. (1994) 'A realist theory of empirical testing', *Philosophy of the Social Sciences,* 24 : 133–58.
Jones, R. and Hagen, M. (1980) 'A perspective on cross-cultural picture perception', in M. Hagen (ed.), *The Perception of Pictures, Volume 2.* New York: Academic Press. pp. 193–226.
Kitcher, P. (1993) *The Advancement of Science.* Oxford: Oxford University Press.
Kornblith, H. (1993) *Inductive Inference and its Natural Ground.* Cambridge, MA: MIT Press.
Kornblith, H. (1994) 'Beyond foundationalism and the coherence theory', in 'H. Kornblith (ed.), *Naturalising Epistemology* (2nd edn). Cambridge, MA: MIT Press. pp. 131–46
Kuhn, T. (1970a) *The Structure of Scientific Revolutions* (2nd edn). Chicago: University of Chicago Press.
Kuhn, T. (1970b) 'Logic of discovery or psychology of research', in I. Lakatos and A. Musgrave (eds), *Criticism and the Growth of Knowledge.* Cambridge: Cambridge University Press. pp. 1–23.
Kuhn, T. (1970c) 'Reflections on my critics' in I. Lakatos and A. Musgrave (eds), *Criticism and the Growth of Knowledge.* Cambridge: Cambridge University Press. pp. 231–78.
Kuhn, T. (1977) *The Essential Tension.* Chicago: University of Chicago Press.
Lakatos, I. (1978) *The Methodology of Scientific Research Programmes, Philosophical Papers Volume 1.* Cambridge: Cambridge University Press.
Lakatos, I. and Musgrave, A. (eds) (1970) *Criticism and the Growth of Knowledge.* Cambridge: Cambridge University Press.
Laudan, L. (1977) *Progress and its Problems.* Berkeley, CA: University of California Press.
Laudan, L. (1981) 'A confutation of convergent realism', *Philosophy of Science,* 48: 19–48
Laudan, L. (1984) 'The pseudo-science of science?', in J. Brown (ed.), *Scientific Rationality: The Sociological Turn.* Dordrecht: Reidel. pp. 41–73.
Laudan, L. (1990) *Science and Relativism.* Chicago: University of Chicago Press.
Laudan, R. (1987) *From Mineralogy to Geology, the Foundations of a Science.* Chicago: University of Chicago Press.
Le Grand, H. (1988) *Drifting Continents and Shifting Theories.* Cambridge: Cambridge University Press.
Leplin, J. (1994) 'Critical notice: Philip Kitcher's "The Advancement of Science" ', *Philosophy of Science,* 61: 666–71.
Lipton, P. (1991) *Inference to the Best Explanation.* London: Routledge.
Lloyd, G. (1983) *Science, Folklore and Ideology.* Cambridge: Cambridge University Press.
Long, G. (1988),'Selective adaptation vs. transfer of decrement', *Perception and Psychophysics,* 43: 207–9.
Longino, H. (1990) *Science as Social Knowledge.* Princeton: Princeton University Press.
Meehl, P. (1992) 'The miracle argument for realism', *Studies in History and Philosophy of Science,* 23: 267–82.
Miller, D. (1982) 'Conjectural knowledge', in J. Levinson, (ed.), *In Pursuit of Truth.* Brighton: Harvester.
Miller, R. (1987) *Fact and Method.* New Jersey: Princeton University Press.
Mortensen, C. (1989) 'Anything is possible', *Erkenntnis,* 30: 319–37.
Mosedale, S. (1978) 'Science corrupted: Victorian biologists consider "the woman question" ', *Journal of the History of Biology,* 11: 1–55.
Munévar, G. (ed.) (1991a) *Boston Studies in the Philosophy of Science,* 132.

Munévar, G. (1991b) 'Feyerabend's free society', *Boston Studies in the Philosophy of Science*, 132: 179–98.
Musgrave, A. (1985) 'Realism vs. constructive empiricism', in P. Churchland and C. Hooker (eds), *Images of Science*. Chicago: University of Chicago Press. pp.197–221.
Nerlich, G. (1992) *Values and Valuing, Reflections on the Ethical Life of Persons*. Oxford: Oxford University Press.
Newton-Smith, W. (1981) *The Rationality of Science*. London: Routledge.
Nitske, W. (1971) *The Life of Wilhelm Conrad Röntgen*. Tucson: University of Arizona Press.
O'Leary-Hawthorne, J. (1994) 'What does van Fraassen's critique of scientific realism show?', *Monist*, 77: 128–44.
Oldroyd, D. (1986) *The Arch of Knowledge*. New York: Methuen.
Papineau, D. (1993) *Philosophical Naturalism*. Oxford: Blackwell.
Polanyi, M. (1958) *Personal Knowledge*. London: Routledge and Kegan Paul.
Popper, K. (1966) *The Open Society and its Enemies*, (Vol. 2, 5th edn). London: Routledge.
Popper, K. (1970) 'Normal science and its dangers', in I. Lakatos and A. Musgrave (eds), *Criticism and the Growth of Knowledge*. Cambridge: Cambridge University Press: 51–8.
Popper, K. (1972) *Objective Knowledge*. Oxford: Oxford University Press.
Popper, K. (1976) *Unended Quest*. Glasgow: Fontana.
Popper K. (1980) *The Logic of Scientific Discovery* (10th edn). London: Hutchinson.
Quinn, S. (1995), *Marie Curie*. London: Heinemann
Riggs, P. (1992) *Whys and Ways of Science*. Melbourne: Melbourne University Press.
Roll-Hansen, N. (1979) 'Experimental method and spontaneous generation: the controversy between Pasteur and Pouchet', *Journal of the History of Medicine*, 34: 273–92.
Roll-Hansen, N. (1983) 'The death of spontaneous generation and the birth of the gene: two case studies of relativism', *Social Studies of Science*, 13: 481–519.
Routley, R., Plumwood, V., Meyer, P. and Brady, R. (1982) *Relevant Logics and their Rivals, Volume 1*. Atrascadero: Ridgeview.
Schmaus, W. (1993) 'Review of Helen Longino, "Science as Social Knowledge" ', *Philosophy of the Social Sciences*, 23: 562–5.
Shapere, D. (1974) *Galileo, a Philosophical Study*. Chicago, MA: University of Chicago Press.
Shapere, D. (1982) 'The concept of observation in science and philosophy', *Philosophy of Science*, 49: 485–525.
Shapere, D. (1984) *Reason and the Search for Knowledge*. Dordrecht: Reidel.
Skorupski, J. (1989) *John Stuart Mill*. London: Routledge.
Smart, J. (1963) *Philosophy and Scientific Realism*. London: Routledge.
Smart, J. (1968) *Between Science and Philosophy*. New York: Random House.
Solomon, M. (1995) 'Legend naturalism and scientific progress: an essay on Philip Kitcher's "The Advancement of Science" ', *Studies in History and Philosophy of Science*, 26: 205–8.
Stove, D. (1986) *The Rationality of Induction*. Oxford: Oxford University Press.
Teeter Dobbs, B. and Jacob, M. (1995) *Newton and the Culture of Newtonianism*. New Jersey: Humanities Press.
Thalos, M. (1994) 'The common need for classical epistemological foundations: against a feminist alternative', *Monist*, 77: 531–53.
Thomas, K. (1984) *Man and the Natural World, Changing Attitudes in England, 1500–1800*. London: Penguin.
van Fraassen, B. (1980) *The Scientific Image*. Oxford: Oxford University Press.
van Fraassen, B. (1985) 'Empiricism in the philosophy of science', in P. Churchland and C. Hooker (eds), *Images of Science*. Chicago, MA: University of Chicago Press. pp. 245–308.
van Fraassen, B. (1989) *Laws and Symmetry*. Oxford: Oxford University Press.
van Fraassen, B. (1994) 'Gideon Rosen on constructive empiricism', *Philosophical Studies*, 74: 179–92.
von Brentano, M. (1991) 'Letter to an anti-liberal liberal', *Boston Studies in the Philosophy of Science*, 132: 199–212.
Watkins, J. (1982) *Science and Scepticism*. London: Hutchinson.

Whewell, W. (1968) *William Whewell's Theory of Scientific Method*, R. Butts (ed.). Pittsburgh: University of Pittsburgh Press.

Winkler, M. and van Helden, A. (1992) 'Representing the heavens, Galileo and visual astronomy', *Isis*, 83: 195–217.

Wittgenstein, L. (1968) *Philosophical Investigations*. Tr. G. Anscombe. Oxford: Blackwell.

Worrall, J. (1989) 'Why Popper and Watkins fail to solve the problem of induction', *Boston Studies in the Philosophy of Science*, 117: 257–96.

Index

Lightning Source UK Ltd.
Milton Keynes UK
19 July 2010

157219UK00003B/27/A